The City as a
Human Environment

Only One Earth Series

Management of Hazardous Agents: Volume 1: Industrial and
Regulatory Approaches
Duane G. LeVine and Arthur C. Upton, editors

Management of Hazardous Agents: Volume 2: Social, Political, and
Policy Aspects
Duane G. LeVine and Arthur C. Upton, editors

THE CITY AS
A HUMAN
ENVIRONMENT

Edited by DUANE G. LeVINE
and ARTHUR C. UPTON

ONLY ONE EARTH SERIES

Westport, Connecticut
London

Library of Congress Cataloging-in-Publication Data

The City as a human environment / edited by Duane G. LeVine and Arthur
  C. Upton.
     p. cm.—(Only one earth series)
  Includes bibliographical references and index.
  ISBN 0–275–94659–2 (alk. paper)
  1. City planning. 2. Urbanization. 3. Urban ecology.
  I. LeVine, Duane G. II. Upton, Arthur C., 1923– . III. Series.
  HT165.5.C58   1994
  307.76—dc20   94–1146

British Library Cataloguing in Publication Data is available.

Library of Congress Catalog Card Number: 94–1146
ISBN: 0–275–94659–2

First published in 1994

Praeger Publishers, 88 Post Road West, Westport, CT 06881
An imprint of Greenwood Publishing Group, Inc.

Printed in the United States of America

The paper used in this book complies with the
Permanent Paper Standard issued by the National
Information Standards Organization (Z39.48–1984).

10 9 8 7 6 5 4 3 2 1

CONTENTS

Foreword   vii
Maurice F. Strong

Preface   ix
Ruth A. Eblen and William R. Eblen

Introduction   xi
Duane G. LeVine and Arthur C. Upton

PART ONE: PLANNING THE BUILT ENVIRONMENT   1

1   Affordable Housing and the Urban Environment   3
   Kathryn Wylde

2   Affordable by Design   13
   Zane Yost

3   The Local Initiatives Support Corporation's Approach   29
   Paul S. Grogan

4   Affordable Housing   39
   Kerron R. Barnes

5   Energy Consumption and Architectural Design   47
   Richard G. Stein

6   A Public/Private Collaborative Process for Achieving
    Energy Efficiency in Buildings   55
    Earle F. Taylor, Jr. and Luisa M. Freeman

PART TWO: IMPROVING URBAN TRANSPORTATION   **71**

7   Transportation and the Environment—Lessons from the
    Global Laboratory   73
    Wilfred Owen

8   The Auto, Land Use, and Transit   83
    Boris Pushkarev

9   Urban Transportation: Progress and Priorities   97
    Mark A. Wright

10 The Role of Rail Transit in Contemporary Cities   105
    Vukan R. Vuchic

11 AASHTO Transportation 2020 Program   113
    David Clawson

12 A Highway Designed to Be Part of the Human
    Environment   121
    Matthew A. Coogan

**PART THREE: SHAPING PATTERNS OF URBAN
LAND USE**   **131**

13 The New York Region Experiment   133
    John P. Keith

14 Constituting a Preservation Plan for Urban Areas   141
    M. Christine Boyer

15 Making Cities Safe for Trees   157
    R. Neil Sampson

16 Living on the Crust of the Earth: Human Ecology and
    Environmental Planning   171
    Sheldon W. Samuels

17 Conclusions   187
    Duane G. LeVine and Arthur C. Upton

Bibliography   191

Index   197

About the Contributors   201

FOREWORD

MAURICE F. STRONG

> As we enter the global phase of human evolution it becomes obvious that each man has two countries, his own and the planet Earth.
> *Only One Earth,* 1972

It had been my great privilege as Secretary-General of the U.N. Conference on the Human Environment, held in Stockholm in 1972, to introduce Rene Dubos and Barbara Ward and to enlist their cooperation in producing, with the support of some one hundred other leaders from around the world, the book *Only One Earth,* which became the principal source of guidance and inspiration for that conference.

I was honored, therefore, to serve as chairman of the distinguished committee of conveners for both Dubos forum programs that not only commemorated the tenth and fifteenth anniversaries of that historic Conference, but also celebrated the lives of Rene Dubos and Barbara Ward. Our objective was to assess the progress made since the Stockholm Conference with a view to developing action agendas for a more hopeful and positive future.

The Only One Earth Forum, convened in May 1987, was the first major occasion in the United States in which an American and international group of professionals and public leaders examined in depth the themes, recommendations, and the analysis of the report of the Brundtland Commission, prior to its being published as *Our Common Future.* The report guided the development of our agenda for that forum in much the same way the Stockholm Conference developed the basic agenda for the world community around the theme of "Only One Earth" fifteen years ago.

Just as the Dubos forum commemorating the tenth anniversary generated the Environmental Regeneration Series, the Fifteenth Anniversary Forum has spawned this Only One Earth Series. The first two books in the series, *Management of Hazardous Agents: Industrial and Regulatory Approaches* and *Management of Hazardous Agents: Social, Political, and Policy Aspects,* are based on the workshop on managing hazardous substances at the Only One Earth forum and the Dubos forum on managing hazardous materials held in 1988. This third book in the series, *The City as a Human Environment,* is based on the Dubos forum (with the same title) held in 1989.

It is hoped that the process begun at each forum will be continued and enhanced by publishing the findings and opinions of scientists and policymakers from all sectors of our society. In this way, the ripple effect of these dialogues begun among a small group of authorities will suggest creative new solutions to the environmental problems facing the human community and thereby help to translate the report of the World Commission into realities in our economic life, in our political life, in the development of our culture, and in our educational systems.

PREFACE

RUTH A. EBLEN AND WILLIAM R. EBLEN

> Cities, dwellings, and the ways of life in them cannot be designed or imagined merely on the basis of available technology. Each decision concerning them must take into consideration not only human needs in the present but also long-range consequences.
>
> Rene Dubos, 1968

In 1989, the Dubos forum on The City as a Human Environment was organized as a follow-up to the "Workshop on Human Settlements: Factors Affecting the Quality of Life" that was held at the Dubos Center's Only One Earth Forum in 1987, under the co-chairmanship of Jorge E. Hardoy, Director, Latin American Office, International Institute for Environment and Development, and Eric Carlson, Special Adviser, International Union of Building Societies and Savings Associations. Four aspects of cities were addressed in the 1989 forum, in light of Rene Dubos's "five E's of environmental management" (ecology, energetics, economics, esthetics, and ethics), in the following four workshops: (1) Planning the Built Environment, (2) Improving Urban Transportation, (3) Managing Urban Wastes, and (4) Shaping Patterns of Urban Land Use. Cross-cutting issues addressed in each workshop included the following key questions:

1. What are the major challenges that are posed by urbanization?
2. What are the significant interactions, contradictions, and trade-offs?

3. What research, legislative, institutional, philosophical, and cultural changes are needed for dealing with the problems of urbanization? and

4. How can public participation in these issues be made more effective in improving the quality of the urban environment?

This book, *The City as a Human Environment,* reflects the Center's continuing interest in urbanization—beginning in 1979 with the forum on Coexistence of Rural and Urban Areas. Three of the four workshops are represented in this volume.

The Center is indebted to the editors—Duane G. LeVine, Manager, Science and Strategy Development, Environment and Safety, Exxon Corporation, and Arthur C. Upton, M.D., Director Emeritus of Environmental Medicine, New York University Medical Center—not only for their conscientious selection of papers to be included from the many excellent ones produced for the forum, but also for their diligent editing and important contributions to the book's content.

Duane LeVine and Arthur Upton also co-chaired the steering committee for the Dubos forum on the City as a Human Environment. The two co-chairmen and members of the steering committee met throughout the year to plan the forum and, among other things, to establish priorities for the forum agenda as well as to make the all-important selections of resource people to write papers and to participate. The success of the forum program was due in no small measure to the expertise of the authorities that made up the steering committee.

Julie Ruttenberg, Alisa Shen, Ann McCooey, Sara Peracca, and Erica Mohan, Dubos Center's staff, did an excellent job of preparing, revising, and organizing the final manuscripts so essential to the completion of this book.

INTRODUCTION

DUANE G. LeVINE AND ARTHUR C. UPTON

The following chapters respond to the need for up-to-date information about three of the major challenges that are posed by urbanization: buildings, transportation, and land use.

Planning the built environment involves integrating all aspects of human life so that an aesthetic, economic, and sustainable system is established. There are innumerable challenges that arise from this endeavor. The primary goal, however, is to provide adequate, safe, efficient, affordable housing for an ever-increasing population. Engineers, utilities, and scientists have joined forces to improve safe and energy-efficient appliances and building structures, and detect air quality problems that have resulted from the desire to construct or retrofit buildings to maximize energy efficiency. Financiers, planners, government, and local community groups have joined forces to increase the quantity, affordability, and aesthetics of housing so that all have equal access to decent shelter. In many cities public-private coalitions of business and civic leaders, the building industry, and local government have been forged to address the problem of financing and implementing cost-effective reconstruction programs at the local level. Probably the most effective projects are those now under way at the state level and those sponsored by private-sector groups. Also increasingly numerous efforts are being sponsored by the nonprofit sector.

There are many challenges for those who seek to improve urban transportation—reducing noise levels, finding usable, cleaner energy sources, improving the quality and/or quantity of public transit, meeting demands for roadways, and improving esthetics. Ultimately, the goal of most transportation systems is to preserve rural access, provide modal interlinks where necessary, and reduce congestion while permitting efficient, comfortable movement for a maximum number of people. These challenges are not new, but innovative approaches are being considered for implementation. The best solutions account for the specific characteristics of each city—population density, current and projected land use patterns, pollution hazards, and commuting habits. All, however, include a plan to improve utilization of automotive and public transportation in line with a strong, individual desire for independent, convenient travel. In addition, traffic management methods include ride sharing, provision of high occupancy vehicle lanes, and use of public transit. Simply increasing highway capacity or expanding public transit is not the answer to improved urban transportation. Experience has shown new capacity is quickly filled and overburdened. Improved land use planning to make communities more self-sustaining must be seen as part of the solution.

To convert chaos into order, to make cities workable, to bar bad development, and to encourage the building of necessary facilities, improved planning must establish better use of land. Overall, current conventional approaches are not adequate to meet the increasing needs of city dwellers around the world. Many planners are currently in search of new creative ways to better utilize human, natural, and financial resources—all of which are in desperately short supply. Local initiative and community participation appear to be the most promising solutions.

I

Planning the Built Environment

1

AFFORDABLE HOUSING AND THE URBAN ENVIRONMENT

KATHRYN WYLDE

The buildings and infrastructure of America's older cities are wearing out, requiring a huge commitment of national resources to accomplish their renewal and replacement. Whether and how to reconstruct urban centers constitutes the foremost domestic challenge facing the nation. The issue is complicated by the increasing cost and complexity of urban redevelopment and by the fact that cities constitute concentrations of poor people whose capacity to contribute to the reconstruction process is limited. Moreover, there is a growing resistance among the American citizenry to virtually all types of development, even when its purpose is to house the homeless, to generate jobs for the unemployed, to maintain urban transit, sanitation, and criminal justice systems, and to re-create value when a built environment has reached the end of its useful economic life.

The magnitude of the challenge facing urban America is greatest in New York City. Almost a quarter of the city's 2.1 million housing units were built more than seventy years ago and must either be substantially rehabilitated or demolished and replaced in the next decade. New York City and New York State have committed funding for a ten-year, $5 billion housing plan to repair or replace about 250,000 apartments—almost all involving city-owned land and buildings. But the capital investment required to adequately address the city's immediate housing needs is easily five times that amount, exclusive of the cost of public facilities and infrastructure that must be reconstructed to support residential redevelopment.

Do urban localities and the nation as a whole have the commitment and capacity to preserve and rebuild America's urban centers? The answer depends, in large part, on how the cost of development is weighed against other budget priorities and against the consequences of allowing cities to disintegrate. High costs obviously discourage local governments from supporting aggressive public development programs. In New York City, a conventionally financed new apartment costs $150,000 or more to build and must rent in the $1,600 per month range. Rehabilitation and refinancing of older apartment buildings costs about $50,000 per unit and requires rents of $800 per month. Even the median price of an existing home in the city is over $190,000. At the same time, median family income is only $27,200, and 98 percent of the population (earning less than $70,000 annually) is priced out of the private housing market.

Homelessness and the housing shortage arc directly related to the fact that it costs more to develop and maintain housing than most people can afford to pay. This "affordability gap" must be bridged by public subsidy, as private capital can only be attracted when market demand permits prices (or rents) that exceed costs. The lead role that public investment must play in rebuilding urban centers presents an unprecedented development opportunity. It should make possible a planning and development process that maximizes achievement of community goals in the reconstruction of cities. This, in turn, can help assure that the "rebuilt environment" of cities is responsive to the needs and expectations of Americans in the twenty-first century.

For example, the change in New York City's economy and labor force—from a manufacturing base to service and financial industries— calls for different housing and amenities. The city's workforce, once housed in tenements, today demands homes with middle-class accoutrements like yards, basements, and parking. The brownstone revival movement, stimulated in part by the impact of the gasoline crisis on the cost of the urban commute, is one way that urban buildings have been recycled to meet this demand, but the city is running out of brownstones. The urban population is increasingly minority—Black, Hispanic, and Asian. As minorities move into the middle class, they are looking for homeownership opportunities and middle-class neighborhood amenities *within* the city, rather than in the suburban ring. This is due to a combination of high prices, absence of ethnic cultural and commercial institutions, and racial discrimination in many suburban communities.

Despite widespread public concern about homelessness and the lack of affordable housing, there is no consensus about where the money will come from to finance urban redevelopment. The federal government, which financed most slum clearance and redevelopment activity in the 1950s and 1960s, faces a national debt problem that will likely preclude substantial assistance for urban development in the foreseeable future. Urban localities are hard pressed to raise tax revenues from business, given the increased competitiveness of nonurban areas and the mobility business enjoys in this era of telecommunications.

The tension between broad-based needs and limited resources has generated public-private partnership initiatives in many cities. These are aimed at encouraging business, civic, and government leaders to work together to reconcile revenue and expenditure needs and to find new ways to attract and leverage private investment and income-generating activity in the city. In the development arena, partnership efforts have focused on reducing costs, thereby narrowing the affordability gap and lessening the financial demands on government. The concepts of Enterprise Zones, which hold out the hope of increasing the revenue base of depressed areas through deregulation and lowered taxes, represents a national programmatic application of the local partnership concept.

The New York City Partnership is a nonprofit consortium of business and civic leaders founded by David Rockefeller and chaired by James D. Robinson III. It has brought together builders, bankers, and the business community with local officials and community organizations to create a common agenda for cooperation in development of new affordable housing. Initiatives include reform of building codes, zoning regulations, and procedures that are obstacles to cost-effective development; the involvement of banks and builders in affordable housing production on a limited profit basis; reutilization of low-cost land in the city inventory; and an introduction of more economic construction technology with the cooperation of unions and contractors.

Because cost is a key factor in determining the scale of urban housing production through the next decade, the potential impact of cost-saving construction systems deserves attention. Urban developers have, in the past twenty years, used panelized wall systems, pre-cast floor systems, and prefabricated structural systems to achieve a more efficient production of high-rise housing and office buildings. In recent years, wood and steel modular systems—pioneered in rural America—have become an important option for low-density urban housing. The application of modular housing has ranged from customized luxury condominiums on Long Island Sound to the Ryland company's creation of a $20,000 single-family home for the Enterprise Foundation in Maryland.

The urbanization of modular, prefabricated building systems got off to a bad start in the 1960s with HUD Secretary George Romney's "Operation Breakthrough" program. The only Breakthrough system to achieve wide urban replication was Forest City's panelized concrete high-rise product with modular kitchens and baths. (This system still has not come to New York City, due to union resistance.) Breakthrough also left a bad taste in the mouths of investors and banks. The project was interrupted by President Nixon's 1973 moratorium on Federal Housing

Programs, bankrupting plans established to provide products through FHA programs and generally discrediting the industry among financial institutions.

It was not until 1982 that modular, single-family ranch homes were introduced in New York City to carry out housing redevelopment projects in the South Bronx, South Jamaica and East New York, Brooklyn. Modular was the only construction method that could bring down housing costs to levels mandated by low FHA appraisals—less than $65,000 for a single-family home. The first wave of modular development did not go well. The South Bronx project ended up in political imbroglio: it took five years and four developers to complete ninety homes at three times their initial projected cost. Moreover, the density of ranch homes on quarter-acre lots was too low to support needed commercial development and public services. Another project was thrown into default based on a combination of developer incompetence and inadequate financing. South Jamaica—a project of about sixty ranch homes—demonstrated the economics and marketability of the typical frame, modular product, but density was too low for this self-contained subdivision to have a positive impact on the surrounding blighted urban area. These experiences suggested that prefabricated housing did not have an urban application.

In 1986, the Stamford-based F. D. Rich Company attempted to use their concrete modular system to help develop homeless facilities in New York. The system had been used effectively in the suburbs for hotels/motels and office buildings. To appease teamster and construction trade unions, project sponsors made Rich transfer substantial work from the factory to the field, destroying the economies of the system. Rich estimates cost overruns at seventy percent and has refused other invitations to bring its system to the city.

The first broadbased and generally successful application of modular housing in New York City has been through Housing Partnership New Homes Program, a joint initiative of the city and the New York City Partnership. Since 1984, more than 1,000 units of modular housing have been erected in the Bronx and Brooklyn under the Housing Partnership. This was the first development of modular two- and three-family rowhouses, built to the city's strict fire and multiple-dwelling codes. Deluxe Homes of Berwick, Pennsylvania, made the investment in engineering the multifamily rowhouse and set up a new assembly line for steel and stud modules built to New York City and New York State code standards.

As a result of this local partnership effort, the problems traditionally associated with modular technology and its application in the urban environment were resolved. Cost savings of about fifteen percent are still achieved through modular construction, even when homes are built to an urban code and design standards. As for union issues, an International AFL-CIO Tritrades Agreement between carpenters, plumbers, and electricians authorizes the use of modular housing that comes from a union plant, as long as one hundred percent of the on-site work is performed by union labor. Plumbing, electrical, and mechanical subcontractors remain unhappy with the loss of customized work, but this could be addressed with a local plant that uses independent contractors rather than in-house personnel. Many areas, like New York, suffer from a shortage of skilled carpenters, but have an unskilled labor pool that, with plant supervision and assembly line techniques, could perform finished carpentry to a standard that they could not achieve in the field. Importantly, even in a union plant, factory wages are substantially lower than the field wages, based on better (indoor) working conditions, fewer journeymen, and regularized employment.

Once the prefabricated, modular product was upgraded to meet urban standards, including adaptation to design and facade needs of infill housing and the urban streetscape, it readily achieved market acceptance. The only instance where the Housing Partnership has been disappointed was with a concrete modular three-family home. The relatively high cost of concrete and of transporting heavy modules, together with limitations on size and finish of the housing, have resulted in little enthusiasm for this product.

Despite dozens of wood and steel modular systems and efforts by a dozen would-be entrepreneurs to capitalize on the New York market, Deluxe is still the only major supplier (more than one hundred units/year) of steel modulars to New York City. Modular production is a manufacturing business, with a fixed overhead and capital cost that requires consistent cash flow. Unlike the conventional homebuilder, whose operation expands and contracts with workload, industrialized housing requires regularized production and sales over a sustained period. Some owners of modular plants have successfully addressed this problem by creating their own development capacity that generates a predictable pipeline; also useful is a relationship with government-sponsored programs that are less dependent on market factors.

It is discouraging to those who have worked to achieve economies through modular construction that a proliferation of new government impositions on development threatens to neutralize cost savings and diminish the leverage of public investment in affordable housing.

Historically, the parochial interests of unions and subcontractors were the greatest source of resistance to factory-built housing. But these problems were almost always negotiated out among people who shared a common interest in getting housing built. Such a shared interest no longer characterizes the parties in controversies over development and, because obstacles emanate from federal law, it has become increasingly difficult to resolve issues at the local level.

It is ironic that, just as a spirit of public-private "partnership" has begun to take hold in urban communities, countervailing forces have emerged to thwart them. Federal and state "special interest" statutes and regulations, along with a growing body of case law that reflects the anti-development bias of most litigants, are emerging as the single greatest obstacle to the preservation and reconstruction of American cities. Environmental laws, often applied in areas that are unrelated to protection of the natural environment, have the most negative impact on the pace and cost of development, but there are many other problem areas. Congress recently passed a Fair Housing Law mandating handicapped accessibility that will increase the cost of housing construction and renovation substantially. Design requirements and delays associated with historic preservation concerns are a major problem in older areas, where virtually every development site is contiguous to a candidate historic property. Development sites that are candidates for the Hazardous Waste list—and this can apply to most of the huge inventory of urban land that was formerly used for manufacturing purposes—are "off limits" in perpetuity.

The component costs of housing are those of land, construction, and financing. Land costs include legal and professional fees, testing and mitigation measures and carrying costs during extended review by multiple agencies. They must include the exactions demanded by the community in return for development approvals as well as public relations and litigation expenses for contested projects. In the past few years, urban land costs have increased at least 100 percent for all development, including affordable housing. And these costs are the same, regardless of the construction technology.

Construction costs have also increased due to the newly mandated specifications. Some of the impositions of the past ten years that offset savings of assembly line production and code reform are:

Water Meters (installed)	$300/house
Toxicity Tests (PCBs, asbestos, etc.)	$500/house minimum
Insurance (including indemnification on hazardous waste)	$250/house
Dumping/Waste Disposal Costs	$1,000/house
Contiguous to Historic District	$8,000/house minimum
Within Historic District	$16,000/house minimum
Wetlands (design and reconstruction)	$10,000/house
Archeological Tests	$250/house

Handicapped Access	$2,000/house minimum
Street Trees	$300/house
On-site Stormwater Retainage	$3,000/house

This list does not include the installation, weatherization or noise mitigation measures (double or triple glazed windows, roof baffles, earth berms, air conditioning sleeves, "r" ratings) that were imposed on housing construction and rehabilitation prior to 1980. It does not make reference to such special interest considerations as minority training, hiring, and contracting, on-site parking and open space, all of which frequently are requirements for development of affordable housing that add to construction costs.

Financing costs of housing are a function of time and predictability. Higher risks and longer time expenditures resulting from special interest laws have increased the return required by investors and developers. The savings of modular housing are primarily due to efficiency, predictability, and standardization (resulting in lower costs for professional fees, financing, security and vandalism, supervision, and overhead). Delays and customized site or environmental requirements remove the biggest advantages of industrialized building systems.

Litigation, growing out of the broad and ill-defined scope of the laws that impact on urban redevelopment, has paralyzed the development approval process in New York City and threatens to do so elsewhere. The courts have elevated form over substance, basing decisions on the process by which development impacts are studied rather than the facts of the case. For example, the New York State Environmental Quality Review Act (SEQRA) mandates land use decisionmakers to take a "hard look" at the impact of a project on the environment. A state court has recently invalidated the city's longstanding process for administering this review, subjecting prior development approvals to reversal.

Laws enacted to protect the environment from over-development are being enacted by advocates of private causes to exact economic or political concessions from government or development interests. For example, citing the National Environmental Protection Act, the courts have recognized "Secondary Displacement"—the inevitable consequence of redevelopment that raises property values in a blighted area—as a negative impact on the urban environment that might be mitigated. (In most cases, such mitigation can be achieved only with more public subsidy.) Litigation based on environmental statutes is increasingly a "last one in closes the gate" or a NIMBY (Not In My Backyard) strategy to keep out unwanted neighbors or uses. Groups that have lost in the public arena turn to the courts, where they can defeat projects by delay.

If we are, as a society, to get beyond the current state of paralysis and

conflict between development and anti-development interests, a combined program of public education and legislative initiatives is required.
This program must address and resolve conflicts between the needs of
the urban community for affordable housing and other cost-effective
development and legitimate efforts to both protect the natural environment and re-create a well-planned built environment in the city.
National coordination of a campaign aimed at Congress and the general public is required. But, constituencies and implementation mechanisms must be established at the local level. One essential ingredient is a strong local land use and development planning process that
incorporates early input from all levels and sectors of the community.
New York is currently going through a Supreme Court–mandated
City Charter Revision that will hopefully cause progress in this direction.

A regional model for consensus-building on development issues is
being tested right now by the Tristate Regional Plan Association (RPA)
of New York, New Jersey, and Connecticut. At the invitation of a new
Bronx Borough President, RPA recently undertook the preparation of a
comprehensive community plan for redevelopment of the Bronx, with
broadbased participation of political, neighborhood, business, institutional, and academic leaders of the Borough. The participatory planning
process will help to define overriding priorities and to reconcile competing interests. The conclusion should be consensus behind a major development initiative that can move forward quickly. This process is coming
up with solutions to classic conflicts: the desire to maximize construction jobs for local residents while keeping housing costs low is addressed by proposing the creation of a local modular housing plant. The
goal of replacing ghettoes with mixed income neighborhoods is to be
achieved by renovating older housing for low-income tenants and carrying out an "infill" new homes construction program serving the middle class.

Beyond local consensus-building, the complexity of the development
approval process requires that states and localities establish an ombuds-
man agency to steer projects through the system and, where necessary,
override special interests within and among government bureaucracies.
At the federal level, HUD should be encouraged to play such a role.
Enterprise Zone legislation may offer a laboratory where community
priorities can be tested—to determine, for example, when historic facades are less important than low-income housing. In New York City, a
Mayor's Office of Housing Coordination has been established to perform an expediting and prioritizing role; at a minimum, it helps get
affordable housing plans to the "top of the pile" in city agencies. Based
on recommendations of a Governor's Housing Task Force, New York
State is setting up a public-private Housing Policy Council, with profes-

sional staff, to promote, expedite, and advocate for affordable housing development.

Outside of government, nonprofit intermediaries must be encouraged to serve as honest brokers between special interests, the courts, the development community and government bureaucracies in order to promote more efficient and fair resolution of conflicts over development and land use. Private developers cannot effectively make the case on behalf of the public interest. The New York City Partnership has met with some success as an intermediary proponent of development. It was able to secure waivers of the more onerous facade requirements for modular houses built in the South Bronx near "Fort Apache," the police precinct building made famous in a movie and, therefore, a candidate for the National Registry of Historic Properties. It negotiated a compromise for relocating a "wetland" to permit a 250-unit affordable housing project to go into construction.

The role of nonprofit groups must also include educating legislators, the press, and the public about the consequences of special interests on the achievement of goals like affordable housing. Legislation should be amended to better define areas of environmental concern, with the goal of limiting discretion of bureaucrats, litigants, and the judiciary to use these laws for extraneous or parochial purposes. Time limits should be imposed on the development approval process and the judicial review process. Cost-benefit analyses, and appropriations of funds where necessary, should be required for legislation and regulations that will add to the cost of residential development. For example, if new sprinkler requirements are enacted, the cost should be balanced against legitimate fire safety concerns; if handicapped access is necessary, there should be some connection to local needs and a fund to pay for accessibility measures in low-cost housing should be established; in the case of asbestos testing and removal, government must assure access to disposal sites. In some cases, laws should be more explicit. They should, for example, state when environmental impact assessments will not be required—as in the case of housing developments that conform to local zoning and code.

At local and national levels, open-minded dialogue must take place among public officials, business leaders, advocates of affordable housing and urban redevelopment, and responsible representatives of special interest groups. The object is to forge public policy guidelines and legislation that will serve the general public interest with respect to controlling development. Former HUD Secretary Jack Kemp expressed a willingness to provide leadership in efforts aimed at improving incentives for low-cost housing and economic development in urban centers and highlighting situations where other federal requirements are imposing unnecessarily on the achievement of development goals. In 1988, HUD co-sponsored a symposium on the topic "Business and the Entrepreneurial American City" with the New York City Partnership and the U.S. Chambers of Commerce. Public and private leaders from cities across the country came together to share their problems and successes in rebuilding urban communities. Their individual projects and experiences offer many models for the larger task of planning and reconstructing the built environment of urban America. The objective is to sustain older cities, based on the conviction that they should continue as centers of culture and commerce in America beyond the twentieth century.

2

AFFORDABLE BY DESIGN

ZANE YOST

In the spring of 1988, the National Housing Task Force released a report on America's housing crisis. Entitled "A Decent Place to Live," it detailed these troubling facts:

1. Throughout the 1980s, rents and housing costs for low- and moderate-income families have been increasing while real income has been decreasing.
2. The national rate of home ownership has steadily declined, reversing a forty-year trend.
3. The Department of Housing and Urban Development has reduced funding for new housing by 80 percent.

Throughout the Northeast, California, and other localized markets, inflated land prices, no-growth zoning, and skyrocketing appreciation have created a gap between income and housing cost. A growing number of people, from first-time buyers to modest-income renters, cannot afford the housing they want.

According to figures from Harvard University's Joint Center for Housing Studies, there has been a dramatic 7 to 8 percent drop in home ownership in the twenty-four to thirty-nine year old age group. This means that two million households who would have been able to buy a house or apartment in 1980 cannot afford to do so today. The first rung of the ladder of home ownership has been removed for the traditional first-time buyer. This in turn restrains current owners from moving up. Even more critical, low-income rents and moderate-income buyer opportunities are becoming an endangered species. Many families are already paying 50 percent or more of their gross income for rent, with rents expected to increase 30 percent by 1992 (1987 People's Bank Study). Further complicating the rental outlook is the economic motivation of many landlords to convert low-income rental units to condominiums. In the wake of federal real estate tax reform (Tax Reform Act of 1986) and the termination of federal housing assistance programs, we are faced with the prospect of continued deterioration of downtown neighborhoods. Owning and for many even renting a home is receding as an achievable dream.

What has brought us to this crisis in affordability?
How can we learn from past successes and failures?

Historically, suburbs have protected community structure and increased their value through zoned scarcity, while cities have systematically destroyed their urban villages by overbuilding. Following World War II, architects saw the housing solution in large isolated megastructures which produced "Pruit Igoe" environments all over the world. Putting thousands of people into high-rise filing cabinets creates inevitable social problems. The inclination of developers is to build to maximum density to obtain maximum yield on their investment. However, to the degree that land is developed beyond the limitations set by environmental factors and human needs, the cost to the community is great and there is a point of diminishing return to the developer.

Only luxury high-rises can justify the expense of replicating the necessary amenities of lower density communities, such as gardens, courtyards, and controllable clusters of housing units. William Levitt is the merchant builder of more single-family houses than anyone in history. Levittowns and Levitshahrs have been built in the United States, Iran, Nigeria, and Venezuela. The keys to his success have been productivity, volume, and community planning. He has proven that the excess profits expected by builders of high-density high-rises are unconscionable. Levitt tacked on a modest 5 to 7 percent profit, which kept his housing affordable for the mass market. The final significant ingredient in his success formula was sophisticated planning of community facilities. Shopping, schools, churches, water supplies, disposal systems, and industrial facilities addressed human needs. Government officials, private-sector leaders, and many professionals endlessly argue that there is inadequate land in urban areas. This is not true. Even in New York City there are vast tracts of abandoned buildings and open spaces.

On October 31, 1982, ground was broken for the first NEHEMIAH home—a three-bedroom, brick townhouse in the Brownsville section of Brooklyn, New York. It sold for $39,000. National attention has focused on the co-operative effort of local churches, community organizers, and the City of New York to build affordable housing without federal assistance under the NEHEMIAH PLAN (named after the Old Testament prophet who rebuilt Jerusalem) in an area so devastated it seemed doubtful that even one house could be sold. Using high-volume techniques forged forty years ago on Long Island by William Levitt, the NEHEMIAH homes are built on large tracts of cleared, city-owned land—in effect, creating suburbs within the city. Efficiency and economy result from production quantity, for example, foundations are poured for a whole city block of houses at one time. The houses themselves are a snug 18 feet wide by 32 feet deep with 1,150 square feet of living space. Each has a 40-foot front yard and a 45-foot backyard plus a full basement. A savings of $6,000 per house was realized by convincing skeptical city officials that instead of a separate street cut for each house to bring in sewer and water lines, one cut could be made for all twenty-eight homes. Connector lines are run under the houses from one end of the block to the other. Soft costs (i.e., legal, engineering, and financing) were reduced from 35 percent for typical conventional projects to 6 percent, or $3,500 per house. The architect receives $204 for each house built. The developer fee is a modest $1,000 per house. Construction financing comes from a $12 million no-interest revolving loan fund contributed by the thirty-six congregations that joined together to form East Brooklyn Churches. To further reduce the cost of the $40,000-$45,000 two- and three-bedroom homes, a $10,000 house loan, in effect a second mortgage, is provided by the city, to be repaid when the house is sold. The city also abates property taxes for twenty years, and the State of New York Mortgage Finance Agency provides buyers with below market rate mortgages. To date NEHEMIAH has been able to deliver 1,250 houses and 250 more are under construction. There are 5,300 names on the waiting list. The maverick developer, I. D. Robbins, contends that there are 30,000 acres of developable land in New York, and that if city officials made sites available, NEHEMIAH could build 2,000 units of affordable housing every year. However, city officials say large tracts of developable land are scarce. The juggernaut continues.

Today, six years after the first residents moved into the houses in Brownsville, streets such as Christopher Avenue and Sachman Street are lined with colorful front yards landscaped with shrubs and flowers. Nearly every homeowner has invested in the security of wrought iron window and door guards. The backyards are a reflection of each owner's version of home. The NEHEMIAH PLAN has put into effect ideas long advocated by I. D. Robbins, a civic activist and construction executive who published his views in a *New York Daily News* column for several years. He believes in low densities and home ownership as the best approach to the reconstruction of deteriorated urban areas; the NEHEMIAH homes are built at twenty-four units per acre, socially much preferable to the one hundred families per acre density, or greater, common to city living. Large cities work best when they are made up of groups of small communities that protect their residents. Approximately one hundred families form a social unit called a neighborhood. Lack of defined scale leads to environments that inhibit the fulfillment of human needs. Families with children should be provided with private yards. In NEHEMIAH homes, mothers can watch their children playing in the backyard through the living room picture window (*New York Times*, May 1, 1983 and September 27, 1987).

As low as the density of NEHEMIAH is in comparison to the typical urban multi-family density, the density chosen by another successful New York City developer, Edward Logue of the South Bronx Development Organization, is much less. The first ninety detached factory-built Charlotte Gardens houses are sited on plots of 6,500 square feet, or about six units to the acre, in the East Crotona Park section of the South Bronx.

These are healthy, cost-effective examples of affordable urban housing accomplished in today's economy. At the other extreme are the sterile, energy-inefficient, out-of-scale and uncontrollable megastructures which have been espoused to meet urban affordable housing needs historically.

Father Panik Village in Bridgeport, Connecticut is one of the earliest projects built as part of America's public housing program. Today, it is the oldest and most seriously deteriorated. Perhaps its greatest liability is its vast size—approximately 1,100 units in forty-six buildings, laid out in monotonous rows. As rental housing, it gives its residents little control over their environment. It has uncontrolled vehicular access, which has destroyed playgrounds and grassy areas and contributed to its high crime rate. Inefficient unit layouts, a poor site plan, high density, and unmaintained buildings conspired to be a recipe for disaster.

Across the street from Father Panik is a twenty-four unit co-op that my office designed under Section 221 D-e over twenty-three years ago. Six stucco three-story buildings in soft pastels are clustered together to form an enclave for twenty-four families. The four-bedroom townhouses have fenced-in backyards. Parking areas, clustered at the perimeter, are located inside a gated fence for security. At the center of the development is a landscaped courtyard which functions as a common play area and social court. Children need the physical and psychological security and controlled small scale that is impossible to achieve in an environment of depersonalization, large buildings, uncontrolled streets, and public spaces. Co-operative ownership has given the residents of Marionville a sense of pride in their homes and control over their environment. Twenty-three years later, trees and shrubs are mature, and the community as vital as ever—while across the street a wasteland is being demolished, and Father Panik's residents relocated, at a cost of $36 million for the first phase, and at an even greater psychological cost to countless families.

While limitations are placed on housing in suburban communities, adjacent cities are burdened to provide that housing for the region's workforce. There are cultural fears and prejudice at work that take the form of no growth zoning and public outrage at any change that might threaten the character of their neighborhoods. As political pressure to preserve "quality of life" intensifies, the responsibility of a housing solution is passed down the line.

In 1966 the mayor of Stamford, Connecticut, Thomas Mayers, formulated a plan to house Stamford's needier residents, mostly African Americans and Puerto Ricans, in garden apartments "scattered around the city from its gritty core to its leafier edges." (*New York Times* 1989). The plan was in keeping with Stamford's disillusionment with high-density, high-rise public housing. One night the mayor came home to find a cavalcade of cars outside his house, horns blaring, American flags flying and hand painted signs reading, "Throw out scatter-site housing and Tom Mayers with it." Within a year, Mr. Mayers was defeated for a third term, and his low-income housing plan was dead—drowned out by the same type of vociferous opposition that would lead Yonkers into federal court twenty years later. No law suit has ever charged Stamford with housing discrimination. Yet, Stamford and Yonkers have a lot in common. Stamford, with 106,000 people in thirty-seven square miles, has slightly more than half the population of Yonkers in twice the area. Both sprang from industrial bases and are surrounded by suburban neighborhoods. Both have a minority population of 18 percent. Like most other cities, Yonkers and Stamford have shouldered more than their share of social costs including low- and moderate-income housing. With 23 percent of the Westchester County population, Yonkers has 43 percent of its subsidized housing. Stamford, with 32 percent of the lower Fairfield County population, has 58 percent of its subsidized housing. Recently however, the debate has moved to housing not only the poor, but the sons and daughters of the middle class and town employees, whose incomes cannot match the soaring land costs of Fairfield and Westchester Counties.

The term "affordable housing" has replaced the term "low- or moderate-income housing." Where neighborhoods once organized to battle subsidized projects, they now use zoning laws and public hearings to block privately built condominiums. In Stamford, the lopsided economic distribution in the 1980 Census swung from a median household income of

$10,889 in the South End to $41,957 in Northern Stamford. The Housing Authority recently turned down a 36,000 square foot housing site because the cost of the land at $1.7 million exceeded their $1.6 million grant. Although Stamford has always prided itself on providing social diversity at a manageable scale, many residents see it in danger of being split, between the rich and the poor—with the middle class pushed out. Surging real estate prices in traditional, ethnic working-class neighborhoods are driving out young families. In a downtown neighborhood, a two-bedroom condominium sells for $219,000. Throughout the city, the average house price exceeds $300,000. Inflating housing costs have economic as well as social ramifications. Corporations, attracted to Stamford during the urban-renewal of the 1970s, are relocating to markets where their middle-level employees will be able to afford to live. This pattern is being repeated throughout the New York metropolitan region. Terry Tondro, a law professor at the University of Connecticut and a member of the Governor's Blue Ribbon Commission on Housing, says, "A large part of the problem is the boundary line, the problem of distribution not within a community, but among communities."

What changes are needed to deal with the affordable housing crisis in many U.S. cities today?

How can public participation be more effective?

In 1975, the New Jersey Supreme Court ruled that each community in a region had an obligation to share the burden for low- and moderate-income housing. As towns in growth areas of central New Jersey adopt affordable housing plans, statewide patterns of future residential development are taking shape. Based on 52,000 approved new housing units, both market rate and fair share, townhouses, a less costly form of construction, will account for a greater share of total housing production (approximately 40 percent) according to Donald Opalsky, director of New Jersey's Council on Affordable Housing.

In higher-land-cost areas, a larger share of that production will be devoted to smaller suburban working households with incomes slightly below area-wide medians. The Fair Housing Act of 1985 allowed towns to transfer out up to 50 percent of their fair share obligations to needier towns in the form of cash payments. The Council on Affordable Housing was established to review town proposals for meeting their total mathematically determined fair share requirement. Because of the transfer of money from prosperous to lower-income communities under Regional Contribution Agreements, housing will be increased and improved in the poorer areas as well. Rather than spreading new construction further out into low-cost areas, where single-family detached houses can be built for the mass market, the new production will be concentrated on more developed higher-land-cost areas, where townhouse construction is by nature less expensive, and can be delivered to a mass market. As of January 1, 1989, just under 10,000 new units of lower income (i.e., Mt. Laurel) or fair share housing had been approved in New Jersey. The bulk of these are 80–20 mixed income developments, in which builders provide one low-income unit for every four at market rate. Higher density zoning is what allows builders to subsidize these lower-income buyers. New Jersey's vast diversity of communities and housing needs made it appropriate to use a wide spectrum of mechanisms to fulfill fair share housing obligations. For example, the Council worked out a formula to give the town of Warren a requirement of 367 affordable housing units. By Regional Contribution Agreement, Warren agreed to pay New Brunswick $4.3 million to take over half of these units. Warren raised this money by charging developers for more favorable, higher density zoning on their land! Most of the money came from one development company that paid $3 million to have a 365-acre site rezoned from one and a half to one acre (i.e., one house per acre).

Hovnanian Enterprises, based in Red Bank, New Jersey, is the second largest attached-housing builder in the United States. It has already completed 2,500 units in Mt. Laurel developments for residents with 50 to 80 percent median incomes. Bonus density allows the company to meet the 4:1 ratio market rate, the low/moderate income formula. At four units per acre, Hovnanian can achieve a 5 to 10 percent set aside, but at fourteen units per acre, the 4:1 formula can be met and exceeded. Low- and moderate-income housing is integrated with market rate throughout Hovnanian's developments. A typical Mt. Laurel development requires 10 percent downpayment and sales are $29,000–$59,000 for the low- and moderate-income units—$95,000–$145,000 for market rate units. Mt. Laurel buyers are typically twenty to thirty-five year old nurses, teachers, or policemen. Low- and moderate-income housing is deed-restricted for twenty years and owners can only participate in appreciation up to the CPI (Consumer Price Index).

Hovnanian's success begins with its sites. It builds along major growth corridors within easy reach of metro area markets. Its townhouses and towncomplexes (townhouses piggybacked over flats) are visually attractive with pitched roofs, turned gables, and dormer windows to vary the roofline. Hovnanian uses construction efficiencies by building ten unit batches on a concrete pad. However, it mixes brick facades with clapboard in the same building and adds shutters, copper roofs on bay windows, and entry detailing that give real curb-appeal. Layouts are standardized, and a computerized cost accounting system monitors each ten-unit building on each project regarding framing, roofing, and siding right through to the finished houses.

Hovnanian Enterprises is currently building 1,200 units in downtown Newark, on an urban site so challenging that when the city put out a bid for proposals, it was the only developer to answer. The community has been presold at $85,000–$95,000 for the two- and three-bedroom market rate townhouses. There is a bonus density in exchange for 10 percent low-income and 10 percent moderate-income units. The development cost, selling prices and loss incurred for the low- and moderate-income housing is as follows:

	Average Cost	Sales	Loss
10% Low-income 120 units	$57,500	$30,000	$27,500
10% Moderate-income 120 units	$57,500	$44,000	$13,500

At an average loss of $20,500 per unit for low- and moderate-income units, the total loss is $4,920,000. Spread over the market rate units, this loss adds roughly $5,000 per unit to their cost! The low/moderate-income units are subsidized by the market rate units, and the project is made economically feasible by the density bonus.

The landmark Mount Laurel ruling has not been cloned by other states, because housing is a local issue that must be solved by each state and community in its own way. Nevertheless, Mt. Laurel has caught the attention of the nation, and dramatized not only the crisis of affordability but the decentralization and shifting of power from the federal government to the states.

Connecticut has begun a voluntary program that commits towns in a region to enter joint housing efforts in return for additional funds for transportation and environmental protection. Although a majority of towns have jumped on the bandwagon, the program was blocked in lower Fairfield county when three towns, including two Stamford neighbors—New Canaan and Darien—refused to participate. One problem Connecticut has is the lack of statutory tools to convince cities and towns to meet local housing needs.

In Massachusetts, on the other hand, the threat of the stick is always in the background. Actually, the Bay State has two sticks. The first, Executive Order 215, issued by the governor's office in 1981, states that a municipality has a responsibility to assure a broad range of housing availability. The order links state discretionary funding to community compliance. Only six communities have had funds withheld. The other stick, a state law referred to as "the anti-snob ordinance" stipulates that if less than 10 percent of a municipality's housing stock meets local needs for low-income, elderly, and mentally retarded people, then a developer who has been rejected for such a project can appeal to the state. A state panel then brings the various people to the table and makes the determination. Over 11,000 housing units have been built under this law.

Recently, states are taking a more deliberate approach and planning for long-term involvement in housing provisions. They are involving local governments, the private sector, and nonprofit groups in the formation of housing task forces, partnerships, and programs to provide incentives for the construction of lower-cost housing.

In the private sector, there is a grassroots movement poised to shape American housing policy for the next decade or more. It has no leader. It's made up of local businessmen, church groups, home-builders, social workers, mortgage lenders, consumer advocates, and a wide assortment of citizen volunteers. Housing problems are first and foremost local issues requiring local solutions, local money and local leadership. We must do it on our own now because the federal deficit will no longer permit the government to subsidize renters and first-time buyers.

That's the challenge being taken up by the affordability movement. A new generation of sophisticated nonprofit housing developers is taking charge, putting dollars from bankers, local charities, corporations and government agencies to work in bricks and mortar. They know how to move the local power structure because they are part of it.

Two nonprofit groups that have emerged from this "new wave" as important models for producing low- and moderate-income housing are located in San Francisco. The Bay Area Residential Investment and Development Group (BRIDGE), founded in 1983, is one of the few nonprofit housing developers operating on a regional scale, and one of the leading nonprofit developers in the United States. Donald Turner, president of BRIDGE, knows the art of the deal. As a case in point, let's analyze Magnolia Plaza, a 124-unit complex in South San Francisco, one of fifteen BRIDGE projects under construction with nonprofit and for-profit builders. First, BRIDGE bought the property from the school district. Then, it convinced the city to buy the property and lease it back to BRIDGE. That relieved a lot of up-front expenditure. Tax-exempt mortgage revenue bonds issued by the City of South San Francisco helped reduce the cost of financing Magnolia Plaza. The 15 to 20 percent developer profit "thrown back into the deal" by BRIDGE also lowered project cost (and ultimately rental and ownership payments). Half of the project's apartments qualified as affordable at $450 per month rent. But that was still too high, so BRIDGE provided tax credits, which were sold to limited-partner investors, with proceeds of the sale used for equity capital. The tax credits dropped the rent another $80 and BRIDGE produced sixty-two more affordable units to meet the critical housing shortage in the Bay Area. BRIDGE converts land development profits into afford-ability. A key element in the company's success has been its high stan-dard of design and construction, which helps make Bay Area communi-ties amenable to granting land use concessions and density waivers for affordable housing. BRIDGE takes raw land through the design and re-zoning process and creates value, which it uses to pay its expenses and subsidize the rental or ownership costs of its projects. Since 1983, BRIDGE has participated in the development of over 3,000 housing units valued at $240 million. About 40 percent of these are affordable to households with incomes between $12,000 and $25,000.

The Low-Income Housing Fund (LIHF) is an example of a new kind of financial intermediary designed to meet the special needs of commu-nity-based developers of low-income housing. Its work is currently di-vided among four programs:

1. *The Revolving Loan Fund*—provides flexible financing at below-market rates.

2. *Mortgage Brokering Program*—below-market-rate loans from other lenders on behalf of nonprofit housing developers—negotiated and packaged by LIHF.

3. *Mortgage Guarantee Program*—encourages private institutions to invest in low-income housing projects.

4. *Interest Rate Subsidy Program*—supported by social investors willing to accept a below-market return. The difference between the investments market rate of return and that accepted by the social investor is used as a subsidy to lower rent and ownership payments.

LIHF is also involved in a pilot program with the Federal National Mortgage Association ("Fannie Mae") to develop a secondary market for small low-income housing developers. If Fannie Mae is willing to buy loans, LIHF believes many more conventional lenders will be at-tracted to low-income housing. Lenders are already actively seeking ways to pump funds into houses targeted to first-time buyers, low-in-come renters, and the homeless. The Community Reinvestment Act prods lenders to put dollars back into their local markets. There is a growing recognition that banks can help create affordability, with spe-cial low downpayments and rehabilitation loans for example, and help their business development at the same time.

There are new rules to the housing game emphasizing sharing of fi-nancial contributions and recycling of funds. The cardinal rule of pri-vate-public partnership is: *Nobody participates or receives benefits who hasn't put something into the pot.* If a local city council wants to provide low-downpayment, low-cost housing for its school teachers and younger residents, it has to be prepared to grant zoning exceptions for higher density units, cut regulatory tape, and revise antiquated code restrictions. That can be a tough hurdle, but it's happening.

HUD's Joint Venture for Affordable Housing (JVAH) links public- and private-sector groups who share a commitment to creating more affordable housing. These activities include:

- identifying innovations in site planning, site development, building, and processing that can reduce the cost of housing;
- demonstrating these innovative techniques throughout the country in developments carried out by local builders, officials, and organizations;
- identifying federal, state, and local regulations—such as building codes, zoning regulations, and processing procedures—that discourage or prevent use of innovations; and
- providing information to builders and government officials on possible improvements and the resultant cost savings.

Homes are being built on JVAH demonstration sites across the country at savings of up to 30 percent over comparable homes.

The target of their efforts are the disenfranchised nurses, teachers, firefighters, city and state employees, librarians, retail workers, and service professionals who are often in their twenties and thirties and the focus of the home ownership struggle.

A 403-acre planned community in Fort Collins, Colorado, will include apartments, patio homes, and townhouses, as well as commercial and high tech businesses. Due to JVAH involvement, Fort Collins officials are working with a local developer on site development, innovative site planning, and building methods. The performance-based zoning regulations in Fort Collins are among the most progressive in the country. The "Land Development Guidance System," formulated for this city of 82,000 in 1979, comes closest of all to the pure form of flexible zoning. Property owners may choose this approach as an alternative to standard zoning. The ordinance spells out absolute criteria (such as neighborhood compatibility) that must be met, and relative criteria (such as location near a transit line) for which points are awarded. If all absolute criteria are satisfied and enough points are earned, the project is approved. Projects can be modified and/or amenities offered to increase point scores.

In Stephenville, Texas, another JVAH demonstration development located near a regional shopping center features manufactured housing placed on permanent foundations. The city council approved special zoning variances to permit single-section manufactured housing to be set up on lots 44 × 100 feet. Current standards require a minimum of 60 × 100 feet. Another variance permits houses to be placed five feet from the property line to allow more open space on the smaller lots.

Salinas, California, was able to reduce processing time from three months to three weeks on single projects. For larger developments, the usual six to nine months period has been cut in half.

Cooperation between city and builder in Everett, Washington, saved an average of $10,047 per house on a detached single family project called SUNRIDGE. Prices were kept down by using PVC piping for water supply, sanitary sewers, and storm drains, and by using narrower 22-foot streets, rolled curbs and gutters, value engineered framing, and an innovative site plan that placed homes on lots as small as 4,500 square feet compared to Everett's minimum lot of 7,200 square feet.

A major reason for the high cost of new construction is antiquated building and materials requirements. For example, an Everett regulation stated that manholes have to be installed every 300 feet. However, that law was written before new equipment was available to clean a sewer for half a mile (2,640 feet) between manholes. Another old code, written before most fire trucks were equipped with a reverse gear, was intended to allow them to make a U-turn. With modern trucks, cul-de-sacs can be smaller, allowing more homes per lot.

Affordable housing can be built by just chipping away at costs. The JVAH has documented cost savings from 2 percent to 30 percent per unit compared to similar homes in twenty-seven cities and communities in twenty-four states. The average savings is $7,000 per unit. Increased density represented the greatest cost saving.

Cluster housing and zero lot line are two land planning innovations that have had a major impact on housing affordability. Clustering conserves land and energy by concentrating dwellings in a particular area of the site. A cluster plan usually maintains the overall density permitted by zoning, while permitting an increase in net density in exchange for open space that is protected by a cluster ordinance. Reminiscent of the New England village center, the cluster plan grows out of the land, concentrating the housing on the most suitable areas of the site. Soil limitations, drainage, a steep slope, wetlands, or a site amenity can easily be accommodated when a cluster rather than a grid concept is chosen. Clustering also allows flexibility in lot size, frontage, and set-back requirements. The engineered plan can save money in infrastructure cost and result in less environmental impact. For these reasons, cluster housing has been well received by most communities.

The zero lot line concept can accommodate up to nine dwellings per acre depending on the size of the houses. Rather than being located in the center of a lot with two side yards, each house is built at or near the property line on one side of a long, narrow lot. There are no windows (except for clerestories) on the zero lot line side, while there is a long yard on the other side. A promising variation, the Z-lot, lays out the lot and the house at an angle to the street rather than perpendicular to it. The front of the house and a portion of the side are visible from the street. The architect can avoid monotonous repetition of garage doors and give variety to the streetscape. In a wide-shallow development, lot widths remain at the traditional 55 feet to 70 feet, but hard costs are decreased by making lots shallow (55 feet to 70 feet rather than 100 feet). A density of seven units per acre can be achieved with the wide-shallow plan that offers the image of a traditional single family home from the street. However, wider lots do add proportionately to site development costs, that is, street, utilities, and landscaping.

Our office has come up with what we call the Northeast's answer to the zero lot line. It adapts well to uneven topography and can be built at two stories without problems of privacy or blocking sunlight. With the FAN PLAN small lots fan out in clusters of four. Two have 60-foot street frontage and are separated by an entry court. Two lots are to the rear (or play lots). Connecting yards are woven in a zipper pattern. An internal court eliminates the row housing look. The FAN PLAN achieves efficient lot utilization (up to seven units per acre), opens up the floor plan with glass on all four sides and shortens the street, thus reducing infrastructure cost by $1,200–$1,500 per house. Land costs can be reduced by $15,000–$20,000 per unit without compromising living space.

If we are going to ask homeowners to live closer to their neighbors, to share walls, lawns, courtyards, and zero lot lines, we must design housing that respects their privacy and lifestyle needs.

Design can be a major cost containment factor through site plan flexibility and value engineered interior space. Good affordable housing is designed to make small spaces *live big*. Fortunately, demographics is on our side—with a prevalence of one- and two-person households and smaller families. How far can architects go in breaking the residential size barrier to create affordable housing for urbanites? Like Honda, with its CRX model automobile, the architect must create an exciting product in a smaller, less expensive package. It has been said that an architect who designs this housing must become a master of the cubic foot. A California architect, Donald MacDonald, evaluated every space needed in a basic home, reduced it to a minimum, and then established different levels of privacy.

In developing STARTER HOME, he determined the optimum footprint to be 20 × 200 feet square, which relates to a standard 25-foot wide lot in San Francisco. The housing was designed to be attached with two stories plus a loft to maximize vertical space and provide separate privacy areas. The floor plans included a one bedroom plus loft with a garage beneath at 600 square feet, or a two bedroom unit plus loft without a garage. The houses have private backyards, and were built slab-on-grade. Plywood siding and plastic pipe were used for economy of construction.

Although housing has been designed to function at under 500 square feet, for long-term livability 600 square feet allows for a separate bedroom which is psychologically more satisfying. The cost of building a bedroom is insignificant. It is kitchens and bathrooms with their plumbing and fixtures that do the most to drive up the cost of a house.

My office has designed a stacked fourplex with floorplans of 600–800 square feet and 1,100–1,2000 square feet using the construction efficiency of back-to-back units. The fourplex can eliminate stairs on hilly sites. There are garages under for the lower flats and garages at grade on the uphill side for the upper flats. To compensate for smaller square footage, there are value-added features such as volume space, 9- and 10-foot ceilings, wrap around clerestory and oversized windows, cantilevered bays, and European balconies. We stress value engineering which means: making design flexible, keeping circulation space at 6 to 7 percent, standardizing materials, and giving unfinished bonus spaces.

Affordability should not be used as an excuse to build basic boxes without architectural character and lacking in memory features. For example, 9-foot ceilings, at an additional $1.50 per square foot, stretch small spaces and give them a touch of elegance. Builders can buy a whirlpool tub for as little as $450, which goes a long way towards satisfying lifestyle needs. Interior space must work overtime with dual function rooms and built-in features. To compensate for downsizing, volume should be increased with cathedral and higher flat ceilings allowing for storage space and lofts. Larger windows will bring the outdoors in and dramatize interiors.

Architects working with builders are rejuvenating over existing stock of older buildings. Old warehouses and mills, railroad stations, factories, and even silos are being adapted for reuse as housing. This represents one solution to the housing problem that also solves the urban problem of decay and disuse.

Every city and mature suburb has small vacant, "skipped-over" parcels of land in otherwise fully developed areas. Some of this land may be located in the inner city and be publicly owned as a result of tax default, urban renewal, or other public intervention. A larger proportion is privately owned and may be located in fully developed suburbs. Infill housing utilizes this available land. Successful infill development makes better use of a community's infrastructure, increases its tax base, and contributes to its overall vitality. Historically, infill has been linked directly to the revitalization of urban neighborhoods. Today, an increased demand for infill has been created by changing demographics and the urbanization of the suburbs. Throughout the country, visionary developers and talented architects are taking on the challenge of infill sites. They are overcoming the constraints of zoning, topography, and cost, and are producing imaginative, neighborly, livable housing.

In 1981, affordable ownership housing in the City of New Haven, Connecticut, was severely restricted. Over 50 percent of housing demand was in the $30,000 to $72,000 range. However, less than 10 percent of residential production met this market need. The wide gap between affordability and cost of existing inventory left few opportunities within the purchasing power of young families and one- or two-person households.

It was in this environment that New Haven's Redevelopment Agency announced a design competition for a four and a half acre stretch of land along the Quinnipiac River in Fair Haven, a section of the city settled in the seventeenth century.

We recognized the potential of this site because of (a) its waterfront location, (b) its quaint historic environment—an enclave within the city, and (c) the role it might play in the area's revitalization.

Our design submission was based on a three-pronged strategy: (1) a design "friendly" to the buildings in this historic neighborhood, (2) a skillful high-density solution with appealing residential forms that would meet market demand for affordability, and (3) a $150,000 developer contribution as an incentive to the city for a riverside park it had promised as a key amenity of this project.

Winning the competition gave us the right to buy the land for $76,000. The reduced land cost, combined with the high density, allowed Riverfront Development to produce upscale housing at an affordable price.

Zoning allowed a density of twenty units per acre or eighty-eight units. The townhouse/flat mix included three-story flats reminiscent of the historic New Haven "triple decker" and townhouses over flats.

Because it was an urban infill site awarded by the Redevelopment Agency, plans had to be in keeping with the goals for the revitalization of the Fair Haven Renewal Area and, in particular, the Quinnipiac Riverfront. Since the site was also located in the Quinnipiac River Historic District, separate approvals were needed from the Historic District Commission and the State Historic Preservation Office. To integrate Riverplace with its historic neighborhood, we chose a distinctive Victorian architecture in a stick style with balconies, bay windows, dormers, tall narrow windows with ornamentation, scalloped shingles, eave brackets, hand-built stair rails, and white picket fences. Inside, the quality feeling is reinforced with recessed lighting, traditional detailing, fireplaces, greenhouse windows, and French doors. Riverplace Condominium Development was a response to the city's affordable housing shortage. Presales opened in June 1984 at $65,000–$85,000. The attractiveness and affordability of the units created a very successful sales pace of ten units per month. Construction cost averaged approximately $42 per square foot. The market has been first-time buyers, singles, and young professional couples who enjoy the convenient access to shopping, churches, restaurants, employment, and public transportation. Riverplace has been a catalyst for intense development interest along the riverfront. By

1986, proposals had been presented that would bring the number of new housing units in Fair Haven to 600. The banks of the Quinnipiac River and the two-mile-square community of Fair Haven have come alive once again.

Demographics may be the strongest force in determining the future course of construction. As our population grows dramatically older, housing choice for the elderly has become a pressing issue. Many want to continue living in familiar surroundings, close to friends, stores, doctors, and churches. We have designed a prototype that will fit on a half acre of vacant land in a city or built-up suburban location. It offers the independence and security of affordable congregate living. Designed to look like a traditional single-family house with porch, gables, and dormers, it has a common parlor or game area, living room, dining room, kitchen, and two handicapped accessible baths, each with a separate shower and tub. There are ten bedrooms, each with a private half bath. One of these can be used for a housekeeper. All of this is on one level, approximately 2,700 square feet with attic storage. The same affordable concept of shared living can be applied to other age groups.

Development standards for affordable housing are changing. Communities are using flexible regulatory techniques such as Planned Unit Developments and performance zoning to ease density requirements, reduce minimum lot size, update antiquated building codes, and expedite processing. They are putting the roof on housing costs with accessory apartments, shared living alternatives, adaptive reuse, and imaginative infill developments.

What makes the new grassroots affordibility movement particularly significant is its clear impact on federal housing policy. The major pieces of legislation now being written on Capitol Hill emphasize local public-private partnerships as the future for housing.

What can you do?

- Learn more about housing costs and why prices are high.
- Talk to local housing professionals to learn their plans and problems.
- Attend local planning board meetings or legislative sessions.
- Get involved in citizen action to change cumbersome regulations and produce more affordable housing.

By insisting on design at the appropriate scale with provision for privacy, security, and individuality, and becoming involved in the housing process, we can all contribute to healthy, responsive communities, the existing ones and those of tomorrow!

3

THE LOCAL INITIATIVES SUPPORT CORPORATION'S APPROACH

PAUL S. GROGAN

As the 1980s draw to a close, America is rediscovering the serious problem of urban poverty and its alarming associated ills, including the dwindling availability of decent low-income neighborhoods and the underclass phenomenon. My purpose today is not to document in any detail the scope of these problems. Instead, I want to talk about the kinds of grassroots institutions that low-income communities throughout the United States are forming to combat these problems. While they are still relatively unknown, these institutions are quietly becoming a primary force nationwide for stabilizing low-income communities and fighting poverty. They are most often called Community Development Corporations, or CDCs.

THE EMERGENCE OF CDCs

CDCs are nonprofit development corporations that are accountable to the communities in which they operate. The ultimate mission for CDCs is to reduce poverty, stabilize distressed or declining neighborhoods, and gain economic power for their communities. Development activity is thus not just an end to its own right, but also a tool for achieving this broader mission.

A 1991 nationwide survey by the National Congress for Community Economic Development (NCCED) indicates that 2,000 CDCs have completed at least some housing, commercial, or business enterprise development activity. Housing development is the most common activity of

CDCs (88 percent of the 1,160 responding to the NCCED survey), followed by business enterprise development (25 percent), and commercial and industrial development (25 percent). Importantly, most CDCs also undertake other related activities in concert with direct development: 70 percent pursue community organizing or advocacy; 75 percent provide tenant and homeowner counseling and housing for the homeless; and more than 60 percent offer emergency food assistance, job training and placement, child care, youth programs, crime prevention, and other social services.

The CDCs' importance as a community institution dedicated to stabilizing low-income communities is particularly relevant in the context of recent evidence of the increasing intensification of poverty in inner cities. William Julius Wilson, perhaps the most widely known and respected analyst of the underclass phenomenon, states that:

The significance of changes embodied in the social transformation of the inner city is perhaps best captured by the concepts *concentration effects* and *social buffer*. The former refers to the constraints and opportunities associated with living in a neighborhood in which the population is overwhelmingly socially disadvantaged—constraints and opportunities that include the kinds of ecological niches that the residents of these communities occupy in terms of access to jobs, availability of marriageable partners, and exposure to conventional role models. The latter refers to the presence of a sufficient number of working and middle class professional families to absorb the shock or cushion the effect of uneven economic growth and periodic recessions on inner city neighborhoods. The basic thesis is not that ghetto culture went unchecked following the removal of higher income families in the inner city, but that the removal of these families made it more difficult to sustain the basic institutions in the inner city (including churches, stores, schools, recreational facilities, etc.) in the face of prolonged joblessness. And as the basic institutions declined, the social organization of inner city neighborhoods (defined here to include a sense of community, positive neighborhood identification, and explicit norms and sanctions against aberrant behavior) likewise declined. Indeed, the social organization of any neighborhood depends in large measure on the viability of social institutions in that neighborhood.[1]

There are two clear ways to relieve this increasing problem: to move the poor out of their present communities, or to make those communities stable, attractive places for working- and middle-class people to live without displacing the poor. Although low-income people should certainly have the legal right to live wherever they choose, any concerted attempt to move poor people to middle-class areas would face strong resistance from poor and middle-income areas alike, would require massive ongoing public subsidies, and would cause the abandonment of inner-city neighborhoods. Stabilizing distressed low-income areas is the more workable answer to the problems that Wilson describes. Restoring institutions—including CDCs and the other institutions that CDCs attract and support—is essential to healthy communities.

CDCs are not a new phenomenon, but only recently have they become widespread. The first CDCs drew attention in the late 1960s and the early 1970s as attractive development vehicles because of their commitment and sensitivity to community needs in selecting, structuring, and implementing projects. In very real terms, CDCs have enabled low-income community residents to take direct control over whether and how development takes place in their neighborhoods. Absent CDC involvement, many low-income neighborhoods saw no development activity at all. CDCs have enabled low-income community residents to define the scope, design, and location of proposed ventures, as well as to participate in the political process through which many development decisions are made.

Federal funding cutbacks in the 1980s focused more attention on CDCs and their role as developers, especially of low-income housing, has grown more prominent. Part of this prominence is attributable to the withdrawal of profit-motivated developers as federal programs were cut back; indeed, CDCs are in many cities the only developers working in low-income neighborhoods. But, CDCs have not simply been good survivors of federal subsidy cutbacks; their number and sophistication actually multiplied in the 1980s.

Several factors explain this growth:

- First, it has been broadly recognized that community advocacy and human development activities, while necessary, are insufficient by themselves to stabilize and empower communities, relieve poverty, or re-establish an institutional presence in these communities. Direct physical development is essential, especially to meet the rapidly rising need for decent and affordable housing. Since they cannot depend on the profit-motivated sector to undertake development for them, many communities have taken on the responsibility for development themselves.

- Second, the ability of CDCs to work collaboratively with a wide range of public- and private-sector institutions has grown dramatically. CDCs have been earning their place at the negotiating table with mayors, bankers, and profit-motivated developers by contributing tenacity, a respected voice for their neighborhoods, and growing technical sophistication. These are very valuable assets in rebuilding communities.

- Third, as CDCs have become more widespread and successful, their activities have become far more visible. So as churches, social service agencies, neighborhood activists, city and state governments, local foundations, and others concerned with distressed low-income communities have searched for new solutions, the CDC model has been much easier to identify, and has been perceived more often as legitimate and effective.

- Fourth, the technical and financial support available to CDCs has grown substantially over the past several years, enabling more CDCs to get started and undertake more complex projects. The advent of nonprofit "intermediaries," such as Local Initiatives Support Corporation, the Enterprise Foundation, and the Neighborhood Reinvestment Corporation, has also helped to expand CDC resources.

The interest CDCs have sparked arises not solely from their increasing number and skills in a period of federal retrenchment. Indeed, CDCs are worth encouraging because of the unique combination of resources they bring to low-income community development.

CDCs have strong community ties, a working knowledge of community housing needs, markets, and opportunities, and the ability to craft flexible and effective programs that respond to these circumstances. The history of the public housing, subsidized housing, and urban renewal programs demonstrated that "top down" or "imported" redevelopment does not work well in poor neighborhoods. These approaches are comparatively costly, and the failure rate is relatively high. Numerous low-income housing projects have failed—even with the best intentioned sponsors, and despite increasing demand. Many failed because the developers, owners, and managers lacked the will, capacity, control, and staying power to make them work. Most projects that succeed work because the developers, owners, and managers have strong ties and roots in the community. And, they and the residents have a clear commitment to maintaining their homes, controlling the environment, and making the community a better place for the next generation. CDCs have roots and a clear commitment, and are more likely to motivate residents to share these values.

CDCs undertake individual development projects within the context of an overall neighborhood preservation strategy. Developing successful projects does not ensure the success of the redevelopment process. Since there are insufficient resources to meet all neighborhood needs, achieving revitalization requires designing and implementing a strategy to secure and deploy project resources in a way that maximizes impact. Private developers are not in the community redevelopment business. Many of the projects that profit-motivated developers consider least attractive—projects that are too small, too risky, insufficiently profitable, and located in areas that are too distressed—are often the most important to community renewal. The public sector can devise strategies, but, in most cases, it cannot implement them. CDCs are uniquely suited to play the roles these institutions will not or cannot.

CDCs use projects to change people's perceptions and behavior. Neighborhood disinvestment is a psychic as well as a behavioral phenomenon, and the two are closely tied. When significant numbers of residents lack pride and hope, the individuals, businesses, and public institutions with resources are reluctant to invest. The process of community deterioration feeds on itself. But, CDCs are proving that this process is reversible. Once project success is demonstrated *and* resident perceptions appear more positive, potential investors perceive reduced risks and greater opportunities. When this happens, behavior changes and reinvestment begins—the redevelopment process gains momentum and starts to become self-fueling. More people are served and have greater opportunities. The community becomes more stable and more attractive to working- and middle-class people as well as the poor. Because CDCs are based in the community and work with it on its behalf, the projects have a greater impact on resident and investor perceptions and behavior than other private or public projects.

CDCs' physical development projects also foster human development and anti-poverty activities.

- First, physical development projects are visible evidence to community residents that they can take control of their environment. Better housing and places to shop are typically the first priorities that residents themselves set for their communities. Once progress becomes evident in these areas, residents can begin to see that improving their lives in other ways are also possible.

- Second, physically deteriorated neighborhoods are difficult (and often dangerous) places for families to live in, let alone grow. It is hard for children to study in overcrowded housing or to dream of a better future in a burned-out neighborhood.

- Third, CDCs' physical development projects often directly involve human development components. Many housing projects have day care centers and offer other tenant services. Providing housing that is affordable to the poor frees up more of their limited income for food, health care, and other essentials. The opportunity of homeownership is a central image in the American dream at all income levels. Commercial development projects provide jobs and critical community services.

- Fourth, human development programs require the same community leadership and broad participation among public and private institutions that physical development requires. Successful physical development enhances the standing and the legitimacy of a community and its leadership among public and private institutions alike. As this leadership and institutional support is built through highly physical development, it can be applied to human development programs as well.

CDCs' project development activities, and the community advocacy work they and other organizations pursue, are mutually reinforcing and equally essential to a community's economic and political empowerment. For example, Community Reinvestment Act advocacy work can cause banks to offer loans in low-income communities, but these commitments are often unfulfilled unless CDCs have bankable projects to propose and can help prospective homebuyers to qualify for mortgages. Similarly, a community's advocacy for more responsive public services and its housing rehabilitation program are more likely to succeed in tandem than separately. Because a well-organized community is often a necessary precursor to strong CDCs, the West Palm Beach program of the Local Initiatives Support Corporations (LISC) started with an intensive community organizing effort. And, conversely, a CDC's capacity to implement successful development projects will increase the responsiveness of a city's political and business leadership to the community needs.

CDCs develop indigenous community leadership. By organizing communities and working as equal partners with a wide range of public and private institutions—which are essential to the community development process—CDCs are natural breeding grounds for community leaders. CDC directors have become congressmen, foundation presidents, and bank executives, and have received MacArthur fellowships. Indeed, it is difficult to conceive of a CDC succeeding without strong leadership.

CDCs have the necessary political and technical skills to marshall community support and to assemble multiple public, private, and charitable resources to make projects feasible. CDCs have honed these skills because it has been the only way to get projects done in a period of severely restricted public resources.

CDCs are committed to serving low-income people on a long-term basis. This commitment is becoming increasingly attractive to policymakers as existing HUD-assisted low-income housing projects become threatened with defaults and conversions to upper-income use.

In short, CDCs are the most appropriate vehicles for revitalizing distressed communities. This realization led to the creation of LISC, stimulated the many other intermediaries and partnerships of LISC and its partners support, and continues to spark new mechanisms designed to help CDCs. In 1986, Congress recognized the importance of CDCs when it set aside 10 percent of the Low-Income Housing Tax Credit for nonprofit developers. In further support of these developers, Congress, in 1990, set aside 15 percent of the funds for HOME Investment Partnerships, the centerpiece of the Cranston Gonzalez National Affordable Housing Act.

Here are a few examples of what CDCs have accomplished:

- In New York City, the Mid-Bronx Desperadoes have developed over 1,100 low-income units and either manage or co-manage about 725 units in a seriously distressed area.
- In Boston, Inquilinos Boricuas en Accion (IBA) has built and rehabilitated 884 units to preserve low-income housing opportunities in a neighborhood experiencing rapid gentrification.

- In Cleveland, the twelve CDCs of the Cleveland Housing Network have rehabilitated more than 800 housing units, many of which are single-family homes for eventual ownership by poverty-level families. The homes are provided on a lease-purchase basis to families that could not qualify for bank financing. The other homes are part of a home ownership program for moderate- and middle-income families.

LISC

LISC began operations in 1980, with the initial capitalization provided in part by the Ford Foundation. Since that time, LISC and its affiliates have raised capital resources of $827 million, virtually all of which has come from 800 corporations and foundations in the form of grants, loans, and equity investments. LISC and its affiliates have used these resources to make grants, recoverable grants, loans, loan guarantees, and equity investments to 875 CDCs. Projects assisted with these funds directly involve over 44,000 units of low- and moderate-income housing, 4,308 jobs, and 7.6 million square feet of commercial space. LISC-assisted projects have attracted approximately $1.9 billion from other sources. CDCs and their affiliates have conducted all of this activity in distressed low-income communities in a period of severely curtailed governmental funding.

LISC's activity has grown rapidly over the past few years. Program output—grants, loans, and loan guarantees—has risen from $6.4 million in 1985 to $23.8 million in 1988, to $38.6 million in 1992. When investments from LISC's affiliate, the National Equity Fund, are taken into account, 1992 program activity totaled $154.7 million. This growth indicates that LISC and community-based development are indeed gaining momentum as a significant force in distressed low-income communities.

While these quantitative outputs constitute a substantial measurable achievement, they do not capture the broader institutional impact that LISC has sought to make in support of community-based development. Community-based development is "developmental" because it seeks to change the behavior of institutions and individuals with respect to low-income communities, not simply to undertake individual projects. Changing institutional behavior can have an impact much broader and longer lasting than any single project.

Accordingly, LISC has devoted much of its energies to creating supportive institutional climates both nationally and locally for CDCs and low-income communities. LISC was created in part as an intermediary that could increase philanthropic participation in community-based development. LISC has expanded this intermediary role by:

- Establishing local advisory committees in each area of concentration, through which funders can participate on a policy-making and programmatic basis in

LISC activities. Local advisory committees serve as a forum through which business and philanthropic leaders learn about CDCs and engage their own and other institutions in the community development process.

- Creating citywide financing programs that foster community-based production systems for certain kinds of projects (e.g., homeownership or multifamily rental housing). These programs assemble a full range of public and institutional partners, drastically cut the time and expense of planning each project, and operate efficiently on a substantial scale. For example, a LISC program in New York involves more than twenty CDCs in the rehabilitation of nearly 3,000 units of gutted tax—foreclosed housing at a total cost of $250 million—the largest single nonprofit housing project to date in the United States. Similarly, LISC's HomeSight program in Washington, D.C. comprises a complete system for developing and financing owner-occupied housing.

- Attracting previously untapped local partners, including public agencies, lenders, businesses, foundations, and religious institutions. For example, the Neighborhood Development Support Collaborative in Boston has made the local United Way a long-term source of core operating support for CDCs—a crucial and scarce form of funding. Moreover, this program is the model for a national demonstration that is already involving other United Way chapters around the nation.

- Establishing the National Equity Fund, through which LISC has raised $567 million in its first five and a half years from major corporations in the form of equity investments that yield a competitive return based on federal tax credits. These funds are invested in CDC sponsored low-income rental housing, enabling CDCs to take advantage of the primary source of federal support for low-income housing development. NEF recently obtained a special ruling from the Internal Revenue Service that will facilitate the permanent use of this housing for low-income residents under community control—a breakthrough in federal tax policy.

- Tapping national capital markets to provide bridge financing for NEF investments. *The Wall Street Journal* reported LISC's issuance of $25 million in rated bonds as "a first for a nonprofit, low-income housing group, and some industry specialists said it could lead to more capital financing for low-income housing" (November 23, 1988, C23).

- Building CDC capacity through training and technical assistance programs. For example, LISC's Houston program has focused on helping CDCs to organize and devise community revitalization strategies. In Los Angeles, LISC operates a coordinated training and technical assistance program to help nineteen groups plan specific housing development projects and bring them to fruition.

- Establishing the Local Initiatives Managed Assets Corporation (LIMAC) to provide a source of liquidity to nonprofit, profit-motivated, and public lenders to CDC projects. LIMAC has begun an innovative pilot program with the Federal Home Loan Mortgage Corporation (Freddie Mac) that encourages investors to put their money into affordable housing, typically considered a risky venture. Through the program, LIMAC buys loans from banks and other loan originators, swaps those loans with Freddie Mac for securities, and then sells the securities to investors. Together, LIMAC and Freddie Mac have committed $100 million for loan purchases, which is expected to generate a low-income secondary mortgage market worth billions.

- LISC launched the Campaign for Communities in January of 1991. As the community development industry's largest fund raising effort to date, it aims to raise $200 million by the end of 1995. These funds come from corporations and foundations in the forms of grants and low-interest loans or program related investments. The campaign is a reaction to the growing number and strength of CDCs nationwide. It will allow for increased research and development on LISC's part; and it will provide CDCs operating in LISC's local program areas with the financial resources they need to move forward as they increase their capacity to build housing, manage property, foster community building initiatives, or address any issue dealing with the stabilization of a community. By the end of 1992, the Campaign for Communities had already raised $105 million.

LISC's approach to program development exemplifies its name: local initiatives support. LISC offers a variety of tools to CDCs, including core operating support, training and technical assistance, project seed grants and loans, intermediate term loans, and loan guarantees. In addition, it offers equity investments for low-income rental housing, a secondary market for community development lenders, and the development and management of complete citywide financing programs that can be used for several projects. But how these tools are applied in a given city depends largely on the capacity and needs of local CDCs and other institutional partners. The key is to respond as flexibly and creatively as possible to local obstacles and opportunities. It is common for LISC to develop a new program in one area in response to local needs and then adapt the same program to other areas. For example, the National Equity Fund was based on a successful pilot program in Chicago, and a Boston program that provides core operating support to CDCs has been replicated in Chicago and, as mentioned earlier, is the model for national programs by the United Way of America. LISC is becoming even more responsive to local priorities as it continues to decentralize program staff. LISC now has program staff on site full-time in all of its areas of concentration. On-site program staff is immersed in the local CDC scene and is responsible for identifying and addressing the needs of local CDCs. LISC's close working relationships with the public and private sectors make it a strategic broker in assembling new resources for CDCs.

These initiatives reflect the LISC's view that perhaps the greatest challenges facing CDCs over the next few years will be to increase the scale of their output, to institutionalize comprehensive community-based delivery systems on the local level, and to attract new financing resources to support this increased activity. These challenges are important because of the magnitude and urgency of community needs, and because achieving growth sends the message that community development works. LISC believes it can and should be an important partner with CDCs in meeting these challenges.

Taken together, LISC's activities have contributed substantially to the maturation of CDCs by expanding CDC capacity, increasing the resources available to CDCs, and building a broad consensus among the public, private, and philanthropic sectors that CDCs are a creative and effective response to the urgent needs of America's low-income communities.

NOTE

1. William Julius Wilson, *The Truly Disadvantaged* (Chicago: University of Chicago Press, 1987), p. 144.

4

AFFORDABLE HOUSING

KERRON R. BARNES

In recent years the need for housing, in terms of supply, has again become a public issue that has risen beyond the special interests of the poor seeking or living in public housing. Today, seniors, young families, middle-class renters, and the homeless alike are increasingly unsure if they will find housing. For the first time in a generation, homeownership is in decline.

As the issue has grown in dimension in the public and media consciousness, there has risen a considerable new debate over the nature of the problem. In general, this has boiled down to two positions. On one side the position commonly supported by housing advocates is that new housing supply is needed, including large-scale production programs. The position supported by many others is that affordability, not supply, is the problem, and that more income in the form of housing vouchers will allow the poor to find shelter as provided by the private sector. The basic position of the first group is that people are homeless because there isn't enough housing to go around; the second group claims that people are homeless because they don't have the money to pay for housing which is there.

The latter theory has been in ascendancy in recent years due to a variety of factors, including a conservative Republican Administration, the perception of poor results from expensive supply programs such as public housing, and the unwillingness of Congress to embark on expensive new initiatives in the face of a massive federal deficit.

A contributing element is that in recent years, much media attention has been devoted to a more superficial aspect of the problem, that of high housing cost. The enormous increase in sales prices, apartment rents, luxury condo costs, etc., has been widely reported, as has the luxury index, which compares the average home price against the average family income. Rarely do the media acknowledge the low vacancy rate or the lack of public or private production of rental housing brought on by the dual government actions of withdrawal of subsidies and tax incentives.

The decade-long lack of any focus on housing as an issue and the general neglect of urban policy and urban issues has led to a multitude of new state and local efforts. While these efforts have lacked both substantial funding and the efficiency and effectiveness of a large-scale production, they have benefitted from being somewhat more grassroots in origin. The trend has led to a proliferation of smaller, less efficient, but nevertheless more appropriate, efforts. An inadvertent result has been the trend toward smaller scale developments, aimed at increasing the supply and maintaining affordability.

Perhaps the most effective group of initiatives are those now under way at the state level—as well as those sponsored by the private sector, such as the Local Initiatives Support Corporation. However, of equally considerable note are the far more numerous efforts now evolving from the heretofore underdeveloped and neglected nonprofit sector. This last sector is late in developing in the United States, but has been in the forefront of the development of affordable housing in Europe and Canada.

The latter's history is a precursor of the trend in the United States, as the Canadian government effectively withdrew from the housing field several years ago, and an enormous variety of nonprofits—including hospitals, YMCAs, and neighborhood organizations—have begun to fill the void.

An important aspect of this trend is that the resulting projects tend to be smaller in scale and lower in density than many of the earlier federally funded efforts. Since they are produced by an enormously varied set of agencies, they tend to spring up at scatter site locations. They are generally on pieces of land or utilize existing structures that are available at low cost because they are less desirable. In addition, such smaller parcels usually have development interest at the community level, as profit-oriented developers rarely have the willingness to devote the extensive resources needed to develop such properties, given their limited return potential.

As we enter the last decade of the millennium, we see that new efforts in producing reasonably priced housing have shifted to the state, county, and local level. There are an infinite variety of successes among these efforts, and an analysis of the common factors suggests several elements that are now required for such a locally based development to produce any sort of housing marketable to the general public. Obviously, prior to enumerating such elements, it should be noted that the relative degree of the local housing shortage, and the resulting interest of the local officials, are key. Many potentially successful projects go nowhere, while lesser efforts succeed due to the relative strength of local political will.

Many of the common mechanisms found in successful housing developments involve ways to solve the cost problem of the equation, as discussed earlier. These mechanisms can bring costs to within rental or purchase range for people of modest means. In general, they seem to deal with the issue of affordability, as the small-scale of production can in no way have a major impact on supply. These programs, however, do not address the issue by merely putting money in the hands of poor people. In that regard, such programs thus relate to supply.

One of the most necessary elements is the reduction of land cost. This is usually accomplished using public land that is unwanted, such as tax-foreclosed or poorly sited parcels. This factor is significant, since it is land costs, more than construction costs, that in recent years have led to price escalation, especially in high-cost areas.

A related element is the need to increase the density for affordable housing. Since land is expensive, it is often necessary to use sites where one acre zoning prevails and build at densities of five to fifteen per acre.

Another common element is affordability by design. This concept involves the premise, developed years ago by Levitt, of using the most efficient design, reducing the space devoted to circulation, and getting the most out of materials that go into a house. Related to this is the need to generally reduce the size of units from the current national average of 1,600 square feet to somewhere between 900 and 1,100 square feet for families, and 500 to 700 square feet for seniors and single persons. Needless to say, such reduction in design and size do not lead to the creation of a *Better Homes and Gardens* dream house, but rather the starter home of the 1980s.

Parallel to this process of cost and size reduction is that of bureaucracy reduction. In recent decades, we have loaded every fear, rational and irrational, on the back of the developer. The starter homes of the 1950s would now be illegal in many communities. Developers must pay all sorts of fees, provide bonds for every piece of pipe, cement wall, and light fixture (which he also must supply), and probably must start every project with a staff person under twenty-five in order to have one member of the development team alive at the completion. In short, a reduction in the length and complexity of the local approval and permitting process has become a vital requirement for new affordable housing. One element of this trend is that some communities now make developers pay an impact fee for housing. This makes private-sector housing even more costly in order to subsidize a few affordable units.

Finally, there are certain soft costs that can be removed from the financing equation. It helps if the sponsor is a nonprofit and does the marketing directly. Of even greater significance is the need for below-rate market financing, generally through tax-exempt bond proceeds. In many cases these interest rates are combined with the ability to pay only 5 percent or less as a downpayment. One feature of such programs in urban areas is the advantage of free infrastructure along with free land.

While there is a tendency to think of vacant or tax-foreclosed inner-city land as less desirable, it often has several advantages, including access to public transportation and jobs, and the presence of water, sewer, electric, and gas supplies.

In many cases, unused suburban areas, especially old industrial sites, have water settings, making them highly desirable for housing development. In these cases a reverse pattern sometimes takes place, in which only the wealthy can afford the housing stock.

One final characteristic found commonly in programs dealing with affordable housing is the involvement of multiple agencies, funding sources, and players. It is not uncommon to have four or five public agencies, a combination of public and private financing sources, a for-profit builder, and a nonprofit sponsor, in addition to the normal development team of engineer, architect, attorney, planner, and several subcontractors. This has become the norm for many projects and, as can be imagined, it adds a complexity that requires a great deal of time and effort to overcome.

As there are numerous segments of the population who need housing, the programs to meet their needs take great diversity. Among obvious need-groups are first-time home buyers, senior citizens, renters, and populations at risk, such as the retarded or deinstitutionalized, and the growing number of homeless.

One result of the withdrawal of federal support for housing for any but middle-class persons is that a diversity of highly focused efforts has sprung up. While many of these tend to be amateurish, they also have the ability to be precisely tailored to local needs and the local market.

In future years, the task will be to marry the grassroots qualities of the nonprofits to the professionalism of for-profit builders to produce a result that is acceptable.

The next task is to identify or create for the nonprofit or public/private housing sponsors sufficient and affordable financing for their developments. This trend is now beginning, with the development of numerous community housing trust funds, to make below-market-interest-rate loans to capable nonprofits.

ORANGE COUNTY, NY—A CASE STUDY

A typical example of the current trend in housing development may be found in Orange County, a semi-rural exurb of New York. A prosperous, fast-developing area, the county estimated in 1986 that it will need 50,000 new housing units in the next fifteen years to keep pace with demand.

In spite of exceptional economic growth, incomes have not kept pace with home prices. There are few new rental units being added to the stock, and housing for lower-income groups is virtually unavailable. The county houses several hundred people, including many children, in emergency shelters and motels. The response of the county has been to address several discrete aspects of the problem from the needs of the homeless to the wants of the prospective purchaser, and the requirements of the various groups of renters in between.

The first action taken by the county in 1988 was to create an infrastructure and a housing loan fund capitalized at $12 million. Because of the prohibition of Article 18 of the New York Constitution against counties becoming involved directly in housing activities, the funds may be loaned only to municipalities within the county. They, in turn, working through the CDAs, housing authorities, or public benefit corporations, may lend funds to limited-profit developers under Article 11 of the Housing Finance Law.

Under the program guidelines, funds may be loaned at as low as 1 percent interest for up to twenty years. The first priority of the program is new rental units that cost no more than 30 percent of family income for people below 80 percent of the county median income. The second priority is senior rental housing followed by new owner-occupied units affordable to families with incomes lower than the county median of $35,200. In 1988, the county again funded this program for $8 million.

In the first year of operation, five projects received approval from the municipal loan commission, which is the governing body of the program. These are described briefly below in order to illustrate their variety and complexity.

HUD Senior Housing—Washingtonville. Sixty-four rental units. Permanent financing through FMHA with rental assistance payments from New York DHCR. In addition, thirteen acres of land were donated by a local developer in return for a density bonus on a nearby townhouse project.

The county has also granted this project $150,000 for infrastructure, and New York State has provided an additional $100,000 grant. Construction was completed in 1990. Phase II of more than one hundred units is anticipated sometime in the early 1990s.

Patrick Campbell Senior Housing—Wallkill. Orange County provided $145,000 at 1 percent interest in bridge financing and $113,900 for twenty-five years at 3 percent interest to complete the financing package for a seventy-five unit rental project with HUD Section 202 permanent financing.

Horizon Heights—Senior Family and Owner—Wallkill. This package combines twenty-eight affordable owner-occupied single-family homes and thirty-eight senior rental apartments on the same site. The project has $964,000 in county loan funds at 1 percent interest for fifteen years, as well as funding from both the New York Housing Trust Fund and the New York Affordable Housing Corporation. In addition, the town of Wallkill has provided a special zoning density bonus to allow for more units on the site.

Walden View, Family Rental—Walden. This sixty-unit project was originally funded under a HUD HODAG grant. The county added $300,000 in infrastructure financing at 1 percent interest for ten years in order to save the developer sufficient interest to install a special electro-thermal heating system that will cut energy consumption by more than one third.

In addition, the project developer agreed to increase the number of units reserved for lower-income persons from twelve to eighteen.

Renwick Row, Family Rentals—Newburgh. The final project approved by the county in 1988 involved a two-phase rehabilitation of twenty-eight apartments. The county's loan of $650,000 was for five years at 2 percent interest with interest only for the first five years. The project has $700,000 in permanent financing from the NY HFA and $312,500 in private funds, as well as rental rehabilitation commitments from Orange County.

In summary, these various loans illustrate the complexity and variety of affordable housing projects that are created when several financing sources can be combined with support from local governments. Together, they illustrate today's mechanisms for increasing the supply of housing and making it affordable.

Transitional Housing

One very ambitious effort on the part of the county involves the use of the existing purchasing power of several programs to create permanent housing for homeless families. This is called the Transitional Housing Program.

In 1988, Orange County and two nonprofit agencies, PODER (Occupational Programs for the Development of the Economy) and RECAP (Regional Economic Community Action Program) developed a program to move homeless families from motels to permanently affordable rental housing.

In addition to achieving these two important housing goals, the program is expected to cost about the same as is now paid to shelter homeless families in motels.

Under the program, the nonprofit sponsors purchase scatter site rental properties. The Orange County Department of Social Services pays rent as it would for motels, and the high cash flow is used over an eighteen-month "transitional" period to reduce the principal on the bank loan. Since the nonprofit sponsors have little cash, the Office of Community Development makes eighteen-month no-interest loans for the 10 percent downpayment and closing costs. If the property needs rehabilitation, the Community Development Office uses its Rental Rehabilitation Program to match private construction financing on a fifty–fifty basis. The Community Development office also provides inspection services prior to purchase and oversees the rehabilitation process.

It is the aim of the program to occupy forty-eight units in its first year, twenty-four each in Middletown and Newburgh. Tenants will be selected jointly by the nonprofits and DSS and will be required to participate in an intensive program of training and counseling. Additional financing was provided through a state grant under the Homeless Housing Assistance Program (HHAP).

It is hoped that the combination of good housing and a high level of attention to the social needs of the participants will enable at least half of those selected to live independently.

At the end of the eighteen-month transitional housing period, the mortgage will have been reduced to a level such that all expenses can be paid with rents at the Section 8 level. Tenants then in occupancy will be given Section 8 Housing Assistance Payment Certificates and will remain in standard affordable housing.

These examples provide a glimpse into the world of affordable housing as we approach the year 2000. The major efforts in this field are at the state and local level. Since a major federal role may not be possible or practical in the foreseeable future, the work now bearing first fruits should be continued.

One of the greatest remaining challenges is bringing together the skills of local sponsors, who tend to be housing novices, and the experience of the private building industry along with meaningful funding to produce affordable housing on a larger scale. The hope is that such a coalition will begin to develop for economic as well as civic reasons, as developers realize the benefits of tapping the pent-up demand at the lower end of the housing market. As this happens, the two groups, often opponents in the past, may find themselves newly allied.

5

ENERGY CONSUMPTION AND ARCHITECTURAL DESIGN

RICHARD G. STEIN

This chapter will concern itself with the city as an energy-using form of human settlement. It is important to realize, however, that the city does not exist for the purpose of using energy or even using energy efficiently. The city exists as a social form because of the various human transactions and interactions that are made possible by this gathering together of great numbers of people. There are many institutions—production facilities, management facilities, educational facilities, cultural facilities—all of which depend on the large groups of people who provide specialized skills and knowledge as well as those who support, use, and take advantage of the educational, cultural, and commercial complexes that are developed. Around all these complexes are the residential facilities that are necessary in order to permit these other activities to occur, grow, die, or change. Although one can understand energy only in terms of the complete functioning of cities, we can allow ourselves the indulgence of examining the energy aspects of a modern urban settlement in its own terms.

Urban energy use and patterns of use vary extensively in cities all over the world. While American cities are not typical for all cities, we have enough data to examine them and arrive at some generalities. One way to look at the city in terms of energy use is to see how much energy a person requires to live in the city when compared to living outside of the city—in a rural setting, for example. For the United States, we can divide the whole national energy use by the number of people and derive an individual budget for each person. That figure is roughly 315

Btu per person per year or, in joules, about 332 billion joules per person per year. In more immediately visual terms, that would be the equivalent of fifty-two barrels of oil per person per year. Each of those barrels would contain fifty-five gallons of petroleum. On average, there are a little more than three and a half individuals per family unit. If the family members were to pool their energy budgets, that would mean that an average family would have available approximately 195 barrels of petroleum a year. Out of this would have to come all of the family's energy uses: transportation, heating, cooling, ventilating, and discretional uses of electricity such as television, stereo equipment, electric games, personal computers, and so forth. The amount of energy for the working members of the family would also have to be accounted for. That is, if the total energy necessary to run the office at which a family member worked was ascertained, the proportion of the complete energy required to run that office divided by the number of employees would be the part of the total family budget that had to go into this particular use. In a similar way, if there were children in school, the total cost in energy terms of operating the school divided by the number of pupils in the school would represent the amount of that 195 gallons that would be allocated for educational purposes. And so on down through the complete inventory of all that the family did to live, move, work, indulge in recreation, participate in educational programs, and so forth. Also, out of the complete prorated budget assigned to each family, there would have to be significant allowances for sustaining the governmental and military apparatuses that are a customary part of our national life. The amount of energy that goes into the support of the military alone is obviously very great. But the amount that is required to sustain the governmental structures and bureaucracies, police forces, prisons and all other commonly supported public enterprises is also accounted for as part of the total national energy use.

We know that energy budgeting is not determined on the basis of the sharing of the energy wealth, nor does extracting the part of this wealth that is expended for public uses leave a remainder that is made equally available to each individual to spend as he or she wishes. We normally have no more socialism in energy use than we do in the economic life of our country. Each person can purchase as much energy, to be used in whatever way he or she wants, as that person's income allows. We know there are significant differences in how energy is used. Nevertheless, there are certain demonstrable truths about energy uses. Even with all the inefficiencies in the way our buildings are built and the way they use energy, multi-story buildings tend to be much more energy efficient in providing basic services than smaller free-standing buildings. The reasons are obvious. A 2,000 square foot free-standing house would have a total exposed surface area (including the roof) of about 4,500 square feet. On the other hand, if the same size 2,000 square foot unit for one family were in a multi-story building, a twenty-story building for example, with elevators, public corridors and services, the average 2,000 square foot apartment would have an exposed area of only about 1,900 square feet, or less than half the area of the self-contained building. Since it is this outside area that loses heat from the inside of the building to the outside, and picks up unwanted heat that must be cooled in the summer, it obviously takes less energy to provide comfort conditions for the multi-unit building than for the free-standing building. In addition, the average amount of energy required for transportation is less for the city dweller than for someone living within a suburban or rural area. It is not unusual for a suburban family to drive their cars 20,000 miles a year. At twenty-five miles per gallon, that would require 800 gallons of gas or approximately ninety-six million Btu. This represents 12 percent of the family's budget. An urban family using mass transportation would, on average, use only half this amount. For heating, cooling, and electricity, the suburban usage would be about 190 million Btu, another 25 percent of the family budget, compared with about 110 million for the urban counterpart. Approximately one third of our national energy use is in governmental and military activities, approximately 385 million Btu of the typical family budget. If we allow an additional fifty million Btu to take care of the work place requirements and 430 million Btu for prorated industrial usage, we will find that the suburban family's budget is exhausted while the urban family's is still at only 90 percent utilization.

Having seen that the urban lifestyle is potentially less energy demanding than the typical suburban lifestyle, we must now come to grips with the real problem, the elimination of all unnecessary energy use.

First, in examining transportation we must understand that even with the very significant reductions in all areas of energy use in the last fifteen years, there still is a significant factor of excessive energy use in the way we live today. Even without curtailing the amount of mileage that we travel, greater efficiency in the vehicles and methods of transportation can probably achieve an additional 40 percent savings in the transportation area. In addition, if we accept the necessity of curtailing liquid hydrocarbon energy use, particularly the use of petroleum in the form of gasoline and diesel fuel, because of its scarcity and the damaging effects its use has on the environment, there can be further reductions based on eliminating some of the unnecessary traveling that is characteristic of the way we live. This will require some changes in attitude. It means that we must be willing to forego some of the convenience of having available individual transportation for any activity, shopping trip or social purpose that we may opt for at any time.

Second, regardless of the improvements that have been achieved in our building standards, construction technology, equipment design, and controls since the mid 1970s, there still is a possibility of lowering energy use as much again as it has been reduced in the past. There are very few buildings that have completely efficient heating, cooling, lighting, hot water, and control systems. The use of natural light and heat from the sun and the use of natural air movement for cooling has barely been exploited, even in new buildings. In addition, the percentage of older buildings that are still structurally sound and in relatively good repair is very high. Yet most of these buildings have not been modified to increase the efficiency of their energy use. As in transportation, there are major savings that could be realized if people were more committed to the efficient use of the facilities at hand. It is unusual to go into any commercial space, any store or office space, and find a correlation between a space in use and whether the environmental systems are on or off in response to that particular pattern of use. Examples abound of lighting systems that cannot be controlled locally or air conditioning systems that must be turned on for an entire floor in order to serve single occupants. The important generalization is that there is probably a 50 percent overuse of systems representing potential reductions above and beyond those that would be achieved through improving the efficiency of the systems.

Third, we can examine the way energy is generated for urban areas. Almost all of the electricity used in cities is generated outside of the cities, sometimes by as much as hundreds of miles. Thus, the cities do not directly suffer from the polluting effects of the actual power generation. In fact, the major victims of pollution from power plants are often those affected by acid rain hundreds of miles downwind from the power plant. Examples of exporting the pollution are well known. The Four Corners generators at the border between Utah, Colorado, Arizona, and New Mexico have detrimental environmental consequences where the power is generated, but the power is transmitted hundreds of miles for use in Los Angeles. Most of New York City's water supply is located a couple of hundred miles away from New York in the Catskills, where the reservoirs have been created through the flooding of farmlands. On the other hand, the use of energy to do work within the limited confines of an urban area also has its environmental consequences. The most obvious is the cumulative effect of all the burning of hydrocarbons contributing nitrous oxides, sulfur oxides, ozone, and other pollutants to the atmosphere. When the individual auto is the primary means of transportation and is used as widely and as intensively as it is in the Los Angeles area, the result is the continuous presence of an unacceptably deteriorated atmosphere. The condition is not unique to Los Angeles, although that city is by far the worst in the United States.

When electricity is converted into work, it also produces heat at the rate of 3,414 Btu for every kilowatt hour that is used for any purpose, whether for lighting, heating, turning over motors, or anything else. During the summer when a major demand on the electrical systems is for air conditioning, the energy that is created at the generator plants outside of the city is converted into work in the city, mainly through the air conditioning machines. It results in an enormous contribution to the heat of the city, which, when coupled with the heat retention capabilities of masonry buildings, the concrete sidewalks, the asphalt roads, and the direct radiant heat of the sun itself, tends to raise the temperature of the city considerably higher than the temperatures of the areas surrounding it, with a scarcity of green areas to counteract the heat buildup. As an example, New York City, which is a coastal city, no longer has the characteristic diurnal pattern of cool breezes at night tending to purge the accumulated heat of the day. We can observe that in all cases, energy use is detrimental to the environmental quality of cities. The greater the use, the greater the damage. The particulates and the acid produced through the combustion of hydrocarbons is damaging to the historic monuments and to the buildings within the city. Athens, Rome, New York, Brussels, London all bear witness to the cultural damage to the artifacts in the city. The quality of the air breathed is damaging to health, particularly for old people and young children.

Accepting the fact that the cities are structurally more energy efficient than the nonurban areas, but that cities, through the concentration of the population and facilities, are also much more vulnerable to the damaging effects of energy use, what can we do to work toward further reductions in the per capita use of energy in the city? Let us examine four major areas of energy use and identify how they can be made to function using less energy than they do now. The four areas are the residence, work place, transportation, and generation.

The residential use of energy can be reduced significantly by improving the quality of buildings, by an educational effort for the more efficient use of what presently exists, and by the improvement of the devices through which energy is used (such as appliances like the refrigerator, stove, television, and water heater). If all of these opportunities are taken advantage of, savings of 40 to 50 percent in this area are immediately feasible.

Turning to the work place, industry has, for the most part, moved out of the cities, and the major work places remaining relate to the city's growing importance as a service center. While large improvements have been made in new construction in the last fifteen years, the actual performance standards that are still used, the grossness of controls for mechanical systems, and the lack of cooperation on the part of the users, all allow for a good deal of improvement. It is interesting to observe that the way people work in offices is now significantly different than it was fifteen or twenty years ago. For example, many office workers use computers and spend most of the day looking into the CRT monitor. The high levels of general illumination that were once called for indiscriminately are no longer relevant. Of course there are certain kinds of work areas, such as filing spaces, where higher levels of light are required when that area is in use. Since lighting is the largest energy user in most high-rise commercial buildings, the re-examination of its role could result in significant savings in the future. With the growth of electronic communication systems, the amount of electrical energy used for what has been termed discretionary uses increases as lighting demands go down. In general, one can say that by particularizing and making more individual the different areas and requirements within commercial space, there should be appreciable energy savings, possibly in the neighborhood of 20 to 25 percent.

In transportation, the versatility of the system is the key to its efficiency. Most mass transportation systems depend on large concentrations of people to justify the original investment in the infrastructure and the rather expensive specialized vehicles that do the actual transportation. In most densely populated cities, the problem is to find effective transportation from the node points served by a public system to the individual destination points. This has still not been successfully solved. In less densely populated cities like Los Angeles, the dependency is still almost entirely on the individual car. Significant improvement in the energy performance of the automobile has been demonstrated in prototypes with mileage of seventy to one hundred miles to the gallon. The widespread introduction of these vehicles has neither been mandated by the government, accepted by the individual car driver, nor made a requirement for cars used in the center of cities.

Finally, we turn to generation, particularly electric generation. Most of the fuel that is consumed directly for building services is used for heating, usually in the form of steam generation. The waste heat from the generation process is dissipated into the atmosphere. There are, however, techniques for using the waste heat for the generation of power or, alternatively, when power is generated, using the waste heat from the process for the heating and cooling of buildings. This process is known as co-generation. Co-generation does not work well with our large remote power generating stations since the cost of transporting the heat energy to the ultimate user in the city is prohibitively expensive and difficult to achieve. It is possible, however, to have much smaller generating units that operate efficiently at one fiftieth of the size of the typical large remote generator station. These smaller generation plants designed for co-generation have the advantage of being able to be located within urban areas. The heat generated or the heat recovered from the electrical system can be economically distributed through district heating systems, enabling a whole district with a varied set of buildings to have efficient heat generation as well as electrical service. Since these smaller units can also be built more rapidly than large ones, and can be located as required by increasing electric demand, they allow the growth of electrical generation facilities to parallel much more closely the demand curve. Moreover, since they would be linked together in networks, they provide a redundancy that does not require the idle standby capability of a backup plant for the typical thousand-megawatt generating stations. In the combined use of energy for heating and electric generation savings of 15 to 20 percent are realistic.

So all in all, while energy is not the reason the cities have developed, using it more effectively can enhance the quality of life within them. It can reduce the amount of damage to the global atmosphere by contributing less to the greenhouse effect, it can produce a more environmentally enlightened population of urban dwellers, and it can contribute to the aesthetic resulting from doing things adequately and elegantly.

6

A PUBLIC/PRIVATE COLLABORATIVE PROCESS FOR ACHIEVING ENERGY EFFICIENCY IN BUILDINGS

EARLE F. TAYLOR, JR. AND LUISA M. FREEMAN

INTRODUCTION

The human environment in urban areas is largely defined by the buildings in which we live, work, and relax. This inescapable feature of the urban landscape is made up of a varied mix of the existing building stock plus the seemingly constant addition of new buildings. These buildings—old and new—can provide for various task uses over time, and include numerous internal mechanical systems designed to support those tasks.

Electricity makes most of the living environment livable within a building. Ventilation, lighting, heating, and cooling can all be provided by electricity. Even in the case of fossil fuel heating, electricity is needed for moving the heat to its destination.

In considering the "City as a Human Environment," we ask:

- How well do our buildings and their electro-mechanical systems support human needs?
- Are they providing the best environment for us to work, live, and play in?
- If not, how can we create a better environment?

These questions are the subject of this chapter, with specific attention to the electro-mechanical systems of buildings, the living/working needs they support, and the energy efficiency with which these needs are met. The emerging role of the electric utility in shaping building

energy use and efficiency is discussed. Finally, this discussion is supported by a case study of a public/private collaborative planning process to demonstrate how the questions above can systematically be in-
vestigated.

BACKGROUND: THE ROLE OF THE UTILITY IN
SHAPING THE BUILDING ENVIRONMENT

Ever since the passage of the National Energy Conservation Policy
Act (NECPA)[1] during the Carter Administration, electric utilities have
been looked upon by energy policymakers as a vehicle for the implementation of energy conservation objectives affecting buildings. While
the industry (perhaps understandably) resisted the responsibility at the
time, leading electric utilities around the country have since adopted
energy efficiency services as good business practice. In fact, for some
utilities, the reduction of building demand for electricity at peak periods
of the day or year (referred to as load management) is more than just
good practice—it is an economic necessity.

Energy conservation, which implies a reduction in the consumption
of kilowatt-hours (kWh), was an anathema to many electric utilities, because it meant that fixed costs would be spread over fewer sales and
thus drive up average rates. However, more recently, a large body of
policy opinion suggests that in a growth area, such as New England,
conservation can be a major resource in meeting future needs. Load
management, on the other hand, does not necessarily mean less use
overall, but it does mean less cumulative demand at any given moment
(measured as kilowatts or kW). The specific concern of load management is in the peak period of use, such as the hottest or coldest day of
the year or the busiest time of the day ("busy" in terms of electricity
use). A goal of load management, therefore, might be to shift variable
electricity-using tasks to off-peak hours. Unlike energy conservation,
load management has been an objective of many electric utilities for
several years.[2]

There are several factors, aside from being in a national oil crisis, why
the electric utility industry has found it prudent to pursue both conservation and load management programs as part of a sound business
strategy. Key reasons include:

- Federal or state mandates
- Good public relations
- Attention to certain disadvantaged customer segments for which the company
  is perceived to have a social responsibility
- A desire to keep customers satisfied (i.e., competition)

- Short-term (i.e., daily or seasonal) limitations in the ability to provide the load demanded economically

- Long-term future limitations in the ability to acquire new production facilities or purchase power economically

- Immediate limitations in the ability to provide the load demanded (e.g., as in the case of canceled nuclear plants)

Whether conservation or load management (or both) are the appropriate responses to these situations depends upon the specific mix of problems to be solved and opportunities for solving them. Conservation may provide some load relief; load management typically does not provide significant energy savings. Most companies finding themselves with many of the above reasons for pursuing a building energy efficiency investment strategy will pursue a mix of conservation and load management services.

HOW PUBLIC POLICYMAKERS INFLUENCE UTILITY PROGRAMS FOR ACHIEVING BUILDING ENERGY EFFICIENCY

If one looked at the above listing of potential utility "reasons" for pursuing a building energy efficiency strategy, it could be viewed as a continuum from externally imposed reasons to strong and immediate internal business reasons as the two end points. Whatever the utility motivation, federal, state, and local legislators, state regulators, and consumer advocates can all serve to influence the extent (in monetary terms) and even the manner in which a utility's energy efficiency strategy is carried out. The primary opportunity for exerting this influence is that afforded to policymakers in utility rate cases.

Whenever a utility has a need to change the rates it charges customers for electricity, it must apply for such a change to the state regulatory body (or the Federal Electric Regulatory Commission in the case of wholesale rate changes). In the ensuing rate case hearings, various groups representing constituencies affected by such rates, or by some related aspect of the utility company's operations, may apply to intervene in the case. (These parties are referred to as "intervenors" and "other interested parties" in regulatory legalese.)

While the subject of a case might be a change in a specific rate, the opportunity presents itself for various parties to comment formally on all manner of utility operations that might in some way affect the utility's bottom line, and therefore indirectly (presumably) the rate being requested. Thus, recent electric utility rate cases have provided a forum for discussions of utility building conservation and load management initiatives, especially where a rate increase is being requested. The typical presumption by those opposing the new rate is that the increase might have been less had adequate attempts been made to reduce demand and/or consumption.

This point tends to be made even more strongly when the construction of additional power plants and/or purchases of power from outside the utility system to meet growth in demand are proposed. Here, the building energy efficiency argument is often posed as a more cost-effective (or "least-cost") alternative in meeting consumer needs: rather than investing in additional supplies of power, the utility might invest in reducing demand (i.e., peak demand) through building energy conservation and load management. While this idea makes sense in concept, the public-private discussion between utilities and their regulators and consumer advocates in the rate case context is often, unfortunately, adversarial. It is only recently that the first successful attempts have been made in Connecticut and Massachusetts to pursue an alternative method of incorporating the ideas of consumer groups into the utility planning process, replacing the usually less productive (and often more volatile) rate-case forum.

THE CURRENT CONTEXT AND SOME EMERGING ARGUMENTS FOR INCREASED ENERGY EFFICIENCY IN BUILDINGS

The current argument of some public policymakers, then, is that encouraging the efficient use of electric energy in buildings is a good idea from an energy resources standpoint. This, in turn, suggests that utility investments in building energy efficiency will keep consumer electric rates lower than they would otherwise be in the long run (assuming that such investments are cheaper than investments in the construction of new power plants). This argument also provides an economic incentive for utilities to invest in building energy efficiency.

But what about the consumer? What are his/her motivations to *participate* in a utility conservation or load management program to make his/her building more energy efficient? Since utilities alone do not have the power to "force" customers to participate in conservation or load management programs, how can we encourage the free market to use less energy? In a related and perhaps more fundamental point, is increased electric energy efficiency consistent with the goals of creating a better human environment in buildings? The answer is a resounding yes!

Experience suggests two observations regarding consumer and societal motivations to use energy more efficiently. First, consumers do not always (rarely?) act like Economic Man/Woman when presented with cost-effective energy-saving opportunities—even when offered incentives that make the returns on investment more attractive.[3] The individual cannot be counted on to pursue the most logical economic choice when given a set of alternatives and will often choose options that provide less tangible perceived "values" for a higher price.

Second, it is clear that the market, when left to its own devices, does not always serve society well. Recent experience shows that the marketplace does not always reflect the true costs and benefits that can accrue to society in the production and distribution of a commodity or service. Several negative examples have been the subject of news broadcasts, such as the Exxon Valdez oil tanker accident. Society will be paying for the consequences of the demand for oil from this region for years to come, with some now asking whether the environmental costs of the damage to the Alaskan shoreline are not too great. More realistically (since society is clearly not going to go without oil) we question whether the true potential costs to society of this commodity are being reflected in prices. Similar concerns are being voiced in relation to issues of the greenhouse effect or global warming, acid rain, and other potential environmental assaults on the global village that may be the indirect or direct result of increasing demand for electricity.

An awareness of broader reasons for considering individual energy-using behavior saw some expression during the previous oil crisis. For example, the oil embargo period of the late 1970s saw consumers responding positively to the call to conserve for patriotic and national defense reasons. Today, the above issues combined with an overall increased concern for environmental preservation are beginning to spur renewed interest in individual electric energy efficiency efforts.[4]

But, beyond externalities and the extremely important issues *du jour*, some forward-looking planners are proposing equally compelling and long-lasting reasons why energy efficiency in buildings should become an increasingly important dimension of the buildings of tomorrow. In the 1988 "International Symposium on Advanced Comfort Systems for the Work Environment,"[5] held at The Rensselaerville Institute in New York, participants considered the concept of the "sick building syndrome," its relationship to efficiency improvements, and the implications for building retrofit and new construction activity in the future.[6] In the background chapter to the symposium proceedings, the editor states that:

First, and most prominently, the sick building syndrome has escalated as an international issue. Additionally, the work environment in buildings has undergone radical changes due to the introduction of computing technologies, electronically enhanced building systems, and shifts in building-use patterns. At the same time, low productivity in the work environment is adversely affecting the

nation's economic competitiveness to crisis proportions. Energy efficiency and
the new issues of whole building performance are becoming increasingly important.[7]

The above suggests that employers of the future (perhaps the very
near future) will need to concern themselves increasingly with not only
energy efficiency, but with the overall building environment. The *environmental* work space could become as much a part of the potential lure
for prospective employees as other parts of a typical benefits package.
In competitive job markets, employers will need to provide not only for
better space conditioning, lighting, and ventilation conditions, but for
other qualitative aspects of the work space, so that the individual
worker can define his/her own environmental space to suit individual
needs and desires.[8]

In spite of advances such as the smoke-free office in the creation of
more human environmental conditions in the workplace, the problems
(or, in business parlance, the opportunities) still appear to outweigh the
gains, as suggested in the quotation above. A few European and American office planning companies are already recognizing the opportunity
in relation to personalized electro-mechanical systems, and are beginning to produce office furniture products that provide for total environmental control by the individual. One example is seen in the TECHNO-
DRANT office desk system that allows for the control of telecommunications, heat and air conditioning, lighting levels and other
features through a built-in panel.[9] The concept of improved internal environmental conditions is just as much a concern and opportunity in the
residential living space as in the workplace.

Is the objective of improved environments consistent with increased
building energy efficiency? It can be argued that the two objectives indeed work hand-in-hand. The achievement of optimal building systems
design in terms of human environmental conditions can be realized
through the simultaneous achievement of nearer-to-optimal energy efficiency. Indeed, it is the "patchwork" addition of system features (e.g.,
air conditioning), new uses of space without consideration of environmental systems redesign, failure to "rebalance" a building's environmental system every two to five years, and other such conditions that
have resulted in both suboptimal human environmental systems and at
times grossly inefficient electricity usage in buildings.[10]

If the technology exists and society cares, why isn't more being done
to improve both the efficiency of electro-mechanical systems and the
indoor living/working environment in buildings? We suggest it is because of the fundamental conflict of different priorities. Like the oil spill
example, the often-conflicting agendas of key decisionmakers don't lend

themselves to agreement on what might be good for society. While the existence of the oil industry may generally be acknowledged as a good thing for Alaska, the oil companies' priorities regarding that issue may not be consistent with the priorities of public policymakers concerned with environmental preservation.

Similarly, those who build and retrofit buildings may not have the same priorities as those who have been put in charge of designing and enforcing the building codes, which have presumably been created to protect society and the consumer. Building code officials, in turn, have their own set of priorities, which may be outdated, may not be consistent, or may even come into conflict with sound principles of energy efficiency. Further, the building code development procedure is a consensus process that involves many groups, and incorporating change takes a significant amount of time. Thus, current codes still reflect a priority of safety and well-being, with energy efficiency requirements lagging far behind what is possible from a technological and economic feasibility standpoint.

In addition to the time lag problem, conflicting priorities exist among those who own and/or finance new buildings, the architects and engineers who design and build them, and code officials. The client's priorities for new buildings are typically short-term and economically driven, the design community is primarily concerned with meeting client needs, and code officials are only concerned with *minimum* compliance standards, not what's achievable. How does society's concern over increased energy efficiency and improved indoor environmental conditions fit into this already complex decision-making process?[11]

Utility regulators in some jurisdictions have determined that electric utilities should take the lead in the interim (i.e., while waiting for building codes to catch up to potential energy efficiency levels). Determining both the appropriateness of this assignment, and how utilities can effectively carve out a role for themselves in the already complex process described above, has been a point of major contention in past utility rate cases—at high cost to both sides, and with little progress. Similar conflicts have arisen regarding retrofit investments. Certainly a more efficient and less contentious process has been needed for bringing the parties together for achieving the common goal of increased energy efficiency in buildings.

AN INNOVATIVE PLANNING APPROACH

Northeast Utilities (NU or the Company) is a major New England electric company with subsidiaries in Connecticut and Massachusetts.[12]

The Company has provided conservation and load management services to its customers since 1980 and continues to be an industry leader in demand management efforts. Even so, in recent rate cases involving cost recovery for expenses associated with the Millstone nuclear power plant, regulators, consumer advocates, and other outside interested parties have intervened and called for increased demand management efforts on the part of the Company.

A key organization that became involved in cases in both Connecticut and Massachusetts is the Conservation Law Foundation of New England. This organization, and its consultants from around the country, pointed out that, in spite of NU's laudable efforts to date, a more aggressive investment program could and should be pursued as a corporate strategy for offsetting the need for future power supplies. It was further pointed out that there remained significant portions of the consumer population that were yet unserved (or underserved) by the Company's broad-based programs. While many of the points being made by the outside interested parties in these cases were certainly worthy of further consideration, their discussion in the rate case hearing rooms seriously interfered with the main business at hand. Because issues were seldom resolved in such forums, they came to be considered counterproductive by most participants, including the commissions and their hearing officers charged with issuing rulings. However, the Company acknowledged that the experience and ideas of these intervening parties could be valuable in helping to shape NU's previous sincere efforts at a significant demand management program.

In an unprecedented show of common sense and cooperation between regulators and a major utility, it was mutually proposed and agreed that NU would work with representatives of the intervening parties outside of the rate hearing process to review all of its building energy efficiency programs and to develop or modify plans where needed. This would be done in a collaborative manner by NU's conservation and load management staff and the research staff and consultants of the Conservation Law Foundation of New England, and the Attorneys General, Consumer Counsels, and other offices and agencies of the two states.[13]

To provide an incentive for this cooperation and to demonstrate the regulators' acknowledgement of the value of this planning effort to consumers in the two states, the regulatory commissions in both states agreed to try to reduce the burdensome amount of conservation and load management litigation in future rate cases and limit the focus to essential issues. This promise alone would save the utility significant sums in paperwork, cross-examination, preparation, and time in these future cases.

HOW THE COLLABORATIVE PLANNING
PROCESSES WORKED

Perhaps the best way to characterize the collaborative planning processes conducted by NU in both states is that they have been "grassroots" efforts, with top management limiting its involvement to oversight activity. This approach has been quite successful at making available a significant amount of valuable planning information and at fostering maximum creativity.

Essentially, the people closest to the customers have been the ones involved in the planning process. NU's conservation and load management staff and field forces worked closely (often on a day-to-day basis at the same long table) with the staff and consultants of the Conservation Law Foundation and other parties experienced in demand management efforts around the country. What the outside parties brought to the table was an intimate knowledge of specific customer segments, such as low-income and disadvantaged residential households, from work done previously around the country.[14] What the utility staff contributed was a first-hand knowledge of the customers in the two service territories, and, perhaps even more importantly, a keen awareness of how to get things done in a large regulated utility business environment.

Perhaps the most valuable thing gained by the outside parties was a greater appreciation of the business environment in a large corporation, one whose first priority is to keep the lights on. Most of the outside firms involved are either very small or even one-person businesses, where decisions can be made and carried out quickly. NU, by contrast, has over nine thousand employees in locations spread over two states and serves over a million residential customers. Thus, while the spirit may be there for implementing an innovative new program, it takes significant time and a series of approvals and training sessions before it can actually be introduced to the public.

As for NU, the Company has learned a great deal from the outside parties as well. Key results of the planning process have shown that a more segmented approach to marketing building energy efficiency programs results in higher success rates. NU's program plans now include specific approaches for reaching customers in various segments of the residential, commercial, and industrial sectors. Another significant finding of the collaborative work was the feasibility of using outside groups in the residential and business communities to deliver services to customers. This approach logically avoids duplication with state and local conservation efforts and provides a more coordinated (and hence less confusing) front to the consumer. Working with an existing infrastructure rather than exclusively using utility personnel makes sense, and simultaneously provides monies for these other groups to play a role rather than putting staffing pressures on the large utility workforce. While some of these ideas had been explored by the Company in small ways, the outside parties showed how they could be made central features of an overall demand management program plan.

The basic approach followed by the two collaborative processes was as follows:

Step 1: Examine the marketplace by customer segment. This involved a careful examination of utility and secondary data on residential customers by category: low-, mid-, and high-income customers, those using electricity for heating, water-heating, or general service. The commercial class was broken into groups such as institutional customers (e.g., schools and hospitals) and was also viewed in terms of size categories. The aim of pursuing this segmented approach to researching customer markets was to identify homogeneous groups of customers who view energy-related opportunities similarly and who have similar decision-making criteria.

Step 2: Identify the key barriers and opportunities for energy savings/load reduction in each group. In this step, the planning groups took advantage of prior experience to identify key barriers to the adoption of conservation and load management opportunities in the past—barriers that would have to be addressed in the new set of programs in order to generate the significant levels of customer participation needed to make the demand management investment strategy successful (i.e., to result in enough peak load reduction to offset or delay the need for new power supplies).

Step 3: Review the existing menu of programs and develop new conceptual plans. Here the group went over the currently existing programs offered to customers in the two jurisdictions. In several cases, only minor adjustments to the approaches taken were recommended, while in others, a whole new approach variation was needed. In a third case, where a special group was identified where no previous program appeared to meet their special needs for building efficiency improvements, totally new programs were developed. At the conclusion of this step, the utility filed the conceptual plans with regulators in the two states with the endorsement of the outside parties.

Step 4: Prepare detailed implementation plans for the new programs. In this step, the work is carried out in the two states. The outside parties remain involved and will continue to monitor progress as the programs are introduced. However, this step involves more work from the utility's internal staff for carrying out the detailed task of making all the arrangements: obtaining vendors where needed, preparing contracts, ordering materials, developing forms, setting up accounts, developing advertising campaigns, etc.

Step 5: Prepare tracking and evaluation plans. An often overlooked but critical task to be performed as a program is being designed is making provisions for the program's progress to be monitored. What will constitute success for each program in terms of goals to be set and achieved? How will we know we are on target? What are the things we need to track? Certainly the number of participants will be counted periodically, but we will also need to know about their load characteristics, their energy-using behavior, and their feelings about the program. For this, data collection plans need to be prepared, databases designed, and analytical needs anticipated, so that evaluations can be made at some point in the future.

Step 6: Introduce the programs to the public. This final step is actually occurring in a staggered manner, since many programs were already available to customers, and since the new programs are not all ready to present at the same time (nor would it be wise to introduce them all simultaneously).

To illustrate the process above for one important customer segment, consider the new housing market. The Company's previous efforts at influencing new electrically heated residential construction had provided limited impact, other than an enthusiastic but limited response to solar home design plan books. The new program being finalized for introduction this year includes a "team" approach to building design, which involves the architect, developer, general contractor, plumber, electrician, homeowner, and other parties who have an influence over the features and products used in the home. Incentives are provided in the form of computerized comparative redesign services, monies for the extra time required of the building professionals involved, and rebates or grants for the incorporation of the energy-saving features identified.

THE RESULTS

The result, in this case, is a new program that includes aggressive incentives and works hand-in-hand with the local building community to achieve the desired building energy efficiency aims. In addition, the Company has a stronger sense of what other utilities' experience has been in addressing this market segment.

This type of knowledge (from previous experience in building energy efficiency programs targeted at low-income residential customers) was captured and structured in one of the more important planning products of the collaborative process: a series of Principles of Program Design for Low-Income Customers. This set of principles recognizes the special barriers that exist within this market segment and that typically prevent such customers from reaping the benefits of conservation and load management programs. These principles are:

- Provide 100 percent subsidy for conservation measures and services
- Utilize existing outreach agencies to identify potential participants
- Utilize existing local outreach agencies to deliver program services
- Provide flexibility in the service to be delivered
- Strive for a minimum number of visits to the customer's home to avoid unnecessary intrusions
- Conduct inspections to ensure quality control
- Provide consumer education along with the measures and services
- Leverage funds available from other programs to extend the amount of measures and services provided
- Use alternative marketing and delivery mechanisms as needed

Other insights were obtained through the collaborative process, regarding other customer segments, which led to similar specific program design criteria. As another example, in the agricultural sector, a special program aimed at farmers in the two states was developed to address the energy savings available in energy-efficient farm process equipment not covered in existing commercial or industrial energy audit or rebate programs.

Aside from the planning and program results of the collaborative planning process, there are a few more general benefits of interest to those considering pursuing a similar activity:

- The previously adversarial relationship between public policymakers and the utility has been replaced with one characterized by cooperation and the mutual desire to have an impact on building energy efficiency improvements.
- There is increased coordination among the various state and local groups who deliver conservation and load management services to customers.
- Resources have been freed from the elimination of previously duplicated services (e.g., multiple trips to deliver services) by transferring the responsibility for those services to local agencies better prepared to deliver them.
- Utility-provided training and funding for vendors, local businesses, and community agencies to carry out conservation and load management services is helping to build the local infrastructure and thus create a stronger building energy efficiency industry. The important role of building codes and code officials is also being considered in the process.
- The participation of local equipment dealers and other retail businesses in utility programs is increasing the stock of energy-efficient equipment and ap-

pliances, while simultaneously increasing consumer awareness of the energy-saving opportunities at the point-of-purchase. A market transformation is in progress.

- The utility has learned a great deal about consumer markets and successful program delivery techniques from elsewhere around the country as a result of the participation of the outside parties and their consultants.
- Regulators and the outside parties have simultaneously learned a great deal about utility service delivery, its complexity, and the concerns, limitations, and opportunities within which a regulated organization operates.

TRANSFERRING THE PROCESS

What has been accomplished in this collaborative building energy efficiency planning process may seem somewhat simplistic, but it was a very hard-won battle. Getting two knowledgeable adversarial parties to sit down, learn about each other, and then share their knowledge with each other toward reaching a common goal is a problem-solving approach obvious to many, but carried out by few. From individual marriages to international policy discussion among superpowers, it is not easy nor clearly seen as advantageous to work together; all too often battles ensue and the problems are solved only later—at much greater expense and with arguably less understanding.

This model for the development of a public-private collaborative planning effort aimed at more effective building energy efficiency programs is one that can be used in other utility-state jurisdictions. However, the successful transferability of such a process will likely depend upon several factors, such as:

- The management and corporate traditions of the energy suppliers
- The management and agency traditions of the regulators
- The skill levels and personalities of the individuals involved
- The resources devoted to the effort and who pays for them
- The comprehensiveness of information used in the planning process

There are undoubtedly other considerations as well. Three primary recommendations that we would make, based upon the experiences described herein, are as follows:

1. Form a type of "contract" between the public and private parties involved at the outset of the process to serve as a set of rules and objectives for the work. This should include work plans, time tables, and work assignments.
2. Seek in good faith to replace the adversarial nature of the prior relationship with one of *shared responsibility* for the planning process and its outcome.

3. Keep the activity at the staff level by letting the planners do the planning, and delegate as much authority as possible to the level where the knowledge lies.

CONCLUSIONS

Finally, it is our conclusion that both groups—public and private—benefitted greatly from the process described in these pages. Each learned a great deal from the other that will make the future efforts of both parties at achieving improved building energy efficiency more effective. As has been suggested in this chapter, the reasons for improving our building stock and the manner in which we use electricity already exist and will only grow in number and importance over time. NU feels that it has pursued a responsible planning approach to that challenge through this collaborative planning process for building energy efficiency programs and invites others involved in energy policy to follow suit.

NOTES

1. NECPA, the National Energy Conservation Policy Act of 1979, was a far-reaching piece of legislation that was a reaction to the oil embargo crisis. This law required, among other things, that the U.S. Department of Energy develop regulations requiring states to develop Residential Conservation Program plans. This state-mandated program was the first whereby utilities were expressly used as a vehicle to provide energy conservation services for upgrading the energy efficiency of existing residential buildings.

2. In the residential sector, peak use hours are usually associated with meal-times before and after the work day. Thus, for example, the aim might be to encourage homemakers to do laundry after 8 P.M., when cooking, dishwashing, and other tasks are completed. A typical residential electric appliance that has been the target of older utility load management programs is the electric water heater. In commercial buildings, the peak hours generally are in the afternoon during the summer and the late morning during the winter. Thus, a primary load management concern in the commercial sector is electric air conditioning use, for example.

3. If consumers respond consistently based on economic criteria, virtually everyone would use energy-efficient light bulbs, water heater insulation wraps, and other conservaton measures that have been readily available for years. There are a variety of measures such as these that offer pay-backs (returns on investment) in reduced electricity costs in a year or less, and yet sizeable portions of the marketplace have not adopted them in their buildings.

4. The results of various recent utility market research projects for conservation and load management programs have revealed such broad issues as consumer reasons for considering participation in energy efficiency programs.

5. Sponsored by the National Science Foundation, Engineering Directorate, Building Systems and Structures; organized by the Center for Architectural Re-

search, Rensselaer Polytechnic Institute; supported by AT&T, Haworth Inc., Herman Miller Inc., IBM, Johnson Controls, Owens-Corning Fiberglass, The Trane Company, and United Technologies Corporation.

6. The "sick building syndrome" refers to environmental hazards that can exist within the interior space of a building that spread through a building's HVAC system or other space conditioning equipment or features. Here the concept is expanded from a more topical limited definition to refer to the "mismatch" of an existing building to the tasks and environmental conditions currently required of it. For example, an old brick structure originally built for light industry may have evolved into a commercial building with shops on the first floor and an added second floor of office space. While the heating system may have been retrofitted to serve the new space, the addition of computers, a later central air conditioning system, and other features may make the internal environment less than optimal from both an electric energy efficiency standpoint, as well as a human work space standpoint. This can lead to lower worker productivity. Typically, task lighting and localized ventilation are prime suspects, and yet, they are less often considered for retrofit than the larger central building systems when the use of a large space is changed. The "sick building syndrome," therefore, can also refer to the relationship between the building environment and worker productivity.

7. Walter M. Kroner, ed., *A New Frontier: Environments for Innovation,* Proceedings of the International Symposium on Advanced Comfort Systems for the Work-Environment, May 1–3, 1988, Center for Architectural Research, Rensselaer Polytechnic Institute, Troy, New York, 3.

8. This consideration of a building space as a human environment has been receiving attention lately in the identification of smoke-free work areas in offices (also in an increasing number of restaurants). In some businesses with large facilities, individuals who smoke are provided desks near exhaust outlets so that the smoke does the least amount of traveling before being diffused.

9. The desk is manufactured by the West German firm Schmidt Reuter, whose brochure refers to "Top performance in modern indoor technology." An American example is being marketed by Johnson Controls, whose PERSONAL ENVIRONMENTS office system is being developed with consulting support from organizations such as the Center for Building Performance and Diagnostics at Carnegie Mellon, Pittsburgh, Pennsylvania, and the School of Environmental Health at McGill University, Montreal, Canada.

10. The process of "balancing" a building's environmental system is essentially the last engineering step performed after a building is constructed, furnished, and occupied. It involves testing the space conditioning systems designed for the building to see how they work now that the lights, window treatments, etc., are in place. The systems are then "set" so that when the thermostat is set or programmed for 68° F, it will indeed be (or at least feel like) 68° F inside. A significant energy-saving opportunity is lost (some say 20 percent) when buildings are not "rebalanced" when a building's function or occupants change. Even the addition of a new computer room with additional air conditioning requirements can unbalance the building's overall environmental systems. Even with no major changes in use or occupants, it is wise to have a large office building rebalanced every five years, according to William C. Abernathy

of the Mechanical Contractors Association of America and the National Environmental Balancing Bureau (Bethesda, Maryland).

11. This task is even more difficult to achieve in the retrofitting of existing
buildings, but then so are the opportunities for improvements.

12. The Connecticut Light and Power Company, the Western Massachusetts
Electric Company, and the Holyoke Water Power Company.

13. The first collaborative process began in Connecticut and was followed by
a multiutility process in Massachusetts, of which Western Massachusetts Electric
Company is the lead utility and member.

14. Several of the CLF consultants are from the Pacific Northwest, where their
earlier work focused on customers of the Bonneville Power Administration and
other Northwest utilities. Several of the nonutility participants had previous
utility experience.

II

Improving Urban
Transportation

7

TRANSPORTATION AND THE ENVIRONMENT—LESSONS FROM THE GLOBAL LABORATORY

WILFRED OWEN

An assessment of the impacts of transportation on urban living produces two sharply contrasting pictures. On the positive side, modern methods of moving are the lifelines of the cities, making it possible to deliver food and supplies for massive concentrations of people and economic activity. Hundreds of millions of workers are able to get to their jobs and home again each day. Industry prospers from the specialization and expanding markets made possible by low-cost and reliable movement of goods and materials. Consumers enjoy opportunities and choices that could come only from the expanding radius of their activities and the ease of travel. Finally, the speed and range of modern transport, combined with telecommunications, have interconnected the great cities of the world in a global network of production, trade, and travel that has brought significant economic and physical change to a rapidly urbanizing planet.

But the achievements of transportation have been accompanied by the increasingly negative impacts of the conflict between mobility and livability. The cities of the world, in both rich countries and poor, are becoming paralyzed by traffic, stifled by pollutants, and visually diminished by blighted streetscapes and the intrusions of traffic into neighborhoods. The functioning of urban society and the role of the city as a focus of innovation and human progress appear threatened by conditions that transportation has created or that poor transportation has helped to sustain.

It need not be that way, for transportation, rather than detracting from urban life, can be a powerful instrument for creating urban environments in closer harmony with human aspirations. The problems and possibilities can be judged by assessing current conditions and potentials in the light of the five categories (or "five E's") that Rene Dubos has suggested as a test—how the cities fare in terms of ecology, economics, energetics, esthetics, and ethics.

TRANSPORTATION AND URBAN ECOLOGY

Transportation technology, combined with rapid growth of urban population, has altered the ecology of human settlements by changing the relation of people to their physical environment and to each other. An immediate cause is the incompatibility of urbanization and motorization. Living in cities is space-conserving, while riding in automobiles is space-consuming. Yet a critical look at the traffic troubles of cities suggests that other factors are also at work. Cities relying on rail rapid transit, such as Tokyo or New York, have much the same traffic congestion as auto-dependent cities, such as Los Angeles or Phoenix.

The explanation lies in the fact that supplying transportation facilities generates feedback effects that fill whatever capacity is provided. Automobiles fill the space available, and structures rise to take advantage of transportation potentials. With urban development largely unplanned and uncontrolled, the demand for transportation always manages to outstrip the supply. Governments are charged with accommodating whatever transport problems by bringing about a manageable balance between supply and demand.

To cite an analogous situation, architects designing a building include in it a transportation system of corridors, halls, stairways, and elevators to accommodate the numbers of people who will be working or living in it, what they will be doing, and what location and arrangement of activities will provide operating efficiency and convenience.

In cities, which are an assemblage of buildings, it is equally important to balance transportation supply and demand but far more difficult when there is so little control over demand. But if cities are to serve human purposes in the face of rapid change, ways must be found to achieve a more satisfactory match between living and moving.

The global laboratory of cities reveals that the search for solutions is under way. It consists of mixed-use community designs that reduce commuting and routine household trips, and that make use of transportation for planned escape from the congestion of accidental cities.

Stockholm is a good example. Transportation by rail rapid transit and expressway leads out of the central city to new communities on the periphery that combine housing, shops, and services in partially self-sufficient clusters separated from each other and from the city by open space. Movement out of the downtown area into the satellite centers has reduced the inner-city densities and permitted redevelopment. The dispersed multi-centered metropolis has upgraded the environment, provided high-speed traffic corridors, and contained much of the daily travel needs of the household within the planned suburbs.

While more office jobs might have been located in the satellites, the Greater Stockholm model provides an excellent illustration of how a partnership of transportation, urban design, and open space policies has helped to bring about an urban ecology that achieves a satisfying balance between living and moving.

The satellite cities around Paris, accessible by regional express railways and highways, demonstrate on a larger scale the multiple objectives of containing much of the growth of traffic to short trips in planned suburbs, providing fast transport connections to the city center, and helping to prepare the heart of Paris for redevelopment.

The planned urban regions of Paris and Stockholm have their counterparts throughout the world, where planned communities containing both housing and jobs in a satisfying mix of open space and development have been made accessible to the city by high-speed road and rail connections. This formula has been successful in creating the modern Singapore regional city and is being applied in metropolitan Tokyo, Osaka, and other parts of Japan, as well as in Hong Kong and Korea. Japan's comprehensive development plan calls for a national network of high-speed guideways and telecommunications to support a dispersal of relatively self-sufficient communities.

In the United States, the dispersal made possible by transportation has led to the creation of one-purpose suburbs that consist of housing without jobs and shopping malls or offices without housing. Transportation is relied upon to compensate for lack of community. But it has become evident that the resulting traffic congestion cannot be overcome simply by building more transport capacity, and planned models such as Reston, Virginia, and Columbia, Maryland, are being emulated by less ambitious efforts to design whole communities on a smaller scale. In these planned suburbs, some part of the resident population will have the choice of working closer to home and shopping or enjoying recreation nearby. These partially self-sufficient suburbs are designed to be transport-conserving as well as to be well linked by road and rail to a major city where other employment opportunities and services are readily accessible. Instead of compulsory trip-taking, it is possible to reduce the number and frequency of some trips by some percentage of the population. Thus, in Reston, 40 percent of workers living in the planned community hold jobs there, and it is estimated that traffic in and out of Reston is 25 percent lower as a result of the mix of land uses. For those residents unable or unwilling to reduce their commuting or other routine trips, toll road and beltway connections help to serve their needs.

A dozen or more suburban cities are locating along Washington's Metro Rail network and Interstate highway system, planned to contain both housing and employment in an environment that includes education facilities, recreation, and shopping—as proposed in the original plan for the nation's capital. Metro rail is providing the basic framework for much of the construction, while highways are literally helping to pave the way to a multi-centered urban region of more thoughtfully planned transport-conserving communities.

ECONOMICS

There are other possible assaults on traffic and its negative impacts that lie in the realm of economics. The faulty pricing of urban transport services accounts, in part, for the choices being made between public transit and the use of the automobile, along with the neglect of economic efficiency in the allocation of street space between the two methods of moving in the central cities. Generally speaking, public policy favors private over public transport, even in heavily congested areas. Urban highways are underpriced, and the motorist, who pays for roads in statewide and national fees and taxes, pays a statewide charge reflecting average costs instead of the actual marginal costs incurred to supply the expensive facilities provided in cities.

A desirable solution is to levy specific charges covering the economic and social costs of driving into the city during peak periods, either by a special license plate or by collecting a toll. The latter can be accomplished electronically without toll gates as vehicle identification systems make possible electronic monthly billing for street use. Meanwhile, the best example of congestion pricing without electronic aids is in Singapore, where cars with fewer than four occupants are charged with entry into the city in morning rush hours. The effect has been to shift commuters to buses and to cause a sharp reduction in the volume of automobile traffic entering the city.

Increasing the efficiency of existing transportation facilities is a relatively underutilized but effective solution for bringing about a sounder economic approach to urban transportation. So-called transportation system management helps to reach a better balance between supply and demand by staggering work hours, reducing free parking on the streets, increasing charges for parking, and providing financial incentives to encourage employees to come by bus or rail instead of driving. Other aids to collective transport include ride-sharing, the operation of van services by employers, transit subsidies, and such aid to transit as the designation of special bus lanes and bus streets.

The growing urgency of adhering to clean air standards may lend additional weight to traffic management methods that increase ride-sharing and the use of public transit. But the economic advantages of the automobile over public transit are so attractive under most circumstances that neither pricing nor regulatory policies are likely to alter consumer choice to a degree that would be decisive. An economically more promising method may come from an entirely different source, namely the advent of low-cost telecommunications as a substitute for many kinds of trip-taking.

The moving of information to people rather than people to information may make telecommunications and computers a major economic breakthrough for traffic-burdened cities. Their role will be increasing as declining cost and increasing quality of transmission contrast with the rising costs and frustrations of travel. The effect will be a shift from commuting to telecommuting, and the widespread use of teleconferencing methods as a substitute for costly and time-consuming travel to business meetings. The economic advantages of electronic transmission over transportation will further the emergence of the new urban ecology of the dispersed regional city, as well as enhance working conditions, productivity, and the quality of life.

For persons who can operate part-time or all the time from a home electronic workshop or a work station in the neighborhood, more time can be spent at home with a family, or made available for hobbies and recreation. The probability that people will be making multiple career changes in the future adds to the advantages of telecommuting, since a job change may not make it necessary to be uprooted from the neighborhood and home. And since communication costs do not increase with distance, the location of decisions of business and consumers in the information age will be more sensitive to the importance of the living and the working environment.

ENERGETICS

Transportation in the United States is more than 90 percent dependent on petroleum, and half of all petroleum use is in the transport sector. What the future holds for transport, therefore, is closely tied to developments in energy, and these, in turn, will have major implications on the environment.

In the summer of 1988, close to one hundred metropolitan areas in the United States failed to meet air quality standards for ozone and carbon monoxide. Motor vehicles were contributing two-thirds of the metric tons of carbon monoxide, as well as substantial amounts of other pollutants contributing to health hazards.

A reduction in energy waste in dependence on nonrenewable petroleum can be achieved, in part, by more energy-conserving cars. The
trend in new car performance shows a gain in fuel efficiency from an
average of fourteen miles per gallon in 1974 to twenty-eight miles per
gallon in 1988, and it is anticipated that the figure may go as high as
fifty to one hundred miles per gallon for some models during the last
decade of the century. The use of alternative fuels such as alcohol may
also rise as the enforcement of clean air standards demands.

In the long run the various environmental hazards resulting from the
use of petroleum-based fuels, together with dwindling supplies and
higher prices, will accelerate the search for energy alternatives. Among
the possibilities is the electric car, propelled either by the fuel cell per-
fected for space applications or by the more powerful batteries that can
emerge from the discovery of new superconducting materials. Experiments with solar-powered vehicles also point to some of the long-range
possibilities.

If a practical electric vehicle is developed, the effect on the environment could be to both reduce air pollution and to hasten the development of electric highways that would increase safety, reduce noise levels, and provide more roadway capacity without taking more land for
highway construction.

Superconductors that increase the power and economy of magneti-
cally levitated electric trains or other vehicles could also introduce a
nonpolluting method of high-speed transport by a guideway that would
help reduce traffic congestion on major routes in providing an alternative to some types of air and highway travel.

Efforts to overcome the wasteful use of energy and to convert to renewable sources will be given added pressure by a host of considerations, from oil spills and atmospheric pollution to energy and dependence on foreign trade deficits. Meanwhile, the need to alter transport
energetics will lend support for changes in urban design that can help
realize the energy-conserving communities of the future. Reducing the
use of energy will likewise hasten the use of energy-saving communication networks and the large-scale economies this will mean for business,
consumers, and the cities.

ESTHETICS

Transportation in the twentieth century has a well-earned reputation
for contributing to negative scenery of urban areas. The detractions from
the urban environment that occur in the process of moving people and
goods affect many aspects of life in city and suburb.

The roster of transport-assisted ills includes dingy subways strewn
with litter, beaches that bear the brunt of garbage dumped by vessels at

sea, smog that obscures the landscape and the sky, the tangle of poles, wires, and signs along commercial streets, and the outdoor advertising that obstructs the view and desecrates the beauty of the countryside on the escape routes from the city.

Since the streets are the major use of urban public land, failure to establish esthetically acceptable standards of roadside development means that the most frequented areas of the city are often the most unsightly. Often there is the added negative impact of curbside parking that dominates the environment, along with abandoned cars and poorly kept parking lots. Elevated highways often have the same effect on housing and neighborhood as the elevated railways of the past, most of which are now removed.

These conditions are by no means inevitable. As witness, recall the tree-lined boulevards in so many cities in the United States and around the world, including urban parkways and the landscaped sections of Interstate highways.

In recent years in particular, cities have been allocating more street and highway funds to trees and other plantings, and to attractive sidewalk pavers and lighting standards. The costly undergrounding of utilities has also begun in many communities. Programs have been undertaken to upgrade commercial store fronts, adopt uniform sign standards, and encourage commercial outlets to landscape their properties. Curbside parking restrictions and a shift to enclosed off-street parking structures have also contributed to the esthetics of the motorized city.

The transportation sector has also been the source of strategically located properties abandoned as a result of changing technology—rail yards and terminals, docks and warehouses, and close-in airports. These have provided an opportunity to introduce new land uses and to contribute to urban redevelopment, the economy, and the beauty of the city.

In Boston the decision was made to tear down the elevated Central Artery to eliminate an undesirable barrier to the harbor. Boston, Baltimore, Norfolk, and many other cities have converted unused docks, piers, and other marine transport properties to parks, restaurants, and condominiums.

An impressive number of downtown developments have been made possible by the use of outmoded railroad facilities and by joint developments of transportation agencies and private enterprise. Penn Center in Philadelphia was built over the rail yards, as was Prudential Center in Boston. Many urban areas have also been embellished by the conversion of railway stations, notable among them the monumental Union Station in Washington, D.C. Large and small cities have made successful conversions of narrow downtown streets for the exclusive use of pedestrians, including at least a hundred urban communities in Europe and many in Japan, Brazil, and the United States.

The quality of life in cities could be improved substantially by a closer partnership between agencies responsible for public works and parks and recreation. Streets can become linear parks, treescapes can introduce shade and space for benches and tables, and the traveled way can make use of plants and flowers to upgrade neighborhoods and combine mobility with livability. It is the ugliness of the cities and the disregard for esthetics in many of the newer suburbs that typifies much of urban America. The transportation sector and appropriate use of the land adjacent to the highway and street systems in particular hold the greatest promise of overcoming the visual pollution of urban areas and the spreading metropolis.

ETHICS

Because most American cities have developed on the assumption that everybody drives, public transportation is often impractical, inadequate, or nonexistent. The result is that many people living in cities and suburbs who do not have a car available have become stranded members of a new transportation underclass. They include young and old, as well as the poor and the physically handicapped. Without the ability to travel, they are denied many of the opportunities and choices available to those who drive. Urban ethics calls for more equal access to the daily needs of the household for all who live in the city and its suburbs.

Efforts to help the transport-deprived are being made through subsidized public transit and by the operation of buses and vans to provide elders and the handicapped with free access to hospitals, clinics, schools, shopping malls, grocery stores, and similar destinations. These so-called paratransit vehicles in the private sector are often more numerous than the fleets operated by municipal transit companies. The latter have been providing a higher quality of service through recent increases in federal and state subsidies, but unlike the transit successes in European cities, the expanse of metropolitan areas in the United States has made satisfactory coverage impractical.

It is in developing countries, however, that the problems of the transport-disadvantaged are proving to be most acute, as the burgeoning cities leave most of their inhabitants stranded far from jobs and services. Where there are trains and buses, they are grossly overcrowded, and most people are unable to pay the fare. For the millions who live in outlying favelas and squatter settlements, the absence of transport or the inability to pay the fare often means denying access to the means of earning a living. When impoverished families in Third World metropolitan areas say that transportation is their principal problem, what they mean is that lack of mobility consigns them to a life of hunger and deprivation.

The transportation plight of the poor can be alleviated either by very large investments in public transit, which is unlikely, or by measures to bring housing and jobs closer together. Self-help communities built around large cities such as Madras and Karachi are frequently located near industrial estates, and facilities are provided within the community for cottage industries that make it possible to establish handicraft industries, repair shops, and retail services. Easier access to gainful employment is the only practical alternative to costly transportation. A transportation ethic for developing countries calls for easier access rather than greater mobility. It is the same remedy suggested for urban America, where the transport-disadvantaged are likewise victims of location policies and transportation gaps that leave them without access to their daily needs.

SUMMARY

Transportation that has helped build the modern metropolis has also built a reputation for negative impacts on the environment. But innovative methods of keeping the metropolis moving could be a powerful means of achieving a higher quality of urban life. What is required is an effective alliance between those who provide transportation and those responsible for urban design and regional planning. Public-private partnership, with the help of new transport technology and the use of telecommunications, could build the multi-centered urban regions of the future that foster both mobility and livability.

A primary need is to match efforts to make people mobile with programs to make the city accessible—relying on convenient location and arrangement of urban activities and not just on building more transportation capacity. Also required are sounder economic practices in transport financing, more effective use of existing transport facilities, and energy sources that are renewable and nonpolluting.

Upgrading the streetscapes could make a major contribution to urban esthetics, and ethical responsibilities affecting the transport-disadvantaged further stress the need for better public transit and greater convenience through community design.

These elements of a transport strategy apply not only to urban America, but also to the planless expansion of greater cities in less developed countries. In a global setting the threat posed by unmanageable cities could have far-reaching impacts on the future of the world economy. The situation calls for cooperative international research and development and greater use of the global laboratory of urban experience to accelerate practical solutions to mutual problems.

8

THE AUTO, LAND USE, AND TRANSIT

BORIS PUSHKAREV

AN AUTO-DEPENDENT NATION

In the decade and a half after World War II, as the United States was tearing up 15,000 miles of streetcar track, a utopian vision gripped the nation: to build an urban society without cities, a form of settlement dependent only on the automobile.

By the mid 1950s, the backbone of the new settlement—the freeway system—was under construction in earnest. Other countries were also advancing the development of freeways; but they—just as young Robert Moses did in the 1930s—saw them as an auxiliary element for intercity and recreational travel. The key feature of the 1950s vision in the United States was its monistic character: the auto would take care of *all* urban travel needs in the future.

By the early 1960s, travel theory advanced far enough to show how the future would work: urban areas would consist of freeway grids spaced in relation to the density of trip ends. In what remained of older cities, freeways would be as close as a mile or two apart; in suburban areas, three- to five-mile spacing would be typical, stretching perhaps to every ten miles in the urbanizing countryside. Four-lane divided highways, which allowed the enjoyment of scenery, would become largely obsolete: dual-dual expanses of pavement up to fourteen lanes wide were on the drawing boards to satisfy projected travel demand.

With ample funding, rigorous administration, and not much concern for visual values, construction proceeded apace: between 1953 and 1973

43,000 miles of freeway were added to the some 2,000 previously built. Traffic congestion seemed on its way to solution: new lane-miles of capacity were added faster than vehicle-miles of travel grew. On longer trips, freeways easily cut travel time in half, which gave them economic justification.

Then something happened on the way to utopia: in the fifteen years following 1973, the annual increment of freeways opened to traffic shrank from an average of 2,150 to 640 miles (the current rate is 420 miles a year). The cutback resulted from a confluence of events: community opposition to the disruption of neighborhoods; environmental impact legislation, which gave the opposition legal tools to block construction; a shift in fiscal priorities from infrastructure investment to social and medical spending; the drop in the birth rate between 1957 and 1974, which led to a sharp downward revision of population and future "needs" forecasts; the oil crises of 1974 and 1979.

But even as the supply of freeway pavement rose by not much more than 20 percent nationwide in the fifteen years from 1973 to 1988, motor vehicle registrations shot up by 45 percent, and vehicle miles travelled by 54 percent! In large urban areas, the contrast was sharper. With the supply of pavement basically fixed and travel demand growing fast, urban freeway congestion became a major issue in the late 1980s, making headlines from New York to Los Angeles.

The public mind seems to be curiously divided: it welcomed the cutback in freeway construction, but it insists on acquiring more autos and then bemoans the resulting congestion. It fails to consider that perhaps the settlement pattern that requires those auto purchases ought to be altered.

Though the freeway network turned out smaller than planned in the 1960s, the monistic vision of the auto as the sole means of ground transport came close to realization. Walking to work dropped from 10.4 percent of all worktrips in 1960 to 4.1 percent in 1983. Travel by public transportation (urban and intercity) dropped from 13 percent of all ground travel in 1950 to below 3 percent in 1986. The average annual auto travel per resident exceeds 300 miles only in ten major urban areas and reaches 1,100 only in New York (with seven suburban counties). Meanwhile, the average annual auto travel per resident nationally is around 10,000 miles.

This degree of mobility by auto has had a profound impact on settlement. A pedestrian walking at three miles per hour can reach, within a half hour, any point in a 2.25 square mile area around him. A streetcar or bus passenger moving at six miles per hour (including waiting) can reach, within a half hour, any point in a nine square mile area around him. In the same time a motorist, even moving at thirty miles per hour, can reach any point in a 225 square mile area around him.

Assuming for a moment that in a mid-sized city a resident needs the potential for contact with 225,000 other people within a half hour travel time, the pedestrian city requires a density of 100,000 persons per square mile; the auto-oriented one, 1,000 per square mile. These are realistic ranges of actual urban densities over time.

They show that successive transportation improvements did not necessarily improve the efficiency of the city as a "human switchboard," a machine for making face-to-face contact with other people. They did enormously expand the land area over which people are spread, hence the consumption of physical resources needed to support them (the energy, the materials, even the water to sprinkle the lawns) and the consequent emissions into the environment. Annual net energy use in the New York Region in 1970 varied from 200 million Btu per capita at exuberant densities of 1,000 persons per square mile to 120 million Btu at urban densities of 25,000 per square mile. In terms of physical resources consumed—which is what matters in the economy of the environment—the spread, auto-oriented settlement pattern is the most profligate yet invented. The tremendous expansion of the accessible land area carried huge social costs as well. The drop in the relative accessibility in the inner city and the increase in the accessibility of rural land caused major, uncompensated transfers of land value and hence of wealth-fostered segregation by income and race.

Both types of segregation fed back to encourage yet more travel, as whites shunned black ghettoes close to their places of work and middle-class people leapfrogged over the expensive suburbs to cheaper land on the distant periphery. Meanwhile, those locked up in the ghettoes lacked the autos everyone else had to get to suitable jobs.

Auto movement on freeways did foster some growth in traditional downtowns. Even in a regular freeway grid, the center of the grid is the most accessible place. But, as such, it also attracts a volume of travel that the grid cannot handle efficiently. Other interchanges on the grid offer slightly lower accessibility and so the grid encourages, throughout the area, a haphazard formation of dispersed employment clusters, unsuited by density and design for anything but auto access. As they build up, the clusters become too dense to be served by auto without congestion, yet neither dense enough nor centrally enough located to support public transit. This leads to still more dispersal and more auto travel.

IMMEDIATE PROSPECTS

The future, left to its own devices, promises little let-up in motor vehicle growth, which depends on (1) per capita income, (2) the driving-age population, (3) the density of areas where this population lives, and (4) the density of its workplaces.

Per capita income is expected to continue its steady, long-term rise. In the New York Region, we expect it to increase from $16,350 (in constant 1984 dollars) in 1987 to $26,000 in 2015. Each $1,000 in added per capita income will add about three motor vehicles per one hundred residents.

The driving age population will exert some restraint on motor vehicle growth as ownership approaches saturation. In the nation's and the region's most affluent counties, the number of motor vehicles registered already exceeds the number of residents aged sixteen to eighty; adding still more vehicles there will add little to travel demand, since it is hard for one owner to drive more than one vehicle simultaneously. But such high income counties are relatively few; most counties in the nation have a way to go before they reach saturation.

Higher development density at the place of residence can also restrain auto ownership by making it both less convenient and less necessary. An increase in density from one to ten dwellings per acre tends to cut auto ownership by about 30 percent, keeping income and other factors constant. In addition, each car kept at a higher density tends to be driven less: about 10 percent fewer miles for each tenfold increase in gross density. Most population growth still occurs in low-density exurban areas, where auto ownership and use are the highest. An encouraging exception is New York City, which from 1980 to 1987 grew faster in population than twenty-six counties surrounding it; but that was a result of foreign immigration.

Whether a person works in a downtown or in a spread suburban cluster also influences his or her decision to own a motor vehicle. The presence of a rail transit station likewise reduces ownership in its immediate vicinity. But again, only a small fraction of the nation's job growth occurs in major downtowns; the bulk is spread across auto-dependent suburban territory, with no rail transit stations.

In sum, even assuming that the nation's rate of economic growth drops to half that of the past, vigorous decade, and that by 2015, the United States will have 290 million residents (the U.S. Census "middle" assumption) and 178 million jobs, the nation should count on *ninety million more vehicles over the coming twenty-five years—a 50 percent increase over the current 182 million.* In the New York Region, the percentage growth would be slightly lower; in a number of fast-growing metropolitan areas, much higher. Judging by recent relationships, *urban* vehicle-miles travelled, particularly those on *freeways*, would significantly outpace this nationwide growth: the former would double in twenty-five years, the latter—in fifteen years.

Such is the context for discussing future transportation policies. They focus on three related issues: (1) congestion, (2) air quality, and (3) energy consumption.

CONGESTION

On many thousands of rural freeway miles even a doubling of traffic will go virtually unnoticed; why those miles were built in the first place may be a good question. But there is critical urban mileage in major metropolitan areas where stop-and-go conditions now prevail for several hours a day.

According to "highway statistics" for 1987, that year there were 4,460 miles of urban freeway with volume-to-capacity ratios of over .95, that is, those that operated under congested conditions. There also were 20,900 miles of arterial and collector streets and roads in that category. In addition, there were 8,870 miles of freeway with volume-to-capacity ratios in the .41 to .95 range, that is, those that, given our projection, are likely to reach or exceed capacity in the next fifteen to twenty-five years. In other words, *a degree of congestion is likely to become a problem on 25 percent of the nation's 54,000 freeway miles.* The question is—to what degree?

A "desirable" capacity for one freeway lane can be taken as 12,000 vehicles per day. At that rate, stop-and-go conditions may only appear during one hour, and a peak flow rate of some 1,700 vehicles per lane per hour is reached. Meanwhile, a number of the nation's most famous freeways, the Long Island and Brooklyn-Queens Expressways in New York, the Bayshore and I-80 freeways in San Francisco, Routes 101 and 405 in Los Angeles, carry volumes in the range of 26,000 to 33,000 per lane per day. The reason they can do it is simple—their peak flow lasts not one, but three, four, even more than six hours per day. Thus, the "actual" capacity of freeways can be increased enormously, if stop-and-go conditions, speeds near thirty miles per hour, are accepted for enough hours of the day.

Note that this defies the original purpose of freeways—to double average speeds compared to the local street network. Note also that *widening offers little remedy*: adding two lanes to an eight-lane freeway will expand its capacity by 25 percent; for a while, this will reduce the number of daily hours during which stop-and-go operation occurs, but at a 5 percent annual growth rate, in five years things will go back to where they started. The only lasting result will be to increase the throughput of people in vehicles in a given corridor. If that, rather than time saving, is the objective, it can be achieved at a lower construction cost per unit of added capacity—with rail transit. Which is why, contrary to the beliefs of critics, the Wilshire subway in Los Angeles is not irrational; during the peak hour it will, when fully completed, carry a passenger volume equivalent to that of autos on a ten-lane freeway.

Diverting traffic to nearby rail lines or busyways can shed some load from congested freeways. But the approach has its limit: the diverted trips must be numerous enough to warrant the capital cost of a transit facility, which means they have to be destined to a major downtown. In our 1980 "Urban Rail in America" study, we found no more than forty corridors, totalling 350 miles, that might warrant rapid transit; even adding the rough estimate of about an equal milage for light rail, the 700 or so miles of new rail we advocated are no match for 13,300 miles of potentially congested freeways. The point is that the bulk of the traffic on congested freeways travels from dispersed origins to dispersed destinations and as such it cannot be diverted to public transit.

The competitive position of fixed-guideway transit relative to freeways would be improved enormously if a fully grade-separated system—offering high frequency and speed—could be built for a fraction of the capital cost of present systems. Were it to warrant several thousand (rather than several hundred) miles of new lines even under light traffic, medium-density areas now consigned to slow and expensive bus service could develop transit grids allowing service in different directions. Such a system, combining two-way traffic on one light, prefabricated, overhead beam, has been engineered by L. K. Edwards under the trade name of "System 21," but still awaits venture capital for a demonstration line.

To get at the dispersed-origin-to-dispersed-destination traffic that cannot be diverted to fixed guideway or bus, various "high-occupancy vehicle" schemes, such as carpools and vanpools, have been devised. The main problem with them is that they eliminate the freedom of arrival and departure times, and some of the speed advantage, that are the main attraction of the private auto. They represent, so to say, public transit with a frequency of once a day. And they still require some commonality of origins and destinations, preferably a large employer at one end. Overcoming the inconvenience of ride-sharing requires strong inducements in the form of time savings in reserved lanes or otherwise, and the number of takers is small. After all, the entire history of auto ownership growth with rising income is one of the new owners seeking to *avoid* ride sharing.

The difficulty of implementing ride-sharing has led some to advocate the penalties for single-occupant use, whether in the form of outright prohibition during selected times in critical locations, or special fees. Both pose severe problems of enforcement and equity; after all it may be quite impossible for me to round up a companion (other than a dummy) for today's trip, even if the trip is essential. If fees are considered, they ought to apply equally to all users at a given time and place. *There is a good case to be made for managing highway travel demand through pricing.*

The cost of congestion is high. Since many vehicles in large urban areas are commercial (to them, time *is* money), and auto occupants have slightly above-average incomes—there are 1.2 to 1.5 of them per car—to take the cost of delay at $20 per vehicle-hour is not unreasonable. On that basis, the annual cost of freeway congestion in the New York Region (*not* counting local and central business district streets) was put at $4.5 billion in 1984, more than the budget of all its transit systems and equal to 1.1 percent of its Gross Regional Product.

That monetary cost is imposed by a minority of drivers on the majority. It is the last, marginal vehicle entering a congested traffic stream that imposes the most delay on the others; cutting the volume near the congestion point by 10 percent increases speed roughly from thirty to forty miles per hour. Charging motorists for the privilege of driving during the most congested times will allow those to whom the trip is most important—commercial vehicles, vehicles on long trips, those with many occupants—to move without impediment, while weeding out those who can easily switch to another mode or defer their time of departure. From an economic viewpoint, allocating scarce highway space by pricing is decidedly more efficient than the current rationing by random queuing.

Highway pricing used to mean a stop at toll booths, which is objectionable from the viewpoints of driver convenience, extra fuel consumption, and pollution. Present-day electronics allow nonstop toll collection: by laser reading of special decals on the vehicle or by electronic transponders purchased with the license plate. The driver can either purchase a permit to use specific facilities during congested times in advance, or be billed at the end of the month on a credit card. The fact that a public agency will know times and places that a specific vehicle went is no more an invasion of privacy than the telephone company knowing which numbers a customer called when, and how long he talked.

There are other, simpler but less direct ways to promote what are basically congestion pricing objectives: an effective one is parking surcharges and the elimination of free parking.

A key consideration in congestion pricing is that the demand elasticity of highway travel is low: rough estimates suggest it to be on the order of 0.1, meaning that a 100 percent increase in the out-of-pocket cost of a trip is necessary to reduce the number of trips by 10 percent. On a ten-mile suburban trip currently without tolls or parking charges, this implies a $1 fee, on a twenty-mile trip to Manhattan, perhaps a $20 fee. For the public as a whole, congestion pricing offers a lucrative source of revenue.

The revenue can be useful in eliminating a variety of subsidies to motorists, improving maintenance and cross-subsidizing desirable alternatives, such as mass transit and high-occupancy programs. Motorist cross-subsidies to competing modes are justified because:

1. Motorists benefit by traffic diversion from highways;
2. They benefit from the existence of large downtown concentrations of activity supported by transit;
3. Motorist revenues for transit keep the transit subsidy within the transportation sector and prevent society from spending more on travel by all modes combined than the market indicates;
4. Insofar as rail operations are at issue, they are an appropriate subsidy target because their marginal cost of carrying an extra rider is typically below their average cost, while the reverse is true of peak hour auto travel;
5. Most commonly cited "benefits" of transit—lower accident rates, lower land and energy consumption, less pollution, mobility for those with low incomes—are benefits only *in comparison* with the auto; they really are reductions in the external costs of the auto. Asking the public at large to pay for them is like asking it, rather than the chemical industry, to pay for toxic waste cleanup.

AIR QUALITY

The two trillion vehicle miles driven annually in the United States produce emissions into the atmosphere that harm people, vegetation, and buildings. Tens of thousands of premature deaths and tens of billions in damages annually have been attributed to motor vehicle-generated air pollution by researchers.

Public policy in the United States has been to attack the emissions at their source—by installing control equipment on motor vehicles. In 1963, crankcase controls were introduced nationwide to reduce emissions of hydrocarbons; exhaust controls followed in 1968 to attack hydrocarbons and carbon monoxide; in 1971, evaporative fuel controls were required, and some nitrogen oxide controls introduced; finally in 1975, catalytic converters were required on all new cars to oxidize unburned hydrocarbons and carbon monoxide and to reduce nitrogen oxides. By 1986, 82 percent of all vehicles were equipped with catalytic converters.

The controls had a major new impact: compared to the uncontrolled cars of 1960, new models now emit 96 percent less carbon monoxide, 96 percent fewer hydrocarbons, and 76 percent fewer nitrogen oxides. This is about as far as the control technology can go, though its performance deteriorates, of course, over the life of the car, particularly if inspection is lax. Also the catalytic converters are least effective when the engine is cold.

A large part of the gain in emissions control was concealed by the near-tripling of vehicle-miles travelled since 1960. Hence, as of 1985, motor vehicles nationwide were still responsible for these shares of air pollutants:

- 69 percent of all lead
- 60 percent of all carbon monoxide
- 36 percent of all nitrogen oxides
- 28 percent of all volatile organic compounds
- 15 percent of all suspended particulates

Lead is being attacked by phasing out leaded gasoline. Carbon monoxide, while highly toxic, is a problem primarily in localized "hot spots," near congested freeways or in city streets, such as in Manhattan, where ventilation is insufficient.

The major regional or "air basin" problem is caused by nitrogen oxides and the volatile organic compounds that in the presence of sunlight interact to produce ozone and "smog"—the brown haze that hangs over Los Angeles or New Jersey for too many days of the year, causing lung damage and bronchial disease, restricting visibility, eroding building masonry, and damaging crops. Vehicular nitrogen oxide emissions are also thought to contribute to acid rain and the degradation of aquatic marine life in Atlantic coastal waters. Eighteen urban areas in the United States do not comply with federal standards for ozone. Los Angeles and New York–New Jersey are among them, though conditions in the former are seven times worse than the latter. Climactic differences aside, both have massive expanses of auto-oriented settlement, with a high density of vehicle-miles per square mile. The emissions per square mile are a function of the vehicle-miles travelled per square mile.

Given that the on-vehicle control technology has reached a point of diminishing returns (it is hard to eliminate more than 96 percent of any pollutant), the only *ultimate choices*—beyond improved inspection and maintenance—*are to reduce total travel or to change vehicle propulsion.*

One should stress that travel under congested conditions consumes more energy and hence releases more pollutants than travel under free-flowing conditions. Therefore, *all measures previously considered desirable for congestion relief will also promote clean air goals. But they are by no means sufficient.* As noted above, congestion now afflicts 8 percent of the nation's freeway miles and some 10 percent of urban arterial streets. It afflicts even fewer vehicle-miles travelled because it occurs only during some hours of the day.

By contrast, *emissions are generated by all vehicle-miles travelled,* even more so by those travelled under congested conditions. Hence, reducing travel for air quality purposes means reducing all travel, not just peak hour travel at bottleneck locations.

Still, the choices for managing travel demand are similar. One can go the regulatory-administrative route: restrict deliveries, restrict access by vehicle type, by time of day, by number of occupants, by special permit, or even by random odd-even license plate rules. The cumbersome and intrusive nature of these controls is evident. Or one can go the market route—through pricing, when people themselves make the choices of what vehicles to take and when and where to go, knowing how much they have to pay for it.

Because the issue is one of reducing total vehicle miles, the techniques are simpler. A flat surtax on gasoline will reduce total miles travelled. Parking surtaxes will reduce travel. The charges must, of course, be coupled with legislation to make sure that the user pays them himself and is not subsidized by his firm or by the government.

Even more than in the case of congestion pricing, the potential revenues are a very large source of potential state and local government income and can be used both to reduce other taxes and pay for transit improvements.

Because the issue is one of reducing total travel by auto, ambitious schemes of grade-separated transit-grids, covering previously auto-dependent areas of sufficient density (say, between ten and thirty-five dwellings per acre) can be considered. Suppression of auto demand in these areas can help fill transit lines, while gas and parking surtaxes can pay for building them.

Considering the drastic nature of such changes compared to the relatively modest and immediate goal—reducing ozone concentrations in the air—*switching to a new propulsion technology* will seem to be an attractive alternative for many. Unfortunately, successor technologies to the internal combustion gasoline engine are not obvious, even if Los Angeles decreed it by the year 2007.

Immediate contenders to replace gasoline or diesel oil are methanol and compressed natural gas. Pure methanol is meant to reduce the emission and ozone-producing hydrocarbons, while compressed natural gas improves fuel efficiency and reduces carbon monoxide and particulate emissions, but not nitrogen oxides.

All fossil fuels produce carbon dioxide along with water vapor as a result of combustion, and hence contribute to the "greenhouse effect." In the long run, there are only two ways to eliminate carbon dioxide emissions: convert to burning pure hydrogen (a cumbersome and dangerous arrangement) or convert to electric cars dependent on nuclear, hydro, or solar primary sources. (Currently, 27 percent of U.S. electricity generation is nonfossil fueled.) Workable electric autos have been around since the beginning of the automobile age, but a century of research has failed to come up with a battery light and powerful enough to give them range and performance comparable to those driven by gasoline.

ENERGY CONSUMPTION

Apart from environmental issues that the energy use of the automobile-highway system poses, there are pure energy issues. Energy use for highways accounts for roughly one-fifth of total energy use in the United States and more than half of all petroleum; in future years, the petroleum will be increasingly imported.

The response so far in the United States has been, just as the case of emissions, one of a "technological fix." From a low of 13.1 miles per gallon in 1973, the average fuel efficiency of passenger cars rose to 19.2 in 1987. Higher fuel prices helped, but the immediate policy tool was the "corporate average fuel economy" (CAFE) legislation that took effect in 1978, requiring the theoretical efficiency of new cars to rise from 14.2 mpg in 1973 to 28.2 in 1987. That improvement has stalled lately, and the actual efficiency of the fleet has lagged behind the theoretical standard, mostly because of older cars still on the road.

Nevertheless, the improvement enabled total miles travelled by passenger vehicles to rise by 32 percent from 1973 to 1987 even as their fuel use *dropped* by 9 percent; total highway fuel use during the period kept growing anyway because the fuel efficiency of the trucks did not change.

Cars with theoretical fuel efficiencies around forty-five miles per gallon are in various stages of development and design, so that an actual fleetwide increase from 19.2 to over 30 miles per gallon is feasible and should be a policy goal. An increase to forty miles per gallon would make the future auto as energy-efficient as today's electric rail transit car. Efficiency improvements of this magnitude would accommodate the projected rise in motor vehicles without increased petroleum consumption.

There are, however, two catches. First, the economic realities of the world petroleum market are likely to require U.S. petroleum consumption to drop, rather than to stay constant. Second, from the consumer's viewpoint, a further increase in fuel efficiencies promises diminished dollar savings. At current prices, for someone driving 10,000 miles per year, an improvement from ten to twenty miles per gallon saves some $500 annually; doubling that to forty miles per gallon promises an additional savings of only $250. Thus, the "technological fix" should be reinforced with higher fuel taxation.

For an oil-importing country, gasoline taxes in the United States are among the lowest in the world; they average 45 percent of the pre-tax price, compared with 56 percent in Canada, over 130 percent in West Germany and Sweden, 178 percent in England, 317 percent in France, and 355 percent in Denmark. These prices are reflected in behavior: lower auto ownership rates despite similar or higher per capita income, fewer miles driven per vehicle, and many times higher percentages of public transportation use.

The case for higher vehicle fuel taxes in the United States is firm: fewer imports and a lower trade deficit; less fuel use and fewer environmental damages from this use; lower costs of congestion; reduced auto travel and hence reduced incentives for spread urban development— with all the secondary benefits that even a marginally tighter settlement will bring: less segregation, lower infrastructure costs, and lower resource costs for a less spread settlement.

FUTURE POLICIES AND RESOURCE NEEDS

1. Improving public transportation remains an important strategy for reducing highway travel demand in heavily travelled corridors to major downtowns. New transit lines are basically a tool of city-building, of creating human environments in which the monopoly of the auto is broken. But their impact on regional travel congestion and total travel demand should not be oversold.

Research needs: (a) behavioral studies to determine rider response to particular improvements in speed, schedule frequency, service quality, station design, fare collection—so investment can be targeted to maximize rider attraction; (b) hardware development to implement grade-separated transit at a fraction of current capital costs (see "System 21"); and (c) institutional approaches to reduce transit labor costs and increase labor productivity.

2. Expanding high-occupancy vehicle programs have broader, suburban applicability, but depend on the incentive of exclusive lanes, among others.

Research needs: generalizing and disseminating the experience of successful programs, devising criteria for exclusive high-occupancy lanes.

3. Congestion pricing appears as the only economically efficient approach to demand management that can deal with metropolitan congestion head-on. It supports both public transportation and high-occupancy policies.

Research needs: (a) testing of nonstop toll collection hardware at existing toll barriers; (b) behavioral studies to determine motorist response to various types and levels of congestion charges; and (c) public opinion studies and public affairs work to overcome political resistance to highway pricing.

4. Raising motor fuel taxes is a desirable way to curb the growth in highway travel demand, the need for petroleum imports, emissions from fuel combustion, and to reduce fuel incentives to more dispersed settlement. However, to be effective, the taxes must be high, as the European experience shows.

Research needs: econometric modelling to trace and quantify not only the immediate effects of higher gasoline prices (higher inflation), but also the beneficial indirect, long-term side effects.

5. Raising new car fuel efficiency and accelerating the search for alternative motor vehicle energy sources. In the near term, raising miles-per-gallon from twenty-eight to over forty can keep fuel consumption—and also emissions—flat despite rising travel; in the long run, a nonfossil fuel energy source is needed to eliminate both localized atmospheric pollution and the "greenhouse" build-up of carbon dioxide.

Research needs: energy storage and related research to make the electric automobile competitive; further development of the nonfossil fuel electricity generation.

6. Reorganizing land-use controls with the explicit aim of attaining a more compact and resource-conserving urban environment. The major principles are: (a) cluster employment in major centers, aiming for at least twenty to thirty million square feet; provide vehicle-free zones and a pedestrian ambiance within the centers; restrain parking; offer short and convenient access to transit; (b) encourage moderate-to-high-density housing in the immediate vicinity of these centers; even a dense center will not reduce auto trips if it has to draw its employees from scattered directions over long distances; (c) away from the centers, cluster housing around stations; within about 2,000 feet of stations, preference should be given to multi-family housing. Raising residential densities will not reduce auto trips if the housing is randomly scattered; and (d) seek to raise development densities within the already built-up area, instead of expanding it to vacant land.

Research needs: institutional arrangements necessary to reorient land use controls toward tighter development at a metropolitan rather than municipal scale. Land value taxation may have applications as a tool for tightening development.

9

URBAN TRANSPORTATION: PROGRESS AND PRIORITIES

MARK A. WRIGHT

Human mobility presents one of the most challenging problems of the urban environment. The movement of people between home and work lies at the heart of the productive economic system in use by most industrialized nations. Because such movement is vital to the survival of modern economic life, our understanding of its day-to-day functioning is imperative. Yet, mobility is largely taken for granted by the commuting public and even many policymakers, even when periods of gridlock-like vehicle congestion cause us individually to wonder at the monster we have allowed to evolve.

Although this book is focused upon the city, we must look realistically at what urban now means within the context of transportation. Most urban areas, at least in the United States, have sprawled outward to create suburbs, which have spread even further to create what planners call exurbs. Indeed, some of these areas have turned into urban cores of their own, dubbed by some as edge cities. The traditional traffic pattern of suburb-to-city has shifted, so that, while the number of commuters traveling into the city has increased, suburb-to-suburb trips have grown even more. These inter-suburb trips represent about one-third of all metropolitan commuting (Pisarski 1987).

This pattern of commuting was identified through data from the 1980 U.S. Census. While the 1990 census is currently being analyzed, the latest data is likely to show an even more pronounced trend toward suburb-to-suburb travel.

Data from 1980 also drew a picture of concomitant changes in workforce patterns and in the number of private vehicles. "Baby-boomers" and women entered the workforce in record numbers, causing a rapid expansion in the number of people traveling from home to work. Moreover, the number of personal vehicles had skyrocketed. Work is underway to determine whether these trends continued through the 1980s, based on the 1990 census.

There is no escaping the fact that cities and suburbs are linked, at least insofar as their transportation destinies are concerned. The people who commute from one suburb to another often use highways that were originally meant to bring suburban residents to central city jobs. The variety of trips undertaken on suburban roads has severely strained the very system on which the city itself depends. As we discuss the city as a human environment, it will help us to keep this link in mind.

More vehicles and more workers take up more space, profoundly affecting the shape, character, efficiency, and livability of urban environments. In his booklet *Rethinking the Role of the Automobile*, Michael Renner (1988) reports that over

60,000 square miles of land in the United States have been paved over: That works out to about two percent of the total surface area, and to ten percent of all arable land. Worldwide, at least a third of the average city's land is devoted to roads, parking lots, and other elements of a car infrastructure. In American cities, close to half of all the urban space goes to accommodate the automobile; in Los Angeles, the figure reaches two-thirds. (47)

The amount of space devoted to vehicle use and the demographic and traffic pattern changes noted above all invite a number of questions. What is the opportunity cost of this space allocation? Could we provide for the movement of people more efficiently, using less space? Or is ease and speed of movement such a priority for us that even more space should be allotted? To what extent are private vehicles necessary for the viability, economic and otherwise, of our cities? How can we best balance the desire of commuters for personal freedom of movement with the efficacy of our current transportation system and the long-term effects on our natural environment, our health, our well-being? Will the trend toward suburbanization continue, and with what ramifications for mobility? Is there an ideal transportation system for any city and, if there is, can that ideal ever be achieved given the constraints of limited resources, personal and institutional resistance to change, and urban infrastructures that are not easily altered?

Ideal answers to such questions elude us. However, the dialogue engendered by those and other questions has grown to include an increasingly broad constituency. Around the United States, employers, federal, state, and local government agencies, air quality management districts, citizen groups, universities and other academic institutions, real estate developers, public and private ride-share organizations, transportation management associations (TMAs), transit authorities, private consultants, taxi and other fleet management companies, a variety of entrepreneurs, legislators, planners, and others have become involved in addressing these mobility issues.

This dialogue has been furthered by the passage of the Intermodal Surface Transportation Efficiency Act of 1991 (ISTEA). The Act itself was, to a degree, the result of diverse elements of our society providing input through various programs about their transportation needs and priorities. Following passage of the ISTEA, a number of programs—local, regional, and national—brought stakeholders together to share information, discuss implementation of the Act and, at least for a time, reconsider the ways in which our society chooses to move people from point A to point B. Such programs continue, as we move into 1993, since the process of change unleashed by the ISTEA requires an unprecedented reexamination of—and in some cases changes in—our spending, our modal priorities, our infrastructure choices, the relationships between land use, mobility options and air quality, and the very planning, communication and decision-making processes employed to shape transportation in America.

The ISTEA compliments the transportation elements of the Clean Air Act Amendments of 1990 (CAAA). The CAAA recognized that the chief source of urban smog in many areas is the gasoline-powered motor vehicle. "Mobile sources," as they are called, can account for over half (and sometimes a *much* higher proportion) of the smog-causing pollutants in urban areas.

To force reductions in single-occupant vehicle use for commuting, the CAAA required employers of more than 100 employees, located in areas identified by the U.S. Environmental Protection Agency (EPA) to be in "severe" or "extreme" nonattainment for federal ozone standards, to increase the average passenger occupancy (APO) of their employees' commute vehicles by 25 percent over the areawide average. Simply put, this means those employers will need to get employees out of their cars and into ride-sharing, transit, or similar low- and no-pollute commute modes. While the very passage of the CAAA and ISTEA represents highly significant change—and, hopefully, significant progress—further changes are needed, as is further research.

RESEARCH NEEDED

Ever since the gasoline crises in the United States sparked the development of vanpooling, carpooling, and other transportation demand management (TDM) techniques, a number of useful studies have been conducted. New research is very much needed, however.

Behavioral Research

What motivates people to choose one transportation mode over another, and under what circumstances? What specific modal features are more or less attractive to identified personality types? What effect does a commuter's perceived social status or income level have on his/her mode choice? Does peer pressure play a role? How are behavior and stress levels affected by different transportation modes? Research into some of these questions has been undertaken over the years, yet the need for new information remains.

Demographic Research

What will be the long-term effects of suburbanization on transportation? (Will traffic congestion mitigate itself to some degree by driving people back toward cities, or at least closer to their place of employment? Will suburbs continue to expand without significant constraint, spreading vehicle traffic throughout an ever-widening area?) What new demographic trends are likely to affect traffic patterns and density? Do working women and new immigrants to the United States bring different preferences in mode choice, or follow the dominant tendency of auto-dependence? Does mode choice vary with age or cultural background? Significant formal research into the demographic aspects of commuter travel would prove very useful.

Technological Research

This area of research has seen significant attention lately. Tremendous federal investment was provided for through the ISTEA into research and development of so-called intelligent vehicle highway systems (IVHS). Some see technology as the answer to maximizing the capacity of our transportation infrastructure, both in terms of vehicle management and information management. However, further research into low-tech and no-tech options would provide additional alternatives that could improve the overall efficiency and cost-effectiveness of our transportation system. In particular, exploring the relationship between information, transportation options, and commuter behavior would prove valuable.

Land Use Research

The link between land use and transportation is better understood today in some communities. However, tremendous tension exists between market-driven land use decisions on the part of real estate developers and local governments' desires to provide increased traffic capacity (or reduced transportation demand). What models exist for balancing transportation and land use needs? How can the commercial needs of a developer be met while retaining adequate local and area-wide mobility and access? Local governments, under increasing pressure from citizens, have implemented trip reduction or adequate public facilities ordinances designed to hold developers responsible for mitigating the impact of their development. Are such ordinances effective? What are their ramifications? Are there successful examples of nonadversarial approaches to public-private traffic management? How can community zoning and design be modified to appropriately balance access? How can parking be used as an incentive/disincentive for mode choices? A good bit of work has been conducted dealing with parking policies and various system pricing strategies to control congestion. Yet practical research showing realistic applications in American communities is essential.

Employment-Based Research

Clean air legislation has clearly placed the onus of trip reduction in key areas of the country on employers. Is this an effective strategy? Are there alternatives that would produce greater benefits? Some suggest employers are bearing an unfair burden in this regard, and push for a system that puts the spotlight directly on the individuals using the transportation system, with pricing mechanisms to govern individuals' mode choices and miles-of-travel choices.

Some research (*Evaluation of Travel Demand Management (TDM) Measures To Relieve Congestion,* COMSIS Corporation, 1989) already suggests that, under the right circumstances, employer-based programs can be very effective. However, there is also some question as to whether success on an individual employer level can translate sufficiently to success at a regional level. In other words, can enough employer programs be successfully executed regionally to provide for an overall reduction in area-wide traffic congestion (or vehicle miles traveled, or emissions produced)?

The "transportation control measures" (TCMs) outlined in the CAAA for use in cutting emissions-producing vehicle trips were evaluated for the EPA to determine their relative effectiveness. Unfortunately, researchers were unable to document with much confidence or reliability the quantitatively measurable effects of most TCMs. Additional research into their effectiveness is extremely important.

LEGISLATIVE CHANGES

Since the Rene Dubos Forum on "The City As a Human Environment," some of the recommended legislative changes have become reality. The Clean Air Act was amended; the ISTEA was passed. Tax equity for employer-provided commute benefits was vastly improved (thanks to language in a comprehensive national energy bill passed in 1992).

Tax Equity

Employers may, effective January 1, 1993, provide employees with transit subsidies of $60 per month tax-free; vanpool subsidies of $60 per month tax-free; park & ride lot subsidies of $155 per month tax-free. In addition, tax-free employer-provided parking was capped at $155 per month.

Financial Incentives

An area yet to be addressed is financial incentives for high occupancy vehicle and transportation demand management (TDM) programs. While the language in the energy bill changed the tax code to allow employers to give more valuable tax-free incentives for vanpooling, transit use, and park & ride lot use, it provides no incentive for employers to do so. A federal tax credit could offer a useful carrot to motivate otherwise unconcerned employers.

Since no federal provisions exist for such incentives, some states have taken action. California provides employers with a tax credit for TDM; it also allows a tax deduction for individuals who receive no employer-provided TDM incentives but use ride-sharing or transit anyway. Massachusetts offers a corporate tax credit to help employers offer vanpooling.

INSTITUTIONAL CHANGES NEEDED

Business

Business, generally speaking, could help mobility through three key avenues: (1) eliminate free employee parking, (2) offer employees direct commuter assistance, and (3) proactively participate in regional transportation planning and decision-making.

Government

Federal: Develop mechanisms to monitor and adjust implementation of key legislation (i.e., the ISTEA and CAAA) to ensure that changes are accomplished in the manner Congress intended.

State: Establish a statewide commitment to multimodalism and mobility evaluation, planning, and system/program funding.

Local/Regional: Adjust land use approach to require parking space maximums rather than parking space minimums; mandate multimodal access for new developments; provide incentives for mixed use development; educate citizens about the relative advantages and disadvantages of mixed use versus single use development.

CONCLUSION

While none of these changes are simple, the fact that so much was accomplished legislatively in a fairly short length of time provides some hope that urban transportation can progress, even if fitfully, toward greater mobility for all Americans. It has been said that our cities reflect the prevailing transportation technology. We have opportunities to affect the shape and character of our urban environments in the twenty-first century by designing mobility options that provide maximum mode choice and flexibility, minimum environmental disruption, and a practical integration of facilities and technologies to balance the needs of individual transportation system users with the needs of their larger community and region.

10

THE ROLE OF RAIL TRANSIT IN CONTEMPORARY CITIES

VUKAN R. VUCHIC

Construction of a metro (rapid transit) system in any city is a major event. It usually represents the largest single investment in a public facility the city has ever made; it greatly improves transportation and population mobility; and it has a major and permanent impact on the character and environment of the city.

For this reason, planning a metro system involves a major multi-year effort requiring not only physical planning and design, but urban planning considerations, financing decisions and, above all, political decisions by the government or, sometimes, project endorsement through a popular vote.

Most cities that have built metro systems in recent years, such as San Francisco, Washington, D.C., Montreal, Sao Paulo, Munich, or Hong Kong, have experienced a period of intensive construction activities preceded by planning and decisions about the character the city should have in the future. Construction of the metro is also an occasion for tremendous civic activities and pride, but in some cases, particularly in our country, of controversy, criticism, and challenge of its results.

Rail transit, particularly a metro system, can have a strong impact on the character and permanence of a city if it is correctly planned and supported by coordinated land use planning. Policies toward a city's development, form, and character therefore strongly influence decisions about building rail transit.

This chapter presents a brief review of recent developments in rail transit and its current role in cities of developed and developing countries. This will be followed by an evaluation of the controversial points on the basis of facts drawn from real world cases. Finally, the impacts of rail transit on the city and the need for a clear urban transportation policy will be presented.

RECENT DEVELOPMENTS OF RAIL TRANSIT

During the 1950s rail transit was at a low point. Streetcars were disappearing from most cities; they were being replaced by the "more flexible" buses and trolleybuses. Rapid transit systems served relatively few cities and some people believed that they would have decreasing importance because of rapid suburbanization and increasing reliance on the private automobile. Commuter railroads were operated unwillingly by freight-oriented railroad companies and served mostly to transport commuters between suburbs and central cities.

This trend has been drastically reversed since the late 1950s. Several significant developments contributed to the revival and expansion of rail transit systems in many cities around the world.

First, numerous technical innovations of rail transit systems have occurred. Rail transit cars today are quiet, comfortable, climate-controlled vehicles. Travelling either in tunnels or on aerial structures with welded rails, they are drastically different from the rail transit vehicles typical of the 1950s. With many new design concepts, rail transit stations are often effective elements of urban design and focal points of commercial developments and residential areas.

Second, city governments and civic leaders have realized that a high-quality transit system is a sine qua non for retention and enhancement of urban areas that are human-oriented, economically healthy, which have a physical character and environment that is attractive, and in which transportation is available to all residents.

Third, to attract people from automobiles in rapidly spreading metropolitan areas, transit must offer attractive, fast, and reliable service. Rail transit can provide this to a much greater extent than buses or other highway transit modes operating on highways and streets in mixed traffic.

Fourth, permanent, fixed facilities, such as rail transit lines and stations, have a much greater influence on urban development and thus on urban form and character, than flexible systems, such as buses on streets.

Fifth, there has been a great diversification of transit systems in recent decades. Through gradual construction of separate rights-of-way and technical modernization, a new transit mode has been developed; the light rail transit (LRT), which represents a transit mode that has somewhat lower performance than conventional metros, but requires a much lower initial investment. Conversion of commuter railroads into a metro-type operation has resulted in the creation of regional rail systems, which have an increasingly important role in most large metropolitan areas.

CURRENT RAIL TRANSIT MODES AND THEIR ROLES

There are presently four major modes of rail transit. Their characteristics are briefly defined here.

Metro or rapid transit systems operate on fully separated rights-of-way and have enclosed stations. This infrastructure requires major investments for construction, but provides for complete independence from street conditions. The trains, consisting of up to six, eight, or ten cars, operate under signal control in a fail-safe manner. Metro systems therefore represent the transit mode that requires the highest investment, but provides the highest capacity and the best overall performance of all modes.

As the mode with the greatest ability to compete with the private automobile and attract passengers, metro systems have been constructed at a rapid pace in recent years. In 1950 only seventeen cities around the world had metro systems; today, there are eighty-eight metro systems.

The dominant goal in building metros in cities of developed countries, such as Munich, Amsterdam, or Atlanta, is to provide a system with high quality service, able to attract people from their automobiles. The main goal in building metros in cities of developing countries, such as Mexico City, Cairo, and Hong Kong, is to provide capacity and economical transportation for very large volumes of passenger travel in these cities.

Light rail transit (LRT) consists of short trains (one to four cars) operating on mostly, but not completely, separated rights-of-way. Requiring a much lower investment, but offering somewhat lower performance, the LRT mode falls between the metro and bus modes: it provides much higher performance than buses, but requires considerably lower investments than a metro.

Light rail transit existed initially only in cities that retained and upgraded their streetcars, such as Hannover, Gothenburg, and Boston. Now, a large number of medium-sized cities have built or are planning to build LRT systems: San Diego, Calgary, Nantes, Tunis, and Manila are good examples of such systems. Not recognized as a mode appropriate for contemporary cities in 1970, LRT is today being planned for more cities than metro systems.

Regional rail systems are physically similar to metros, but they are typically operated by railroad companies on their lines. Thus they serve larger suburban areas with high-speed lines, long station spacings and high-speed travel.

Regional rail systems mostly utilize existing railroad lines, such as the Long Island Rail Road in New York, the British Rail lines in London, and JR lines in many Japanese cities. In many cities, old regional rail lines have recently been converted or new ones built as large-scale, regional metro systems: examples are BART in San Francisco, S-Bahn in Munich, and RER lines in Paris.

Automated light rail transit, recently opened in Vancouver and in London (Docklands), utilizes modern technology to drastically decrease operating personnel; this distinction—a high degree of automation—makes small-scale metros, which these systems are, economically feasible. This mode is likely to be developed in more and more cities in the foreseeable future.

EXAMPLES OF RECENTLY BUILT RAIL TRANSIT SYSTEMS

The role and achievements of rail transit systems can best be assessed through a review of several different cases. Real life facts represent the best test for examining some controversies that exist about rail transit. A few examples of recently built rail transit systems are presented here.

The *San Francisco BART* was created in the early 1960s with inadequate design expertise, and led to numerous technical difficulties and low system reliability for several years. Now, with the technical difficulties solved, BART plays a major role as the basic regional transit carrier in the Bay Area. The sharp criticism of BART by several academics was shown to be theoretical extremism when the population voted approval of $2 billion in taxes for an extension of the system. Now, controversy is not about the value of BART, but about which part of the Bay Area should get its extension built first!

Lindenwood Line, serving the New Jersey suburbs of Philadelphia, was designed for economical but high quality, reliable operation, and it has achieved that: it recovers 80 to 90 percent of its operating costs from fares. Its more than 12,000 park-and-ride spaces are heavily used every day. The line has, together with BART, proved that rail transit can serve very low-density, high-income suburbs with high auto ownership if transit service is of high quality.

The *Washington Metro,* also a target of criticism during its planning and initial operations, has revolutionized travel in that city: an extensive but confusing bus system and unreliable taxis have been replaced by a metro system with bus feeders that are comfortable, reliable, and easy to use. The result has been that the bus system ridership has remained basically constant, while Metro ridership has increased to over 500,000 per day; this means that Metro ridership is generally newly attracted, rather than diverted from buses. Investments in land use developments in station areas already amount to several billion dollars.

The *Miami Metro* has a much lower ridership than projected. Indications are that a smaller system (lower capacity but more frequent trains, lower-cost right-of-way, and stations) would have been a better, more economically justified choice of mode.

Toronto continues to be a classic illustration that a region with a well-organized metropolitan government, and a rationally and effectively implemented policy, can afford and reap huge benefits from a transit system with heavy reliance on rail modes. Its ridership has been increasing steadily over the last thirty years, and the city is more human-oriented than its peer cities that have pursued more auto-oriented policies.

Mexico City and *Sao Paulo Metros* are being built in countries extremely short of capital. However, with ridership on individual lines reaching 600,000 to one million per day, metro represents not only the only physically possible means, but also the most economical mode, of transporting people. Without their Metros, these two cities, with populations exceeding ten million, would have been suffering from a total paralysis and economic decline.

San Diego and *Calgary light rail transit systems* have demonstrated that LRT can provide an economical transport solution and attract large passenger volumes from their automobiles even without building any tunnels.

The Lindenwood Line and San Diego LRT have some of the highest ratios of revenues to cost of all transit systems in the United States.

REVIEW OF ACTUAL EXPERIENCES WITH RAIL TRANSIT SYSTEMS

Major experiences with the above mentioned and other recently built rail transit systems can be summarized as follows:

- Rail transit, including several modes with a broad range of performance/cost characteristics, can represent the key element for an effective solution to urban transit problems. While in large cities with heavy passenger volumes, rail transit is usually the optimal mode, its domain also encompasses many medium-sized cities. High-density development favors rail modes, but with good organizations of feeders, rail lines can also serve low-density suburban areas typical of North American cities efficiently.

- As a large public infrastructure project requiring a major investment, rail transit must be planned carefully with respect to its functional applicability and economic effectiveness for each particular corridor and for each city. Conditions that contribute to the success of a rail transit system are: (1) Rail transit is planned together with land uses and with other transportation systems.

Integration with buses and park-and-ride is particularly important; (2) The region and the city have a clear, rational, and effectively implemented transportation policy; and (3) The rail transit system is competently designed (avoiding overdesign or underdesign) and integrated with its overall environment.

- The rail transit has a significantly stronger passenger-attracting capability than other transit modes.

- While rail transit requires much higher investment funds than buses and other transit modes, well-planned and designed rail systems can have considerably better operating ratios than most bus systems.

- Rail transit can significantly contribute to shaping, growth or revitalization of cities (particularly if planned in coordination with urban planning) in both developed and developing countries. However, its role in the two types of cities differs: In developed countries rail transit is built to increase the *quality* of transit service, attract potential auto drivers, and reduce congestion and excessive demands for construction of highway and parking facilities that can be destructive for cities. In developing countries the primary *raison d'etre* of rail transit is to provide *high transporting capacity and basic mobility* for millions of urban residents who otherwise spend large portions of their days in exhausting travel through congested streets.

- Flexibility is not an asset for a major transportation system. To the contrary, *permanence* is the feature that strongly influences urban development and it should be provided wherever that is economically feasible.

- The opinion that "rail transit is too expensive" cannot be simplistically generalized. Correct for lines with low ridership potential or excessively high construction costs, this statement is incorrect for many cases where rail transit carries large passenger volumes and has major, permanent positive impacts on an urban area's economy, social equity, energy efficiency, good ecology, and human-oriented environment.

IMPACTS OF RAIL TRANSIT ON CONTEMPORARY CITIES

By its very nature, rail transit has a strong image and a much stronger "identity" than other transit modes. Cities with rail transit therefore have a stronger public transportation system and better overall mobility than cities relying on highways, private automobiles, and buses only.

Because of its important role in cities, rail transit has a very strong impact on each one of the "five E's." A brief review of these impacts follows.

Ecology. Cities relying on rail transit have a character that is open, with great attention to its preservation of nature and "fitting" of man-made facilities to it; cities relying excessively on private transportation are more closed, private with a "club-type" way of life. Social life and mobility are much higher in Boston and Munich, cities with extensive rail systems, than in Houston and Detroit, relying on highways only.

Economics. Carefully planned rail transit systems should result in a decrease of operating costs per passenger trip; attraction of travelers from private automobiles results in additional transportation cost reductions. Moreover, rail transit, when supported by coordinated planning and policies, usually brings numerous indirect economic benefits to the city: increased land values, diversity of urban form, and increased activities due to higher population mobility.

Energetics. With respect to energy efficiency, rail transit has two types of impacts. First, direct energy consumed per passenger-mile is usually considerably lower than on any other mode of transportation (except for buses under certain conditions). Second, data indicates that cities developed with rail transit have a much lower energy consumption per capita for all purposes than auto-based cities. The indirect impact of rail transit on energy efficiency can be large because it is permanent.

Esthetics. Due to its high capacity, small space requirements, and the absence of any exhausts, rail transit can be integrated into urban development better than any other mode of urban transport.

Ethics. Presence of a good transit system represents one of the basic social services in a city. Without it, urban residents lacking an automobile are practically relegated to the position of "second-class citizens." How much provision of rail, bus, or some other mode of transportation results in a more ethical distribution of funds and services depends heavily on specific local conditions. There are a few examples that large amounts of funds have been spent for a rail system with a low ridership and limited other benefits; however, in most cases, from New York and Toronto to Moscow and Manila, investments in rail transit represent one of the most socially oriented and equitable allocations of public funds.

The present U.S. national policies strongly favor automobile over transit and highways over rail systems, instead of fostering integrated multimodal systems in which each mode performs the function it is best suited to provide. With respect to these policies, our pro-highway bias is stronger than in any of our peer western countries. This difference in policies explains why the United States has fallen far behind its peers in the development of urban transit, but particularly rail transit systems.

The preceding discussion shows that our biased policies against rail transit are not only damaging to our urban areas because of their negative ecological, economic, and aesthetic impacts, but that they cannot be justified on the basis of social ethics either.

POLICY IMPLICATIONS AND NEEDED ACTIONS

Neglect of our urban transit systems, symbolized particularly by the current underutilization of rail transit, is one of the causes of the overall crisis most U.S. cities are facing.

Lack of clear understanding of the problems and issues is one of the problems underlying this crisis. The importance of good public transportation (rail transit being its strongest representative) for the ecology, economics, energetics, aesthetics, and ethics in our areas is not fully appreciated.

Consequently, the first major issue that requires immediate attention is how to bring facts and professional knowledge about transportation systems and their impacts on metropolitan areas to the attention of the public and decisionmakers. The second issue is to urge the formulation of rational urban transportation policies. The third step should be vigorous implementation of such policies.

11

AASHTO Transportation 2020 Program

DAVID CLAWSON

INTRODUCTION

Transportation 2020 is a bold new transportation initiative of the American Association of State Highway and Transportation Officials (AASHTO) in conjunction with other major national organizations concerned about the nation's transportation system and its future. This multi-year initiative is a four-phase process to examine transportation needs and issues, to develop alternatives to meet transportation needs and challenges, to reach a consensus regarding the best transportation program for the nation, and then to work together to implement this program. The overall focus of this effort is the year 2020, with a major interim target being the next authorization of the Surface Transportation Assistance Act by the U.S. Congress.

The thirty-two year time frame of the Transportation 2020 program is similar to the major transportation activity that launched the nation's Interstate Highway program. The "Clay Committee," named for its chairman, Lucius D. Clay, was appointed by President Eisenhower to develop recommendations for the implementation of a major highway network known as the Interstate system. With over 43,000 miles of the Interstate now open to traffic, this major lifeline provides a system that serves the many vital economic, defense, recreational, and related activities of the nation every day.

The Clay Committee provided a vision for America that resulted in the largest public works investment in the nation's history. As the interstate system nears completion, national transportation leaders agree that the time has come for the country to develop a new vision to serve as a goal for the next thirty-year time period. A major factor that led to the start of the Transportation 2020 program was a conference held in August 1986 at Smuggler's Notch, Vermont. The report of that conference, *Understanding the Highway Finance Evolution/Revolution*, raised many of the issues that are now being examined in the Transportation 2020 program.

A second factor that led to the Transportation 2020 program was the difficulty in obtaining passage of the Surface Transportation Assistance Act of 1987. This legislation passed only after the Congress was able to override a Presidential veto by one vote. Transportation leaders realized that they needed to work together more closely to develop a consensus-oriented transportation program for consideration by the members of Congress and the President. AASHTO and eleven other major organizations involved in Transportation 2020 have joined together to form the Transportation Alternative Group, known as TAG, which provides a forum for the development of consensus on major transportation issues. This new transportation consortium has been meeting over the past year to discuss transportation issues and is now moving in the stage of consensus development. This consensus development, in addition to its long-range focus, seeks to provide positions for consideration by Congress and the Administration in the development of the next surface transportation authorization. The member organizations of TAG include:

AASHTO

American Automobile Association

American Public Transit Associations

American Trucking Associations

Highway Users Federation

National Association of Counties

National Association of Regional Councils

National Association of State Legislatures

National Governors' Association

National League of Cities

U.S. Conference of Mayors

In addition to the TAG members, several other organizations concerned with transportation issues serve on a Chairman's Advisory Committee (CAC) and provide additional information and raise issues for consideration by the TAG.

ACTIVITIES TO DATE

As an initial Transportation 2020 activity, sixty-five public forums were held around the nation in 1987 and 1988. A large number of individuals and organizations expressed their concerns regarding transportation needs and issues. A report entitled *Beyond Gridlock*, which summarizes the highlights of these forums, was produced and distributed.

FUTURES CONFERENCE

The Transportation Research Board (TRB) held a Futures Conference in June 1988 to examine transportation-related issues to the year 2020, including fuel availability, air quality, demographics, changes in vehicle-related technology, and related subjects. A report entitled *A Look Ahead: Year 2020* presented the findings of that conference.

BOTTOM LINE REPORT

In September 1988, AASHTO released its *Bottom Line* report, which is an assessment of highway, transit, and modal interlink needs for surface transportation through the year 2020. This report indicates that investment in highways by all levels of government totaled $66 billion in 1987. Similarly, investment for transit totaled $14.5 billion, for a total highway and transit investment level of $80.5 billion.

The report then provides low and high ranges of investment levels that indicate the need for substantial investment in highways and transit. The report estimates that just to maintain the current system would require an annual investment level of $80 billion for highways and $15 billion for transit. To accommodate growth and improve service, the report further estimates an annual funding requirement of $100 billion for highways and $16 billion for transit, a 43 percent increase in funding. These figures do not take into account the effects of inflation.

NEW TRANSPORTATION CONCEPTS FOR A NEW CENTURY

AASHTO recently released the February 1989 edition of its report entitled *New Transportation Concepts for a New Century*. This document provides AASHTO's policy recommendations regarding the federal role in the nations's surface transportation system.

This is a living document that continued to be revised throughout 1989. The policy recommendations included in the report do not constitute AASHTO policy. Changes to AASHTO policy will require separate action by the Policy Committee.

TRANSPORTATION ALTERNATIVES GROUP (TAG)

As indicated earlier, in order to develop a consensus among major organizations interested in the future of transportation, the Transportation Alternatives Group (TAG) was formed. This allows other organizations an opportunity to provide input to the TAG.

The TAG is working to develop consensus positions on a variety of surface transportation issues for consideration by the Congress, the Administration and others, with particular focus on the next authorization for surface transportation.

FUTURE DIRECTIONS

AASHTO Policy Recommendations

As outlined in the AASHTO document *New Transportation Concepts for a New Century,* AASHTO proposes that the major highway and transit programs be changed to a categorical and flexible program structure.

The categorical program will focus on the major systems of national significance. Funding for all other projects beyond these systems of national significance would be provided through a flexible program.

Specific recommendation by mode are as follows.

Highways

The AASHTO Transportation 2020 policy recommendations included in the February 1989 edition of the *New Transportation Concepts for a New Century* report offer the following key recommendations regarding the future federal highway program:

The federal highway program would be divided into two major sections—the Categorical Highway Program and the Flexible Highway Program.

Categorical Highway Program. The Categorical Highway Program would include the Interstate system and a portion of a redefined Principal Arterial System, which together would form a Highway System of National Significance (HSNS). Eligible projects to be funded from the Categorical program would include reconstruction/rehabilitation, additional urban capacity, pavement preservation, additional mileage needs, and bridge needs. Also eligible to be funded would be planning/research, safety, emergency relief, federal land highways, and a discretionary bridge program. The program would include contribution of ½ percent minimums. The Minimum Allocation would be increased from its current level of 85 to 90 percent.

The AASHTO proposal recommends that the next Surface Transportation Assistance Act include language to provide a "hold harmless" provision to ensure that each state does not receive less than its FY 1991 funding level (minus any amount over ½ percent minimum for the Interstate program).

AASHTO recommends that the federal share for the Categorical Program be approximately 85 percent.

Flexible Highway Program. The Flexible Highway Program would consist of a grant to the states to fund remaining highway needs beyond the HSNS. The states in conjunction with regional/local decisionmakers would apply funds to meet urban, suburban and rural mobility needs.

Eligible projects to be funded from the Flexible Program would include construction/reconstruction and rehabilitation/preservation to address such needs as urban/suburban mobility, rural access, modal interlinks, and bridge needs. States would receive funds in relation to the amount paid by their respective state to the Highway Trust Fund. That is, there would be no donor/donee relationship. The state matching share would be determined by each state on a project-by-project basis.

As its name implies, the Flexible Program is to be designed to provide a more adaptable program with the ability to spend highway funds on a variety of types of projects.

Transit

The AASHTO Transportation 2020 policy recommendations included in the February 1989 edition of the *New Transportation Concepts for a New Century* report offers the following recommendations regarding the future federal transit program:

The basic structure of the federal transit program and distribution of federal transit funds would remain unchanged with one exception. The exception involves the distribution of Mass Transit Account funds beyond the current level funds provided for the Discretionary Program (approximately $1.1 billion).

Under existing law, the STAA of 1987, Mass Transit Account funding above $1 billion is distributed half to the Section 3 discretionary program and half to the Section 9B formula program.

Under the AASHTO recommendation, the programs currently funded from the Discretionary Program would be held harmless at a level of approximately $1.1 billion, with any Mass Transit Account funding provided above to be distributed on a formula basis to the states. These formula-distributed funds could be used for transit projects under a broadened definition of public transportation that includes high occupancy, shared ride, and related services.

Under the AASHTO proposal, the structure of the UMTA program would remain unchanged, in that the basic elements would be a Discretionary Program and a Formula Program.

The Discretionary Program would come under AASHTO's "Categorical Program" heading and would fund major bus/rail rehabilitation needs, new starts, elderly/handicapped transportation, and transit planning/research. This program would, as now, be funded from the Mass Transit Account.

The Formula Program would come under AASHTO's "Flexible Program" heading and would fund on-going capital and operating needs. This program would, as now, be funded from general funds of the U.S. Treasury.

AASHTO proposes that the existing flow of federal funds to the state or local level remain unchanged. That is, transit funds would be distributed by UMTA just as they are currently distributed, either to state transit agencies or to local transit systems as appropriate. Similarly, the decision-making role regarding the use of these funds, matching ratios, etc., would remain as currently structured.

AASHTO recommends continuation of general funds for the transit and the current Mass Transit Account/Highway Trust fund Revenue relationship.

Rail

The AASHTO Transportation 2020 February 1989 edition of the *New Transportation Concepts for a New Century* report offers the following recommendations regarding future rail programs.

The report states, "A balanced multi-modal transportation network is essential for strong economic growth. Railroads are an indispensable element of this network. Only through coordination among all modes, achieved with the help and support of the states and federal government, can these issues be resolved."

The goals of future programs are:

1. Preserve rail service where it is in the public interest.
2. Develop the ability to anticipate the economic and social impacts of railroad abandonments on shippers and highways.
3. Implement programs that invest in railroad projects that are justified on their own merit and/or as cost-effective alternatives to other improvements.

Recommendations

There is an appropriate federal role in funding rail-related projects. Any comprehensive federal surface transportation program should include funding for track rehabilitation and acquisition, construction of rail/truck transfer facilities, new rail connections, and industry relocation. This proposal meets the objectives of the Transportation 2020 process to preserve rural access, provide modal interlinks, and reduce suburban congestion.

Congress should review the body of law governing the rail industry in the same manner it addressed economic deregulation through the Staggers Act, the Rail Retirement Act, the Railroad Employment Insurance Act, and the Federal Employer's Liability Act. A redrafting of these laws is essential to allow the rail industry to remain a viable part of the transportation system to the year 2020.

Amtrak and certain intercity high-speed rail passenger capital projects are appropriate federal responsibilities and in the national interest. Any comprehensive federal transportation program must address rail passenger service needs.

Congress should compare the laws, government policies, and user fees impacting the various transportation modes. Where a disparity is found, Congress should strive to create an equitable balance.

Any future comprehensive federal transportation program must continue to provide funds for separating or otherwise protecting railroad-highway crossings. In addition, a federally funded state/federal partnership of railroad safety inspections is required to assure that the rail industry complies with federal safety standards. Also, federal research and development funding is essential in the areas of improved warning systems (such as radar and sonar systems) and hazardous and nuclear materials transportation.

THE SURFACE TRANSPORTATION PROGRAM IN THE POST-INTERSTATE ERA

The AASHTO recommendation, as currently developed, proposes a simplified surface transportation program with fewer categories and greater flexibility in the use of funds.

In addition to a simplified program structure, the policy recommendations as currently developed would also support additional transportation research, including the examination of new vehicle and related technology. AASHTO proposes that transportation research be a priority at all levels of government.

AASHTO has supported public input into the development of the post-Interstate program through the sixty-five public forums held throughout the country to discuss major transportation issues and the components of a future surface transportation program. AASHTO continues to support this input from individuals and organizations as the new surface transportation program develops.

As the Congress begins consideration of new surface transportation legislation, AASHTO will make available its findings and the recommendations to the Congress for consideration.

The past thirty years of the federal/state/local partnership has produced vital transportation improvements for the nation's economic and mobility needs. AASHTO seeks an equally strong future program not only to maintain this system, but also to improve it to meet the nation's future transportation needs to the year 2020.

12

A HIGHWAY DESIGNED TO BE PART OF THE HUMAN ENVIRONMENT

MATTHEW A. COOGAN

This chapter has been organized to help the reader understand the nature of Boston's Artery/Tunnel Project and to relate that subject to the four questions structured for the forum on "The City as a Human Environment." In order to accomplish the first objective, a series of fact sheets have been attached to this chapter. These fact sheets are quite self-explanatory, and present the nuts and bolts information about our multi-billion dollar infrastructure investment. The original text of this chapter, at the suggestion of the forum's organizers, is presented as a series of responses to the four key questions.

INTRODUCTION

The Commonwealth of Massachusetts is now proceeding with the design and construction of the largest single Interstate highway project in history. After the monumental Washington, D.C. Metro Project, it is probably the largest urban public works program in the country—if not the world. The program calls for the completion of Interstate I-90 by an extension of the highway from its present terminus at South Station to its final terminus at Logan International Airport, about three and a half miles to the east. The program calls for the completion of Interstate I-93 by the reconstruction of a presently substandard three and a half mile section through downtown Boston, commonly referred to as the "Central Artery." Both elements of the full project are part of the national Interstate System and are eligible for 90/10 federal funding.

The project will create four new lanes of highway capacity on an east-west axis (along I-90), and four new lanes of capacity on a north-south axis (along I-93), effectively doubling the throughput capacity in both cases. I-90 will take the form of a four-lane sub-aqueous tube under the Boston Harbor, and I-93 will take the form of an eight- and ten-lane tunnel through the heart of the historic downtown area. In addition, the project will create several miles of bus-only and High Occupancy Vehicle (HOV) lanes forming a network of exclusive and priority access roadway facilities.

At the same time, the Commonwealth, through its Executive Office of Transportation and Construction (effectively the State DOT) is coordinating the reconstruction of the airport, the seaport, and the mass transportation system, all of which are touched and restructured by the Artery/Tunnel Project. The goal of this coordination is to bring about the improvements to the transportation facilities in a manner consistent with the Commonwealth's strongly held policy that the inner core area must be primarily served by public transportation services.

THE FOUR QUESTIONS

Key Question 1: What are the major challenges in transportation, as revealed by the experience of the Artery/Tunnel Project?

As noted in the introduction, the Artery/Tunnel Project will increase both north-south and east-west highway capacity by four lanes in each case. For me, and for other policymakers who have been working on transportation policies and strategies over the past two decades, the most serious questions (challenges) concern the very desirability of increased highway capacity in the core of the metro region. In the following pages, we will argue that this particular expansion of highway *does* make sense, in terms of its direct impact on the environment.

First of all, let us establish the geographic context of this discussion. We are discussing the policy decisions made in one older, northeastern American city. The observations and conclusions may or may not be relevant to any other city or type of metropolitan area. For Boston may be unique in that it has clearly spelled out its goals in relation to the issue of density and urban development: we are for it.

Back in 1971, Boston made a difficult decision to scrap its program of creating additional radial highway capacity, and opted instead for a policy that the downtown core area must be served primarily by public transportation and not by low occupancy private auto. (As a historical note, this decision to kill the remaining radial interstate construction was made one year before Congress created the so-called "Interstate transfer" legislation that enabled many other American cities to follow Boston and opt not to complete their interstate programs in dense urban areas.)

In the years since the decision not to build any more radial highway capacity into the core, several major transit lines have gone ahead. In the Southwest corridor, the original location of I-95, a combination of a new heavy rapid transit system and an expanded commuter rail facility have been constructed and are in revenue operation today. In the Northwest Corridor, a new transit line and expanded commuter rail has been implemented.

The stated policy goal for transportation investment is to reinforce and support the role of the high density downtown areas with the technologies most appropriate to them.

Here, then, lies the key question. How does the transportation system serve the land use pattern so universally desired by the community? How does the transportation strategy work to support this downtown-oriented growth strategy?

There are those who, observing the near crippling state of congestion on Boston's Central Artery, argue that the downtown, and (more relevantly) the fringe of downtown, should not grow anymore. But the downtown economy is the engine of the regional economy. Continued downtown growth means precious jobs accessible to all, it means a widened tax base for the city with the greatest burden of housing the poor, and, most relevant to this discussion, it means even greater diversity at the center of the region.

There are those who, observing the propensity of new highways to fill up and themselves become congested, argue that it is futile to expand the roadway capacity as we propose to do.

What then is our answer to this challenge?

There are *three* critical elements to our strategy. First, and perhaps most important, the Artery/Tunnel Project does not tend to increase radial capacity from the suburban areas to the core. The decision not to expand radial capacity to the core has not been seriously challenged since it was made. Our Interstate expressway system currently allows about four lanes from the north, all defined at about a four-mile radius from downtown. We propose to make no increase in general purpose capacity at these points. (In most cases physical barriers exist to highway widening at critical points in each of these corridors.) The existing capacity at each of these points serves as a natural bottleneck, which in effect serves to meter the flow that can proceed towards the core in the inbound A.M. peak direction.

Second, we propose to add capacity to the core expressway network to allow it to process those volumes that have been metered through the radical bottleneck points. At the present time, the center of the expressway network cannot possibly process the volumes entering from the radials. South of the Central Artery, seven inbound lanes try to merge into three lanes in the predominant direction of the flow. The result is straightforward and easily predicted by modern methods of bottleneck analysis. Traffic backs up for twenty or thirty minute queues that stretch back for miles. The air pollution implication of these back-up queues are staggering.

Thus, the key to our regional expressway strategy is to create a road-way system which is *in balance;* the downtown expressway system must be capable of processing that traffic volume that has been metered past the radial bottleneck points.

The third integral element of the total transportation strategy is the need for a parking control strategy. In simplified terms, our purpose in building the additional highway capacity is to provide for mobility needs *for those other than low-occupancy users to the transit-rich downtown.* In Boston's Central Business District (CBD), we expect another 50,000 jobs to be created while we build the new highway capacity. Clearly, if all those people drive in low-occupancy mode to downtown, there will have been no effective increase in capacity for those trip makers who have no alternative but to drive. The answer—the only answer—is the creation of a truly effective parking freeze in the transit-rich downtown areas.

The creation of a reasonable parking control strategy is not particu-larly controversial in the transit-rich financial district. Indeed, fully two-thirds of CBD workers come by public transportation, and there is no reason why that mode split will not grow to the 80 percent enjoyed by Chicago. Our more difficult policy dilemmas occur in the establishment of parking control strategies for the "ring" immediately surrounding the existing CBD, where explosive levels of growth are now occurring. This zone, which has been called the "fringe of core" area, or the "extended downtown," is the area most affected by the transportation changes and strategies of the Artery/Tunnel Project.

Within this ring of a one-to-two-mile radius from downtown is lo-cated our airport, our seaport, our medical centers, and our educational centers. In addition there are several underdeveloped tracts of land im-mediately adjacent to the CBD that seem to be logical locations for the expansion of the financial district itself. (They are the Fort Point Channel development area and the Charleston yards development area.)

There are two predominant characteristics of the development cur-rently occurring in this fringe of core area. First, in terms of density, many areas are at a density similar to or greater than traditional parts of the CBD. (Kendall Square and the Fan Pier Project come to mind.) Second, these areas are only tangentially served by major fixed transpor-tation services.

The public consensus about urban form is very strong. Bostonians *like* their dense urban center and do not oppose its further development. (Indeed, the host cities have spent massive amounts of money to induce activities into this area.) The transportation planner and the land use planner alike understand that, over the long haul, this ring of near-CBD development must be served primarily by public transportation services. (Remember, our regional highway plan does not include any increase in general purpose radial highway capacity.)

Here lies the dilemma, and the basis for the present controversy. Limits for parking levels must be established in advance so that each developer understands the constraints of the site at the time of his investment. One approach is to allow for a fixed number of parking spaces based on the ultimate build-out of the area, but to allow for all those spaces to be built initially. Thus the initial "pathfinder" developer has only moderate risk, but later the free market will reallocate those spaces over several development projects.

In sum, the major challenge for Boston is to create additional highway capacity where it is needed, without undermining or destroying the basic transportation strategy of the region, which calls for public transportation services to serve the dense urban core. Based on the years of study and modeling that we have done, we believe that we have developed a highway project that will serve to improve air quality, reduce volumes on local residential streets, lower noise levels, and increase public transportation usage. This is the greatest challenge to the project.

Key Question 2: What are the significant interactions between the four areas, as revealed in the experience of the Artery/Tunnel Project?

As we discussed above, under question one, the most significant interaction is between desired land use (the form of the built environment) and the transportation needs to serve it. Many transportation theoreticians would argue that the most "effective" land form would be one based on a vast grid of north-south roads meeting east-west roads. In such a featureless plane, there would be no need for congestion, because there would be no center; all routes would have immediately adjacent alternate routes, and traffic would spread evenly over this multinucleated grid.

This is exactly the land use pattern that our citizens do *not* want. Our citizens value the historically developed core of the region, with its character and its diversity. And there is great political support for expanding this downtown land use into the adjacent development areas. Residential density in this enlarged core will be very high, with condominium towers poised high over the Charles River, over the edges of the harbor and in entirely new enclaves. Based on recent market trends, we can conclude that Bostonians like living in these highly urban subcenters.

But at the same time, they would like to have highways that flow and infrastructures that work. The kinds of densities that are being proposed simply cannot function without a solid base of public transportation services to accommodate the majority of the flows. With the conclusion of the Artery/Tunnel Project, we will have no more rights-of-way available for highway expansion, and it is highly questionable whether we should build such highways even if we could. Thus, the desired urban form of the built environment demands that a public transportation infrastructure be created simultaneously with the development activity, particularly in the new fringe of core ring of development.

The essential contradiction, then, between the desired form of the built environment (land use) and the form of the transportation system is resolved by a decision to invest in public transportation infrastructure simultaneously with the development in the fringe of core area. But the capital demands of most forms of public transportation (i.e., the cost) renders this solution highly unworkable.

The dilemma that remains is to find a method that will incrementally build up the public transportation infrastructure, at reasonable increments of cost, while simultaneously developing the new land at the fringe of the core.

Key Question 3: What research, legislative, institutional, philosophical, and cultural changes are needed for dealing with the problems discussed here?

Let us start with research. So far, we have established that there is a desired land form, with high-density characteristics, and an absolute need for high-quality public transportation services to be implemented simultaneously with the increments of development of this dense land form. We have also established that we do not have the capital resources to sink vast sums of money into a rapid transit infrastructure in areas that are largely undeveloped at this point.

Boston has been blessed by the existence of a high-quality fixed rail system, which has made possible the density of trip ends we now enjoy, and which we now intend to expand upon. Indeed, we have spent the last decade expanding upon this great resource, with several billion dollars invested in rail improvements. But, over this period it has become increasingly obvious that the new expanded core ring will demand a transit technology which is capable of operating at grade (with at grade intersections with local streets), in addition to its operation along discrete rights-of-way.

There are only two available technologies for us to pursue: light rail and advanced bus technology. About light rail we know a great deal, thanks to the resurgent interest in this approach that occurred during the 1970s (before the lights went out). About the high-technology bus, we know shockingly little; and there is no excuse for this. Transportation researchers have been looking to the high-technology bus as an exciting solution to this dilemma for more than two decades.

It is clear that the developing high-density zones will need a technology that (1) effectively connects back into the regional transit network and (2) can reach the relatively dispersed trip ends that characterize the present land uses in this area. Over the long run, this same technology should develop into a full, high-capacity grade-separated system.

This approach should surprise no one who has studied the history of transit development in this country. For America's first subway was built in Boston, as a light rail system that grew incrementally into the Back Bay as that new land mass developed. In effect, this philosophy of incremental investment is what we seek to follow in the fringe of the core ring of development.

The Artery/Tunnel Project includes several elements consistent with this strategy. A central part of this project is the creation of several miles of "bus highways" or HOV lanes which will serve both advanced and regular bus technology. More specifically, our project includes the creation of a new bus-way at Logan airport, specifically designed for high-technology buses. This bus-way will allow for a new kind of "across the platform transfer" between the Logan shuttle bus and the Blue Line rapid transit service. The inbound bus will be designed with "high platform" doors on its left side. The rider will step through the left hand door, across the platform, and onto the rapid transit car without ever having to step up or down. The wheelchair-based rider will be able to make this transfer instantly, with no delay to the transit operation. The same high-quality transfer will occur on the outbound platform.

This new bus vehicle has the potential to operate in downtown tunnels (in "platoon" formation) with station dwell times that rival rapid transit in efficiency. At the same time it can benefit from the billions of dollars already invested in HOV and in general purpose highway lanes throughout the country. An early prototype of this approach has been adopted by the City of Seattle, although a last minute decision was made there to delete the high platform aspect of the concept. Nevertheless, the Seattle downtown project stands as the single most innovative American transit improvement of the later half of this century.

The Artery/Tunnel Project will create several major rights-of-way appropriate for the high-technology bus concept. These range from highly traditional HOV lanes to underground rights-of-way that could only be used by buses of the Seattle concept.

The lack of interest in advanced bus technology in this country over the past nine years is somewhat pathetic. Major advances in this area have been made in Germany, France, and Sweden, just to name a few. (The Seattle bus is being built in Italy, for example.) Clearly, a small amount of research into the development of the dual-mode bus, a bus capable of on-street (non-guided) operation and in-tunnel (guided) operation, could reap significant rewards in a relatively short time frame.

Secondly, there is a need for an increased awareness on the part of all institutions that build and own roadway surfaces that they are in the business of moving people, not vehicles. All of these strategies to make maximum usage of existing and future roadways require an increased institutional awareness that these facilities will have to be carefully managed in order to maximize their effectiveness. To this day, funding agencies have a greater interest in putting money into a lane that will carry two thousand persons per hour (in general purpose flow) than the same sized lane which can carry thirty thousand persons per hour (as part of a carefully designed bus highway facility).

Finally, in terms of cultural changes, it is important to emphasize that it is a characteristic of the land patterns that we value—that people have to travel in collective units, rather than in individual units. Much has been written on this subject. If we insist upon looking at public transportation services as a lower-class phenomenon, then we will not succeed in building the kind of density patterns we are discussing in this paper.

Key Question 4: How can public participation in these issues be made more effective in improving the quality of the urban environment?

I would suggest there are two kinds of public participation in project development—real and pro forma. The Artery/Tunnel Project includes the creation of seven new acres of public park in East Boston because of public outcry at the possibility of the highway degrading the park environment. Based on this concern, the design was changed and now the park will be larger and more accessible. The Artery/Tunnel Project includes the creation of an entire network of truck roads in the South Boston seaport area, largely because at meeting after meeting the citizens argued for the need to totally separate these large seaport trucks from the life of residential South Boston. The project includes ramps that will cause traffic to bypass local streets in the South End, largely because of the dogged perseverance of local community leaders there. Clearly, then, real meaningful public input can exist and can make great improvements to projects.

Rare is the public administrator who has not been dragged through a public meeting to seek community input, knowing full well that the designs were already produced, the deals already made, and the outcome already determined. At the Artery/Tunnel Project we have (inadvertently) stumbled onto a two-EIS process. In the first EIS (Environmental Impact Statement), we established the basic need for and system design of the project. Then, because too much time had passed since the creation of the first EIS, we started going through the process again: this time focussing on the ramps and the local street connections. The result has been a gold mine of successful improvements to the project that literally could not have occurred at the earlier stage where go/no-go and basic corridor decisions were being made. Of course, there have been those who have criticized the process with the standard responses: "they can never make decisions," and "they just like to plan things, they don't know how to build anything." On the whole, however, this self-imposed, two-hearing, two-EIS process has allowed citizens to focus successfully on the actual decisions at hand, rather than the tour de force of the pro forma process that so often does occur.

This largely accidental documentation process may be a significant precedent for future mega-projects of this scale. The citizen gets the opportunity for macro observation first, followed by a direct ability to participate in the design refinement process with the power of the EIS regulations on his side for both steps.

In any case, the basic requirements do not vary significantly. Whether under the umbrella of the EIS process or whether acting under the more relaxed rules of gentlemanly fair play, the public should be informed of the facts to the extent that they are known at any particular step in the design process. This is often painful for the citizen, who really does want to know the hour of the day that the bulldozer will arrive, when the agency has not chosen the corridor for the alignment. It represents a major personal challenge for the public official; for the public does tend to believe in your omniscience and your infinite ability to hide the facts from them. How do you overcome this problem? I just don't know.

Finally, I think it is only fair to note that in certain of the situations described in this chapter, the public's wish list is that of a child. They want to live in high-density condominium towers, working in still higher density office towers, living in a world of infinite urban diversity, and, by the way, they want the highways to be free flowing for their own personal use at any hour of the day. While it may be well and proper for the maid to arrive by public transportation, surely such an indignity is below their desired lifestyle. It must be stated that it is the responsibility of the public official to tell the truth about the transportation options as they are known; it is not the responsibility of the public official to create the desired world in which no trade-offs exist and everyone attains his or her unconstrained desires.

III

Shaping Patterns of Urban Land Use

13

THE NEW YORK REGION EXPERIMENT

John P. Keith

The Tri-State Urban Region is an ongoing experiment in the use and abuse of land. It reflects the American experience, though in an overly magnified fashion. It exhibits two phenomena of urbanization in the extreme: one is density of development epitomized by Manhattan, the other is looseness of development exhibited by the very large-lot development pattern of suburban and exurban counties of the region.

THE REGION DEFINED

1929 Region

The region was defined as "New York and its Environs" by the 1929 metropolitan plan of that name. That plan was drawn by a predecessor committee of the Regional Plan Association (RPA). It encompassed an area of almost 7,000 square miles within a radius of fifty miles from Manhattan, home to eleven million people in twenty-two counties. The area was seen for the first time by the Plan as a single economy, magnetized by the Manhattan Central Business District (CBD), operating within three states and hundreds of municipalities.

1968 Region

The Second Regional Plan, published by RPA in 1968, encompassed another tier of counties—thirty-one in all, swinging the radius of the

Tri-State Region out seventy-five miles from New York City Hall and enveloping 750 municipalities. Today, in that 13,000 square mile region—running from New Haven to Trenton—19.8 million people reside. It is a vast commutershed, with perhaps 1 percent of its employees crossing outer boundaries to work.

THE REGION'S URBANIZED LAND

Sixty years ago, 470 square miles of then smaller New York Region were urbanized. In 1963, 1,875 square miles were urbanized. In a report entitled *Spread City*, the RPA projected that if the region's land development policies were not altered, the amount of land that would be used up in the forthcoming twenty-five years would be equivalent to that urbanized in the 325 years of the region's previous history.

Squandering the Land

And that has just about happened. If anything, the development policies of the Tri-State Region today lead to much more squandering of the land than in the earlier decades of this century. And in quantity (though not just within the geographical confines of the first region), the amount now urbanized is 3,900 square miles!

In fact, during just the one decade of the 1970s, approximately 350 square miles, or 3 percent of the Tri-State Region, were urbanized—this within a decade when the region's economy boomed and population grew once again. Though not as robustly as during the 1980s, the region is now projected to grow moderately to at least 2010.[1]

Vast Urbanization Ahead

The implications for the abuse of land are clear. If land controls are not strengthened, and public acquisitions and private reservations accelerated, land consumption will go on apace. If it does, it would be safe to predict that today's 13,000 square mile region would be largely urbanized during the twenty-first century, except for public and private land reservations. Today those reserved lands are some 1,500 square miles in extent.

WHY SUCH VORACIOUS USE?

What drives the appetite for such voracious use of the land in the Tri-State Region? Popularly, the response is: "The desire to own a single-family home of your own in the country." That's obviously a cause, but one aided and abetted by others. Planning itself is among the culprits; so are tax and housing policies; so is exclusivity on the part of the business and homeowners.

Planning's Role

The 1929 Regional Plan's prime objective was overcoming the "cheek-by-jowl" squalor of the tenements of the old core of the region. It called for decentralizing the population into smaller concentrations. The highway network of the plan was intended to provide a parallel system to that of the existing rail system. Actually, because of the inability of the private economy to maintain and enlarge the mass transportation system during depression and war, it was not prepared to handle the explosive growth of the region's economy and population in the post–World War II years.

On the other hand, the plan's highway and parkway proposals had been built as part of the depression "pump-priming," and they were ready to accept the surge of post-war autos. They became like "can-openers" to the countryside. Also, encouraging the suburban growth of the 1950s and 1960s were government housing finance programs that favored new rather than rehabilitated housing. Fueling all this new auto and home ownership was rising per capita income in the region. And so the rush to suburbia was on.

Property Taxation and Zoning

As the homes for veterans and others spread across the region, exemplified by Levittown, which blossomed from the potato fields of Long Island, municipalities quickly felt the tax implications. These new homes meant children—and children meant schools—and schools meant increased property taxes.

The solution soon devised was to enlarge lot sizes, cutting back the number of homes to be accepted and, hence, of children and their schools. Another gambit in this fiscal zoning was to attract and zone for industry and commerce to help with the tax burden. It wasn't long before it dawned on homeowners and industry alike that large plots had an additional advantage—exclusivity. Lower income people and businesses couldn't buy in, so segregation could be accomplished by economic means.

And so a tool of planning devised to ensure the health and safety of communities by separating land uses was subverted to achieve other ends, and the stage was set for a spread city with its profligate use of the land.

The Second Plan

The association's Second Regional Plan intended to channel the spreading regional development, so clearly underway throughout the 1960s. It had as its premise the location of regional activities (i.e., major offices and stores, educational, health, and cultural institutions) in centers large and small, from Manhattan to village scale. It proposed linking the main regional centers by public transportation, in particular linking them with the Manhattan CBD. And it recommended—as had the first plan—capturing large tracts of open space to preserve special regional features.

Open Space Results

The second plan was perhaps most successful in the last stated of its objectives—the preservation of open space. It was responsible for the public acquisition of ten major national and state parks such as Gateway, Delaware Water Gap, Fire Island, Minnewaska, and Great Piece Meadows. It also stimulated the provision of federal and state park acquisition funds and the addition of substantial holdings by counties and municipalities.

Center Successes

As for its intention to guide recentralization in a spreading metropolis, the second plan stimulated multi-millions of square feet of office and other development in regional subcenters such as White Plains, Stamford, Newark, and New Brunswick. It encouraged the revival of the Manhattan CBD, and more recent growth in downtown Brooklyn and Jamaica, Queens.

Public Transportation and Renovation

Moreover, the second plan managed to establish a climate for the rehabilitation and refurbishment of the transit systems of the Tri-State Region, which were in a state of near collapse in the mid-1960s. Agencies such as the Metropolitan Transportation Administration, for the New York and Connecticut sectors of the region, and New Jersey Transit were formed to stabilize and improve service. Much remains to be done: capital financing is still short, planning is still insufficient, and operations require further improvement. Despite these shortcomings, an alternative transportation mode to the motor vehicle exists within the Tri-State Region that can be upgraded—unlike some other major metropolitan areas in the United States.

Spread Continues

Nevertheless, the scattering of activities goes on apace across the region's landscape. More than half of the several hundred million square feet of regional activities (enumerated above) built during the past decade have been located willy-nilly. Individually many of these offices, shopping malls, colleges, etc., on campus sites are of good design and attractively landscaped. The collective result, however, in terms of the region's development pattern, is inefficient, exclusionary, and abusive of its land.

ARE THERE ANY ANSWERS?

Control of land and its uses seem to be difficult indeed, no matter the system of government. Asian countries report similar problems. Some metropolitan areas in relatively mature European societies, exemplified by Braunschweig, Germany, are opting for a "no-growth, back-to-nature" approach, thereby stressing the land less. That approach is unrealistic for most of the Southern Hemisphere metropolises, which are growing at dizzying rates as agrarian people seek economic advancement in urban areas (Keith 1988b). These certainly are not simple nor universal solutions to conserving urban land.

Tri-State Region Experience

Experience in the New York metropolitan area leads to some possibilities for ameliorating the land consumption rate. They fall under several headings: regional form, state assumption of power, direct intervention, and tax sharing.

Regional Form. The form of a metropolitan area—or its pattern—in itself can be resource-conserving, especially of the land. If the development is allowed to spread without restraint across the landscape, it can be wasteful of land and other resources, such as energy (Regional Plan Association 1974).

Concern for its development pattern has been evident in Connecticut in the State Plan adopted sixteen years ago, though that plan only applies to actions of government. Similar concern has emerged in New Jersey, and a new State Plan is now before local governments for "cross acceptance." That plan calls for land use tiers, from intensively urban to rural agriculture. New York State no longer plans.

There is need now to encourage New York State to recommence planning and to bring the state planning efforts together regionally. There have been two abortive attempts to do so: the Metropolitan Regional Council, which began in the 1950s, and the Tri-State Regional Planning Commission of the 1960s.

The MRC was unwieldy. Because of elections, its local government membership turned over too frequently to achieve continuity of program, and its staff was not capable of filling the vacuum. Finally, it was folded into Tri-State. The interstate compact agency proved to be an important source of data, but not of policy. It collapsed when Connecticut withdrew during a budget cutback, and no constituency rose in its support in any of the states.

In the late 1950s, RPA proposed that a Tri-State Secretariat should be organized to focus the planning efforts of the states regionally. Now, with growing political concern for the lack of regional approach to issues of regional importance, that proposal should be reconsidered. RPA might itself act in this role, initially, to test its validity.

Promulgation of the concept of conserving land form for the region is imperative. In order to achieve it, state planning must be pursued vigorously by the region's three states interconnectively. Certainly, RPA will continue its civic leadership in that direction.

State Assumption of Power. When the consequences for integration of the spread development pattern were realized in the 1960s, several organizations, such as Suburban Action, began actively to litigate. The Mount Laurel suits I and II, in New Jersey, achieved the most striking results. New Jersey's Supreme Court ordered that low-income housing be accepted by each New Jersey municipality in accordance with the "regional needs" of its area.

These cases are indicative of the increasing willingness on the part of the courts to direct the state to reassume its power over its land. Except for federal land holdings, the states hold the reservoir of power over their land under the U.S. Constitution. Universally, however, they have delegated much of that power to local governments.

If land use is to be shaped in the best interests of the state and of great interstate regions, some of that power will have to be recaptured. New Jersey's new planning act allows its state planning agency to overrule its localities if cross acceptance proves infeasible—and if that proves politically feasible! Comparable steps have been taken by Florida, Oregon, and a few other states. More of the same is to be anticipated in the Tri-State Region.

Direct Intervention. New York State, during the Rockefeller Administration, created a state Urban Development Corporation (UDC). That agency's primary mission was to build low-income housing. It did so rather well across the state until the Nixon Administration severely cut federal housing assistance, magnifying management deficiencies. The agency, and indeed the state itself, were nearly towed under financially.

Since then, and also because of the economic recession of the 1970s, the UDC has concentrated on economic development projects. It still retains the power to spin off subsidiary authorities, such as the New York City Convention Center Corporation. And it still retains the power of eminent domain.

Tax Sharing. The Hackensack Meadowlands Development Commission (HMDC) is the region's best example of tax sharing. New Jersey enacted legislation forming the HMDC in 1969, largely based upon the RPA's recommendation. Its purpose was to allow the fourteen municipalities incorporating the Meadowlands within their boundaries to plan and locate industrial, commercial, and housing developments rationally within an area the size of Manhattan Island—instead of each municipality looking to its own tax needs—and to do so in an environmentally constructive way by protecting segments of the meadows.

The Meadowlands have been the recipient of large-scale growth in subsequent years, not all planned as RPA would have it, but nevertheless the commission represents an important tax-sharing principle. Each of the towns is doing better tax-wise than it could have going it alone, and certainly the Meadowlands pattern is too. It must be said, however, that housing, transportation, and environmental elements of the HMDC plan have been neglected, and office/service activities overly encouraged, but that is another story. The essential point is that HMDC offers a direction.

THE POSSIBILITIES

Land control possibilities at the regional scale emerge from the above-described state experiments in defining regional development patterns, directing housing locations, intervening with specific developments, and tax sharing. Locked together, these sorts of state action could lead to be a land-conserving development form for the Tri-State Urban Region.

Widespread and growing concern over traffic jams in the countryside, disturbing housing shortages, despoliation of air, land, and water, and other regional problems may be opening the political door to an amalgam of such rigorous proposals, now considered politically too risky.

Public understanding is needed to provide a climate in which political leadership can take such difficult steps. RPA has considerable experience with public involvement via self-help planning exercises at the county level and on television town meetings at the regional level. They serve as two-way educational processes between the public and the planner, and they provide a background of public understanding with the support of which officials can take action.

The decade of the 1990s will be telling as to the course the Tri-State Region will take with respect to its remaining 7,300 square miles of open land. And the course taken will determine the shape of the region far into the future.

NOTE

1. Regional Plan Association. 1989. *The New Century* 1.

14

CONSTITUTING A PRESERVATION PLAN FOR URBAN AREAS

M. CHRISTINE BOYER

INTRODUCTION

The preservation of historic centers in American cities is a land use movement with only a fifty-year history. Charleston, South Carolina, was the first American city to attempt to regulate development pressure on its historic Battery. In 1931 when a new city-wide zoning ordinance was created, it embedded within the zoning regulations a set of design guidelines and alteration controls for the Old Historic Charleston District. This innovative use of historic area zoning gingerly transferred control over the architectural wall or the streetscape from the private to the public domain. But it raised a host of problems testing the concept of public control that both regulated private property for purely aesthetic reasons and forced new architectural designs to be consistent with specified historic standards. To avoid some of these problems, in 1937 the City of New Orleans created the Vieux Carré Historic District by passing a Louisiana constitutional amendment. Again, these regulatory controls were controversial and property owners sued. By upholding this preservation ordinance, however, the courts eventually described and expanded the legitimate terrain for aesthetic controls over private property. The importance of streetscape, already outlined in Charleston, was now extended to the "tout ensemble," and consequently the distinct historic ambience created by the spirit of place or "genius loci" came under regulatory control. As preservation activity continued to gain support in cities across the nation, joining forces with the swelling environmental land use crusade by the 1960s, the federal government finally joined the preservation game by proclaiming "that the historical and cultural foundations of the Nation should be preserved as a living part of our community life and development in order to give a sense of orientation to the American people," and so passed into legislation the National Preservation Act of 1966.

But just as the process of historic preservation finally came of age and was beginning to be accepted, a separate development was taking place within the process of city planning. Planners in the 1950s and 1960s wanted to become urban policymakers inside of government where political power resided. They wanted to separate the process of city planning for the act of creating a physical plan. To direct all of a planner's energy towards the publication of a static document that predicted the form of a city years in advance meant that short-range and immediate problems of urban sprawl, strip development, reckless suburban expansion, and neighborhood blight continued without regulation or guidance. Since governmental intervention in American cities during the 1950s and 1960s, in the form of urban renewal and transportation schemes, tended to promote private real estate capital and center city business and administrative concerns, this in turn created unknown social effects such as the removal of ghetto residents from inner city neighborhoods, the replacement of sound communities with new governmental or cultural facilities, and the cordoning off of slum territories from more profitable center city land uses. These ruptures politicized the process of planning and pushed it still further away from the considerations of aesthetic and physical reform. The Harlem and Los Angeles ghetto riots of 1964 and 1965 merely gave witness to what the profession of planners had been experiencing during the 1950s. It was clear that America had become two separate and unequal societies, and this alone made any concept of comprehensive physical planning that saw real estate development and land use order as ends in themselves an irrelevant and atavistic concern. As city planning turned away from its physical base, however, it left none in charge of the general process of spatial restructuring, a vacuum that historic preservation eventually would fill producing questionable and negative effects.

During the 1970s and 1980s, historic preservation became one of the major instruments the private market used in the redevelopment or filtering up of downgraded and devalued inner city territories. In many cities, especially those that have experienced massive real estate development in the last two decades, city planning and historic preservation are fragmented land use instruments given separate and jealously guarded jurisdictions. Neither of them offer either a comprehensive look across the physical restructuring of city space or the ability to monitor the path of real estate revitalization in more than an ad hoc manner.

So cities under the siege of real estate development experience spatial restructuring that entails spreading waves of inner city residential gentrification, the re-evaluation of abandoned territories for upscaled market redevelopment, luxury entertainment and tourist centers spreading out across the city, and high-rise condominium towers randomly sprouting from the base of historic structures. Most of these redevelopments are associated in some manner with historic preservation or the nostalgic allure of traditional architectural styles.

These land use actions, moreover, are said to be the natural and inevitable outcome of the successful real estate market and lie beyond the jurisdiction of city planning controls. The fact that they are causing the gap between rich and poor neighborhoods to grow ever wider, that non-luxury land uses are being squeezed outside the core of the city, that the center of the city is becoming an enclave of the rich and the powerful, are concerns, we are told, that also lie beyond the interest of planning. So it is argued, this spatial restructuring that center cities have experienced during the 1970s and 1980s, is simply the result of private market re-evaluation of center city real estate and does not require governmental intervention or regulation. Nevertheless, this private market activity is cut across by government subsidization in the form of tax benefits, sometimes economic development projects carried out by public-private corporations, and protected by historic preservation land use controls. These implicit and hidden government subsidies underwriting private market activity, including the relationship between historic preservation and real estate development, begs that we reconsider a process of planning that monitors the spatial reterritorialization of cities by the private market and shapes this movement through its regulatory and fiscal powers towards a more equitable and humane distribution of land uses. The issue to be addressed is not the value of historic preservation in the provision of a humane urban environment; that battle has already been won. The question this time is how historic preservation has been used as a major development tool in the spatial restructuring of American cities during the last two decades, and how the negative effects that this application has generated might be mitigated.

TAX INCENTIVES AND HISTORIC PRESERVATION

Suddenly in American cities across the nation, it appears as if all the backwater areas of central cities, their abandoned waterfront, neglected wholesale market areas, low-cost working-class residential areas, shoddy retail shopping streets and entertainment zones have been transformed into upscale market developments accompanied by offices, hotels, conference centers, luxury residences, shopping and entertainment facilities. This process of economically revaluing land from which real estate capital has recently withdrawn is most apparent in cities such as New York that have achieved world class status and are experiencing a major upgrading and expansion of their employment base in the financial, insurance, and business service sectors. The development of New York, for example, as a super-service employment center in turn creates uneven results: capital withdrawing from some territories of the city while upgrading and revaluing others; real estate development pushing some property values skyhigh while allowing others to plummet until they reach a level where in comparison they appear attractive to new investment and the process of reterritorialization begins over again. Although this chapter will cite New York examples of spatial restructuring, the process is also taking place, albeit in less dramatic appearance, in spotted sections of many other American cities and is the result, as will be argued, of basic economic and governmental restructuring.

During the 1950s and 1960s, municipal governments, aided by the federal government, focused on the many related issues that poverty and racial inequality posed. Their intent was the revitalization of economically obsolescent areas of the city and the provision of low- and moderate-income housing. By the 1970s, however, the emphasis of city governments had shifted at first toward general revenue sharing in which it was suggested that communities target their limited resources to those areas of the city that were the most likely to respond to economic revitalization; that is, those areas that lay close to older urban renewal projects, adjacent to institutions that generated low-skill service employment such as hospitals and insurance companies, or inner city neighborhoods with historic or well-constructed housing where subsidies for infrastructure improvement and code reinforcement might generate a wave of private rehabilitation and restoration work. By the end of the 1970s, the stimulation of private market revitalization and economic growth in center cities' neighborhoods was the name of the reinvestment game. And now municipal governments relied on property and income tax abatements to trigger this reinvestment. These tax abatements are never thought of as government subsidies but simply appear as private market incentives, even though they exacerbate the gaping hole that widens between municipal revenues and municipal needs, a void that makes areas of the city with the greatest need for government subsidies even poorer and economically viable areas even richer.

In New York City the spatial effects created by shifting attention away from social welfare issues to what has been called fiscal welfare hidden within a variety of tax incentives and abatements have been unmonitored to date, and it generally is not noted that historic preservation activity has abetted this transformation. Many historic districts of the city have been revitalized through the process of property and income tax abatements. For example, the Revenue Act of 1976 began the process by enabling property owners of historic structures to apply for income tax deductions on certified rehabilitation work. Early applications of these tax incentives for restoration work took place on the Fraunces Tavern block in lower Manhattan, the Woolworth Building, the Chrysler Building, the Plaza Hotel, and three townhouse renovations in Greenwich Village Historic District. These tax incentives, we should note, indeed promote the restoration of historic properties, but they are used primarily by business corporations where income tax shelters have the most effect. On the other hand, property tax abatements for rehabilitation work in New York City have experienced a wider application, and they inadvertently have spurred on the process of residential gentrification, especially on the Upper West Side of Manhattan.

In this revitalized neighborhood above 59th Street, over the last two decades residential rents and condominium sales have soared, townhouses for sale are just about unheard of, and commercial rents for boutiques and restaurants have reached the peak that is demanded for more luxurious locations on the Upper East Side. The West Side Renaissance, however, is not just a recent real estate miracle; it goes back to the mid-1950s when the twenty-block West Side Urban Renewal Area began stabilizing the territory between 87th and 97th Streets just off Central Park West. The renewal project to the west side of Broadway between 62nd and 68th Streets is where the Lincoln Center for the Performing Arts now resides. Having secured the northern and southern borders of the area through these urban renewal projects, selective rehabilitation of townhouses and rooming houses during the 1960s began to draw upper-income residents back to the city. Since the Upper West Side side streets were originally developed in the 1880s and 1890s with rows of townhouses, property tax abatements on substantial rehabilitation work secured their revitalization and restoration in the 1970s. In addition, many large apartment buildings and residential hotels, erected throughout the Upper West Side in the early decades of the 1900s, had deteriorated into single room occupancy or SROs. These too began to be renovated in the 1970s, and slowly what once was an economically and racially integrated neighborhood began to show signs of becoming a gentrified district. Little attention was paid to these property tax abatements, for their original intent was to secure the upgrading of cold water flats. But during the years of the fiscal crisis, the mid-1970s, when the doors of the municipal bond market were closed and there was no federal money available to continue the process of neighborhood revitalization, tax incentives became the only real estate game in town, and developers eagerly took advantage of them to garner windfall profits by renovating abandoned structures, rundown hotels, underutilized office buildings, row houses and luxury apartments, and even restoring facades on historic landmark structures. While this policy of windfall property tax abatements for rehabilitation work no longer applies to Manhattan real estate, this restriction is too late to reverse the process of spatial restructuring that created the West Side Renaissance.

By the late 1980s, rampant development was roaring up the spine of Broadway turning every sleepy two-story structure into mammoth new apartment houses in emulation of their twin tower cousins along Central Park West. The extremely tall spire of the Park Belvedere, visible from all over the Upper West Side, has dared to raise its head over the landmark Museum of Natural History and Manhattan Square at Columbus Avenue and 79th Street while a cluster of new luxury apartments and television studios adorn the Lincoln Center Special District. To the south lies the controversial development on the old Colosseum site, casting its probable shadow over Central Park, and to the west extending along the Hudson River below 72nd Street stand the air rights of over seventy-six acres of Pennsylvania Railroad yards that the developer Donald Trump currently controls. In addition, there are many landmark churches scattered throughout the Upper West Side, some on Central Park West and others elegantly adorning the side streets, whose congregations have dwindled over the years. Some of these churches intend or at least want to retain the option to sell their development rights to speculators who would erect tall towers over their sanctuaries.

Of course many long-time residents and newcomers have opposed many of these transformations. An active citizens' protest has driven more than one developer to modify his plans and to erect more community-oriented and historically sensitive structures. But these citizens' voices cannot stop the thrust of development nor turn back the process of gentrification. Faced with the failures of city planning, the creation of a large historic district appears to be the only approach to channel the real estate market and preserve the architectural ambience and residential quality of the Upper West Side. The City Planning Commission has responded too late and too weakly by tinkering with zoning so that it currently prohibits high-rise structures on the mid-block townhouse sections below 96th Street. But New York's residential districts are left with few procedures to combat speculative real estate pressure that slowly eats away at a neighborhood's integrity, reducing its more spontaneous mixture of economic classes and land uses, until its original residents are displaced and a homogenized luxury enclave appears.

Inevitably, when gentrification has run its full course and pushed property values towards the sky, historic preservation will seem a reasonable procedure to stop further development and to protect the architectural ambience and economic values of an upscaled and higher priced community. In the process, however, one more neighborhood will have been protected from downgrading land uses and people, and secured instead for the city's valued and courted service sector executives and employees.

ECONOMIC VITALITY AND HISTORIC PRESERVATION

Another governmental effort to leverage private reinvestment in selective areas of the city was the Federal Urban Development Actions Grants (UDAG) of the late 1970s. Millions of dollars were allocated to neighborhood recycling, adaptive reuse and historic preservation projects in formerly abandoned territories that were worthy of being designated historic, if a city could demonstrate firm financial commitment from the private sector. The revitalization of New York's derelict East River waterfront, as the South Street Seaport became known, was one such restructuring project. Since shipping activity on the New York waterfront had dwindled and declined, what better way to recapture its glory than by creating a living outdoor museum recreating the ambience of its "street of ships" out of four blocks of old houses on Schermerhorn Row as its historic centerpiece. A plan was proposed as early as the late 1960s to develop the area with a mixture of residential, retail, office, and museum spaces in restored and reconstructed buildings. The city, of course, had its own ideas that it began to implement. By creating the Brooklyn Bridge Southeast Urban Renewal District in 1969, it hoped to develop a residential community at the waterfront edge of Fulton Street, yet still preserve some of South Street's historic milieu. Although it was now empowered through eminent domain to condemn private property in the Renewal District, the city began to take a second look at this prospect. Most of the South Street Seaport area contained low-rise structures of three or four stories in height, while its zoning allowed for high-rise commercial development more in character with the Financial District that Wall Street financial interests eagerly wished to exploit. There seemed to be no justification for confiscating the development rights and freezing the Renewal District with small-scale historic development.

Some compromise between Wall Street development and historic preservation had to be found. Consequently the city created a Special South Street Seaport Zoning District in 1972. This would allow the district to remain open to the waterfront, to set aside several of its streets as pedestrian promenades, to ensure the preservation of some of its valuable historic properties, and to guarantee through its design guidelines that in the midst of high-rise development, the South Street Seaport would remain a special retreat. If New York's 1961 zoning ordinance allowed a developer to transfer developable air rights from open plazas to a backdrop tower, then why not allow the transfer from smaller historic structures to other specified parcels in close proximity? So an inventive system allowing the sale of transferable air rights was achieved to mitigate the development pressure hanging like a cloud over the Seaport and hopefully to finance, at the same time, the necessary restoration work. An agreement allowed development rights to be transferred from the low-rise historic blocks along Fulton Street to three receiving blocks to the north along the Brooklyn Bridge, to the block west of Schermerhorn Row, and to blocks south of Burlington Slip and along Piers 15 and 16. In addition, the city decided in 1970 and 1973 to close certain streets in order to create a pedestrian mall in the heart of the Seaport Special District and to enhance the selling of air rights from large development sites that now included the streets as well.

Just as South Street Seaport became a historic district in 1977, a new public-private partnership sprang up as well. And now the meaning of preservation was stretched beyond protecting the rich history of New York's nineteenth-century maritime development to include economic vibrancy as well, and that specifically meant the creation of a twenty-four-hour-a-day tourist attraction sustaining commercial and residential development. By 1979 the Rouse Company had joined the fray, offering to turn South Street Seaport into a festival marketplace based on the model of Boston's Faneuil Hall/Quincy Market and Baltimore's Harborplace. On property leased from the South Street Seaport Museum, the Rouse Company would develop a 100,000 square foot Festival Markethall followed by the construction of a new pavilion on Pier 17. The Federal Urban Development Action Grant, awarded to the city in 1981, would enable it to reconstruct Pier 17 and to carry out street improvements and pedestrian infrastructure within the Urban Renewal District. This in turn would place the city in a position to leverage private investment for the development of an office tower with first- and second-story retailing at the Fulton and Water Street entrance to the Seaport. And indeed with the focal point set on Fulton Street and Schermerhorn Row, the entire South Street Seaport Urban Renewal District might be reterritorialized from its downgraded wholesale fishing activity into a twenty-four-hour-a-day luxury community with marinas, hotels, offices, apartments, and a variety of entertainment.

By the time the South Street Seaport officially opened in 1983, three quarters of its museum exhibition space had been reassigned to Cannon's Walk, an interior arcade lined with shops. Besides a museum whose cultural program had yet to be financed, a few ships rehabilitated and reberthed at its slips, cultural resuscitation stalled while redevelopment gained an advantage. The new Fulton Market Building opened in 1983, new Pier Pavilions in 1985, in addition to a thirty-four-story office tower called Seaport Plaza. To put it another way, New York's maritime culture had become a valuable commodity, and the story doesn't stop there. The Museum's real estate wing has leased a total of thirty-five acres from the city, roughly half of which comprise the four blocks on which the Marketplace is focused. The rest are thirteen buildings containing wholesale fishing concerns that the Museum wants to convert into retail and residential uses more in line with the festival theme.

Meanwhile property values have spiralled, making even five- or six-story new construction projects financially unfeasible. Nevertheless, the Landmarks Commission has been zealous in maintaining its curatorship over the ten-block historic district and, in spite of real estate economics, has rejected every proposal for tall tower development. As the economic value of land in the South Street Historic District has continued to climb, however, a potential problem has arisen over the privately owned blocks to the north of the Seaport Marketplace. At least one of these blocks was excluded from the designated Historic District in 1977. Ten years later, however, its property owners and the consortium of Wall Street banks that bought the development rights from the low-rise structures along Fulton Street began to pursue plans for developing the site, while others fought them back hoping the block would be placed under landmark control. In 1987, half a million square feet of these air rights, at an estimated value ranging from $15 million to $25 million, remained to be sold and the contested block was the only receiving site left as originally proposed. At this price it was inevitable that once again a compromise would be negotiated between development and preservation issues, and some high-rise development is sure to succeed. While our eyes have been focused on the Fulton Street centerpiece of South Street Seaport, all around the historic tableau developers are creating another luxury enclave for offices, hotels, residences, and entertainment facilities.

There are many other negative effects that occur when real estate development is allowed to prevail over historic preservation. As revenue is used to subsidize or stimulate private market development, it is withdrawn from needed areas. In the poorer sections of town, infrastructure decays, police and garbage service erodes, the quality of education declines. But in the revitalized areas, the forfeited revenues are targeted to private corporations who profit immensely from these subsidizations. In the case of South Street Seaport, the public gains a few renovated historic structures and an outdoor seaport museum, but the benefits stop there. Quite clearly, South Street Seaport is not a public space to which the greater community of New York is welcomed with open arms. There are no homeless wandering about, no ruffian panhandlers nor spontaneous street performers, and even the former artists who resided in Schermerhorn Row have been displaced, and the hurly-burly Fulton Fish Market is under continual pressure to relocate. The public space of South Street Seaport is closely surveilled by the Seaport Museum and the Rouse Company, and even its signage and logos are carefully scrutinized to maintain its proscribed historic milieu. But in addition this historic composition places the act of consuming at its very core: the money used to preserve its historic structures and maintain the ambience of its street of ships comes from its share of the revenues that this street of shops can produce. The Seaport is in reality an outdoor advertisement that narrates a story about trade and commodities and blurs the distinction between the atmospheric stage set and the commodities being sold. So in the end, the public space of South Street Seaport is one more example of how the public is underwriting private market consumption.

DEVELOPMENT RIGHTS AND HISTORIC PRESERVATION

In addition, New York's financial and business service employment has expanded over the last two decades until nearly one third of its total work force can be called urban professionals. During the same period of time, New York's manufacturing employment has declined dramatically, eroding by 28.1 percent since 1979 and losing approximately 15,000 jobs in 1988 alone. Many therefore simply write New York off as a center for manufacturing, even though two sectors show sporadic growth—the style-conscious garment industry and printing/publishing enterprises. Although Manhattan still contains about 206,600 manufacturing jobs, even these are being squeezed for space, pushed outside of Manhattan as former manufacturing lofts in Soho, Tribeca, and Ladies Mile are upgraded into luxury residential, business services, and high-grade retail spaces, and eventually even these warehouse and loft districts, once rid of their original uses, are protected as valuable historic properties behind the regulatory controls of the Soho Cast Iron Historic District, a proposed Ladies Mile Historic District, a community-sponsored Tribeca Historic District, and even a West Village Historic District along its manufacturing water edge. At the same time manufacturing employment continues to decline, in 1988 causing the garment trades to lose 4,800 jobs and the printing/publishing sector to lose 4,200. Obviously, a mismatch occurs between an impoverished working class whose employment opportunities dwindle and disappear and a new historic city that rises glimmering with wealth and allure.

As the need expanded for more office, residential, and hotel space to accommodate New York's world class citizens employed in the growing financial and business service sectors, midtown Manhattan has experienced an incredible building boom. With the benefit of development rights transferred from landmark structures, mega-structures have sprouted out of historic bases in the oddest of configurations. Developers have found that working their tall structures around pieces of history provides their new towers with a competitive edge and contextual historic appeal. So the Palace Hotel raises its head over the landmark Villard Houses on Madison Avenue between 50th and 51st Streets, a tower appears at an odd angle next to Carnegie Hall, another beside the Museum of Modern Art, and a gigantic new office, residential, and retail tower thrusts skyward on top of the low-rise Coty-Rizzoli facades on the west side of Fifth Avenue near 56th Street. At other times towers are built to the side or in back of a landmark structure such as behind Saks Fifth Avenue Department Store, opposite St. Patrick's Cathedral on 50th between Fifth and Madison Avenues, or the Trump Tower on Fifth Avenue and 56th Street whose neighbor is the landmark Tiffany building. In general, as New York recovered from near bankruptcy in the mid-1970s and its newly achieved status as a world financial capital arose on the horizon, a new development era saw gigantic corporate headquarters shoehorning their towers onto overcrowded midtown blocks on the East Side until some fifteen additional towers neared completion in the late 1980s. And once again the public gained some historic preservation, but along with it came super-development in the most densely zoned part of the city as air rights are piled up as high as the sky, while the streets are clogged with traffic and pedestrians can hardly move.

Perhaps the controversy really began in 1968 when plans were announced to erect a fifty-nine-story air-rights tower designed by Marcel Breuer & Associates directly over Grand Central Station's Waiting Room. Once again the villain was the city, for where was the plan to prevent defacing such a worthy landmark and regulating the ad hoc development of office towers in an already overcrowded district? Grand Central Station was one of the city's recently designated landmarks, having received that distinction in 1967 over the objection of its owners. Consequently, the New York City Landmarks Commission, itself a newly created legislative body formed only in 1965, denied permission to erect a tower atop the terminal. Eventually the issue was settled after the Supreme Court of the United States in 1978 recognized the legal right of New York to regulate urban space in its three-dimensional envelope. Thus the hole in the sky created by the low ceiling boundaries of the station and the tower walls that surround it came under public control. But this ruling also allowed the station's development rights to be transferred (TDRs) to contiguously owned but more appropriate sites. Penn Central Corporation's air rights over Grand Central Station amount to 1.5 million square feet and are worth an estimated $82 million. Consequently, Grand Central Station would be back in the news in 1986, and the future of its densely built-up blocks once again at stake. Incredulously, Penn Central Corporation now was proposing to transfer its development rights underground along the railway tracks to the block between 46th and 47th Streets, Madison and Vanderbilt Avenues. On that small site, First Boston Corporation plans to squeeze a gigantic seventy-four-story retail and office tower. The building will be twice the size that zoning otherwise allows, but the developers argue New Yorkers cannot have it both ways: if they want to save the low-scale ambience of historic landmarks, such as Grand Central Station, then they have to expect, in the super-charged atmosphere of Manhattan real estate, super-development in other locations.

There are other lessons to learn from the Grand Central Station case for the rational use of preservation controls, or so the court deemed, depending upon a prior question of whether there exists a plan against which these apparently ad hoc regulations can be tested. If the answer is yes, and the court felt that the selection by the New York City Landmarks Commission of thirty-one historic districts and over 400 individual landmarks constituted planned forethought, then preservation regulations are not an unfair taking of private property irrationally applied to isolated historic properties. The trouble is, however, that real estate developers and property owners do not necessarily accept that inventorying historic resources, setting aside landmarks and historic districts, and specifying the public purposes embodied in a preservation policy constitute a preservation plan. Controversy erupted in New York City again in 1984 when real estate developers decided that landmarking procedures, far from constituting a plan well known in advance, were instead ad hoc and irrational. Consequently, they requested a procedural review to bring some certainty into the historic designation and development contest. The mayor appointed a Landmarks Committee in 1985 to accomplish this review. Reporting within the year, the Committee proposed an elaborate reshuffling of the preservation process by suggesting that a comprehensive list of the city's potential landmarks be completed as soon as possible and then frozen, thus enabling developers to know that if a building was not on that list, it could not be added for three to five years and that under threat of immediate demolition a structure not on the list could not be suddenly landmarked.

Even though this proposal has been modified, and its threat to preservation removed, development interests still continued to pressure the mayor for greater certainty in the landmarking game. In the spring of 1988, "Study Areas" were proposed in which the entire fabric would come under the jurisdiction of the Landmarks Preservation Commission for at least a year. After that period of review, the Commission would publish a "protected-buildings list" from which it could designate "landmarks." Yet it would forfeit control over the non-listed structures that would remain ineligible for reconsideration for five to ten years. In addition, any owner of a listed property could demand a landmark decision within a period of ninety days. In the early months of 1989 another revised landmarking proposal has been offered by the Historic City Commission: it suggests that the commission be required to publish a list of potential landmarks and historic districts four times a year and hold public hearings on those sites within three months, moving to landmark a structure within a year and a historic district within two years. Whatever the eventual outcome, these procedural maneuverings reveal over and over again the delicate balance that is easily upset between the desire to protect as a public right our collective heritage embodied in historic architecture and the development rights of private property seeking the maximum profit and highest use of the land. The Supreme Court has chilled the preservation enthusiasts even further by suggesting in its June 1987 land use ruling that property owners might receive compensation retroactively from historic regulations deemed by the courts to have deprived them of reasonable use of the land. Obviously some mediating device—call it a preservation plan—is increasingly necessary to guide the normally ad hoc and open-ended process of landmark preservation toward some systematic and predictable policy.

WHY DO WE NEED A PRESERVATION PLAN?

Over American cities in general, well-designed historic districts are carving their metropolitan areas up into fragmented districts planned or redeveloped as autonomous wholes. Manhattan, for example, has large historic districts already designated for Soho, Greenwich Village, and the Upper East Side, and public hearings have been held for two Upper West Side historic districts and Ladies Mile near Union Square, while historic blocks of Tribeca and the West Village have been researched by citizen groups and are waiting to be given a hearing. Cordoned off from the rest of the city by special district design codes and preservation controls, these historic areas of the city are cut out and juxtaposed against the metropolitan whole. Predominantly areas of low-scale historic structures whose streetscapes are frozen in time, they contain very few developable spots where new modern architecture may be tolerated. Yet just outside their borders the pressure to develop cannot be contained: the West and East Villages, for example, are hot territories that developers and institutions are exploiting, the Broadway spine and Columbus Circle on the Upper West Side have run-away development, Union Square is sprouting its towers, and to the east and south of the Upper East Side Historic District, super-development reigns. Yet no one suggests a preservation plan that might mediate between too much development and no development at all.

And there are even more serious reasons to suggest some form of preservation planning to negotiate a path between development pressures and the uses to which historic preservation recently has been exposed. Millions of dollars in benefits accrued through real estate tax incentives, special energy cost savings, and bonus development rights have been given to large corporations in order to persuade them, so it has been argued, to stay in Manhattan and develop new corporate headquarters. The city claims that it makes good business sense to underwrite the leading sector of private employment in major corporations and service industries. And in the competition among cities, New York must offer special attractions to lure corporations away from other locations. So the American Institute of Architects and the Royal Institute of British Architects claimed in 1988, "Businesses and individuals—increasingly free to locate where and when they want—select cities with the finest features and benefits. They look for history, culture, safe neighborhoods, good housing, shops and education and progressive government. Cities are competing, and their edge is livability." Every city has to appear upbeat and innovative, supporting creative lifestyles and a range of cultural entertainments if they are going to compete in this game. But these are short-term market responses, in which a city's image-ability, its advertising adeptness, its historic and cultural allure play most important roles.

In a worldwide economy in which satellite communication makes corporate locational decisions more flexible than ever before, minute differentiations in spatial attractions gain in importance. As a two-page *New York Times* advertisement by fourteen major corporations explained, "Smart businesses never forget location is everything. Precisely why these companies—and thousands more—will tell you that being in New York City helped put them on the map" (*New York Times*, April 10, 1989:D6–7). In order to attract these corporations, as described in this paper, New York has developed new consumption and entertainment spaces such as the South Street Seaport, Battery Park City, and Times Square redevelopment integrated with new office and hotel complexes, restaurants, theaters, and cultural facilities. The expansion of corporate and service employment in turn has created multiplier effects that have seen the gentrification of Soho, Tribeca, Ladies Mile, the Upper West Side, and the East and West Villages into luxury residential and retail enclaves.

From a citizen's point of view, on the other hand, it might appear reasonable to expect the city to demand some community contributions from these corporations in exchange for the benefits they freely obtain. Not only are there no planning controls to modify the crowded streets, sidewalks, and subways and the extra costs of police, garbage, and fire protection that corporate growth engenders, but in this development game the benefits of historic preservation, as argued in this chapter, primarily accrue to the large corporations, the well-to-do homeowners, retail companies, tourists, and the upper middle class. At the same time,

the needs of poorer communities are explosive and infrastructure maintenance requirements have largely gone unmet. In addition, it appears
in the spring of 1989 that New York may not realize the expected return
of corporate and business underwriting. Receipts from corporations
and sales taxes have not expanded as expected. Consequently, further
sacrifices may be needed to avert a budgetary crisis, that is, service
reductions among police, sanitation, and education employees. Those
communities already suffering the most will once again have to bear the
burden and underwrite the cost of turning New York into a world class
city.

Nevertheless, in the roar of corporate glamour and world class competition that New York ascendant has recently achieved, and in the fear
of returned fiscal crisis and budgetary deficits that New York so recently
overcame, historic preservation offers an aura of stability in complex
and uncertain times. But the fragmentation of the city into historic fief-
doms, super-developed areas, and neglected interstitial lands fatally
weakens the ability to plan for the metropolitan whole and develop equitable policies to deal with uneven development, the needs of poorer
neighborhoods, the unmet crisis of homelessness, drug wars raging out
of control, mounting pyramids of garbage, the unemployed, the drop-
outs, the undereducated. Rather than respond to long-term planning
needs or mediatory devices that would ameliorate the development
pressures distorting the meaning and value of historic preservation, the
city is focused on the short-term effects of its corporate image-ability,
allowing the values of tradition, continuity, and place that historic preservation exhales to play important new roles in its economic development game.

There are some things that are not right in the heart of American
cities—city planning departments looking like real estate development
arms of the municipal government; historic preservation commissions
understaffed and ill-equipped to deal with larger land use and development issues; residential and commercial gentrification driving long-term
residents and uses outside of the city; the usurpation of traditional architecture and historic milieus by retailing and advertising media. This
chapter has suggested that some form of preservation planning should
be invented, or the process of physical planning re-constituted and
given new life, in order to provide a metropolitan-wide perspective on
spatial restructuring left unmonitored in the last few decades. Some
public voice is necessary to give expression to the spatial effects engendered by pro-growth coalitions in control of the policies of municipal
governments, the media networks, and the corporate and service sectors. Is it too much to request, as we enter the last decade of the twentieth century, that a hands-off public fund be set aside in exchange for
some of the benefits that pro-growth constituents have obtained, so that

a public voice outside of government, beyond media control, and representing a city-wide viewpoint might be established to guide the spatial restructuring of the city toward a more equitable application of economic policies, service provisions, land use regulations, and taxation controls?

15

MAKING CITIES SAFE FOR TREES

R. NEIL SAMPSON

INTRODUCTION

People are forest dwellers. The evidence is all around us—not in some theoretical book about human origins, but in the way we choose to live our lives. From pioneer families moving into a sod hut on the prairie to today's young couple anxiously contemplating the mortgage on their first home, the same instincts prevail. As soon as possible, just about everyone plants trees around the dwelling place. Shade trees, fruit trees, windbreaks, ornamentals, all aimed at "marking" this place as home—a place where life is pleasant, both inside and outside the four walls, and where the dwellers are secure with their place in the world around them.

Today, more than ever before, Americans are city dwellers. It has been estimated that the 1990 census will find 75 percent of all Americans living within fifty miles of our nation's coastlines, most of them within the confines or orbits of large urban areas.

This urban environment can be many things. On one extreme, it can be sterile and mechanistic—concrete, stone, iron, and copper—with square buildings, each a lot like the ones on either side, connected by a complex system of pipes, wires, tunnels, sidewalks, and streets.

But when that same cityscape is softened and buffered by trees, parks, boulevards, flower beds, curved walkways, and shady river banks, it becomes a habitat—a place where people and a lot of plants, birds, and animals *live*. Thus urban trees are far more than a visual amenity. They are the essential bridge that can make our communities liveable. We are, therefore, faced with the not-so-small challenge of making our cities liveable for trees.

The challenge, of course, is not to abandon urban design or workable systems. The challenge is to merge the designed, manmade environment and the managed, natural environment so that neither is destroyed in the process. Like the pioneer family of the nineteenth century, the urban family of the twenty-first century will be happiest and healthiest when it feels safe, comfortable and at home in its surroundings. Since those people will still be forest dwellers in their deepest instincts, that means that the urban forest will remain an essential part of their environment.

That fact will remain true whether the people in question are American, Canadian, Chinese, French, Indian, or Russian. All over the world increasing urbanization is occurring, as is growing concern over global environmental conditions. The increase in atmospheric carbon dioxide, possible global warming, the ozone holes in the stratosphere, and other forms of air and water pollution may not affect every section of the globe with equal symptoms, but they constitute a common concern to all nations. These are not issues that can be solved by improving the living conditions in cities. But working to improve city environments is a logical step in solving them. By making our cities more comfortable and pleasant, we make a small positive gain on improving the world environment. And by mobilizing citizens to do that job, we teach the essential lesson that it is people, carrying out positive environmental management and restoration, that hold the key to a liveable future.

BENEFITS OF TREES IN THE CITY

Cooling the Heat Island

Cities create an artificial heat island—the downtown temperature on a summer day is likely to be five to ten degrees higher than the surrounding countryside. The reasons for this heat buildup are several, ranging from an increase in dark-colored, heat-absorbing surfaces like asphalt and dark-painted structures, to the heat output of automobiles, air conditioners, motors, and lights. The results of the heat island are reflected in excess death rates during heat waves, particularly among the elderly and those suffering from hypertension, heart and lung disease, or diabetes (Spirn 1984).

Increasing the number and size of trees has been shown to be the most cost-effective way to reduce the heat island effect in most city situations. Along streets and parking lots, in parks and vacant lots, and in natural forest areas, stream corridors and other greenways in the city, large trees can significantly lower overall temperatures through cooling due to evapo-transpiration as well as impact on wind currents, humidity, and albedo (the ability of the earth's surface to reflect incoming heat rays). One large tree can evaporate up to 100 gallons of water a day (provided the water is available) and, in the process, produce a cooling effect similar to five average room air conditioners running for twenty hours a day (Federer 1971).

Obviously, trees that provide shade to dark surfaces like streets, buildings, or parking lots are the most valuable, so this means that older, larger trees are more important than smaller ones. Parker (1983) showed that large-canopied trees in south Florida could, in combination with hedges adjacent to walls, reduce west-wall temperatures on buildings by as much as twenty-eight degrees Fahrenheit. In addition, he demonstrated that the location of one or two trees to shade outdoor air conditioning units could increase their efficiency by as much as 10 percent. The lesson to be learned is that trees can, if properly located, be of significant value in changing the cost of cooling homes in many parts of the United States. Every tree, however, is of some value as it affects air currents, cools the air through transpiration, and shades the ground from the summer sun. In the average urban setting, creating a better climate for some parts of the community has positive effects through a far larger area.

A 1979 study done in Dayton, Ohio, indicated that the existing tree cover (which was about 37 percent of the open land in the city) was reducing the city's temperature about 20 percent below what it would have been without trees. It was calculated that modest increases in the tree canopy cover could raise this figure to 26 percent—a drop of about two degrees Fahrenheit—and in some neighborhoods, the effect would double that amount (Rowntree and Sanders 1983).

Research at the Lawrence Berkeley Laboratory indicates that planting trees within urban areas can reduce carbon dioxide production for a cost of about 0.3 to 1.3 cents per pound of conserved carbon. This compares very favorably with a predicted cost of 2.5 cents per pound if we improve the efficiency of electrical appliances, and 10 cents per pound if we improve the efficiency of automobiles (Akbari et al. 1988).

Placement and size of trees are important, of course, but the final measure of effectiveness is the total amount of forest "crown" that covers the ground and the city's rooftops. Many cities have 25 to 50 percent crown cover, with 30 percent being average. A minimum of 60 percent is usually possible, and achieving that difference can have significant effects on the local climatic conditions (Moll 1989).

Around homes and small commercial buildings, well-placed trees can cut home air conditioning bills by as much as 50 percent (Akbari et al. 1988). This cuts energy needs and, in most parts of America, that means less fossil fuel burned for electrical production and a resulting savings in air pollution and carbon dioxide production.

Because the biggest savings occur on the very hottest days, trees act to cut "peak" energy usage, most of which is produced by the electric power industry's most out-of-date and inefficient power plants (which are intentionally kept off-line except during peak demand times). Thus, the benefits of additional shade help both homeowners and energy companies significantly, as well as contributing to the global need for reducing energy consumption and carbon dioxide production.

On the other side of the energy conservation equation, properly placed trees can also reduce winter heating costs by 4 to 22 percent (DeWalle 1978). This requires, of course, that windbreaks are placed and maintained so that they curb winter winds without shading the house itself. Heisler and DeWalle (1984) found that tree windbreaks can typically save 10 to 12 percent on a homeowner's energy bill, and that a Pennsylvania mobile home in a small opening in a deciduous forest would use about 24 percent less energy year-round than one in an open field.

Air Pollution Reduction

The air in many of America's big cities fails to meet air quality standards much of the time, although many cities have made significant improvements in recent years. In Los Angeles, the air was classed as "unhealthful" about one-third of the time in 1979; this was down to only 100–110 days a year by 1983. In New York City, unhealthful air was recorded over 150 days in 1979; down to only eighty in 1983 (U.S. Council on Environmental Quality 1984). Clearly, in spite of intensive efforts and pollution control, and some gains, the quality of the city as human habitation is threatened by air pollution.

This is a complex problem, demanding major attention to reducing the sources of air pollutants. But there is a role here for trees as well, because trees can help ameliorate some of pollution's effects and perhaps even help prevent pollution formation. Akbari, Rosenfeld and Taha (1989) estimate, for example, that as much as one-third of the smog problem is directly related to the heat island effect, and that reducing the heat island can be helpful in lowering smog formation.

The most basic pollution-reduction value of trees and forests is the conversion of carbon dioxide to oxygen through the process of photosynthesis. An eighty-foot beech tree has been estimated to remove as much carbon dioxide as two single-family dwellings produce (Kielbaso 1988). In this process, air is purified and temperatures are moderated through the cooling effect of evapo-transpiration.

In addition, significant amounts of particulates are removed from the air by the filtering effects of tree leaves and needles. Bernatzky (1978) estimates that a street lined with healthy trees can reduce airborne dust particles by as much as 7,000 particles per liter of air. Thus, each healthy tree is a freestanding air conditioner and purifier that is doing its part toward making the world habitable for all life.

Some chemicals in the air can be removed by foliar uptake. Some nitrogen oxides (NO and NO_2) and airborne ammonia (NH_3) can be taken up by foliage, with the nitrogen going to plant use. Trees can also utilize some sulfur dioxide (SO_2) and ozone (O_3), but many species suffer severe damage from exposure to high concentrations (Smith and Dochinger 1976). Most of the pollution reduction ability of trees is, however, finally related to the forest soil since pollutants are either washed to the ground from leaf surfaces or fall directly as the result of having collided with tree structures or entering wind eddies caused by the vegetation. The ability of soils to neutralize pollutants and prevent subsequent water contamination varies considerably.

Trees are not, moreover, able to filter or absorb all pollutants without damage to the tree itself. Species vary in their sensitivity to different pollutants, with some handling high pollution levels reasonably well while others serve as sensitive indicators of the degree of environmental deterioration. In addition to species differences, cultivars within a species have been shown to exhibit different tolerance levels to certain pollutants.

Thus, it is possible to utilize trees and other vegetation as part of a pollution reduction scheme, but only within limits. Such a strategy cannot replace efforts to reduce pollution at its source. Where trees and forests have been stunted or killed by pollution, the basic environmental life-machine has been reduced in capacity, and all life on earth is placed at risk as a result.

Water Quality and Hydrology

Trees intercept falling raindrops and moderate their passage to the ground. This reduces runoff, prevents soil erosion, and slows the buildup of peak flows during an intensive rainfall. In an environment largely dominated by concrete, asphalt, and rooftops, this can be a significant problem. Water flows concentrated by these impervious surfaces can hit unprotected soils or stream channels with terrific force, causing accelerated soil erosion and significant water pollution along with very high flood flows. Trees that shelter impervious areas can cut the rate at which water hits the surface, and tree roots can provide protection that slows water flows and reduces soil erosion. Moll (1989) estimates that a city with 30 percent tree cover has a leaf and branch surface area that adds up to four times as much intercepting surface as provided by the city's buildings and concrete. As a result, cities with maximum tree cover can experience significant reduction of peak flood flows. This translates into less construction needed for floodways and storm sewers, less instances of overflow and resulting damage to life and property, and less pollution flushed into rivers, lakes, and estuaries.

The pollution of water bodies such as the Chesapeake Bay can eradicate important economic fisheries, destroy recreational opportunities, and even poison the drinking water supplies of millions of people. These problems can almost always be traced to the use and management of the land in the watershed. Saving the integrity of these water bodies for the future is a land management problem. And many estuaries, such as the Chesapeake, are highly urbanized. Thus, the condition of the trees and forests in urban, suburban, and urbanizing areas is a regionally significant factor in the water quality of the Bay.

Forested areas in urban regions may also become significant in waste water treatment. Partially treated urban waste water has been sprayed on forest lands with good effect in several cities. This not only provides a least-cost way of providing tertiary water treatment, but also has beneficial effects on forest productivity, aquifer recharge, and stream flow. In State College, Pennsylvania, for example, Sopper and Kerr (1978) reported that sixteen years of spraying partially treated sewage on a forest watershed did not contaminate groundwater, while returning 90 percent of the water to the aquifer. Different forest ecosystems, different soils, and varying aquifer characteristics have to be factored into such a program, and intensive monitoring is needed to assure that performance is meeting health standards, but this method of waste water treatment is almost certain to appeal to more and more communities as water supplies get scarcer and conventional waste treatment facilities more expensive to operate.

Wildlife and Recreation

It is a well-documented fact that forested areas are increasingly sought as recreational locales. What is less well understood is that, for many of America's urban population, the most important recreational forest (either by choice or necessity) is the forest that is around them every day. Dwyer (1982) pointed out that, in addition to providing many urban residents with most of their forest-related recreation opportunities, the urban forest is particularly significant for the elderly, the poor, the young, and the handicapped.

Forest and park managers are faced with the fact that not all people want or need the same kind of experiences. One study showed that people in downtown Chicago preferred more intensively developed and managed parks as a location for visiting and other social interaction, while suburbanites wanted more natural, undeveloped areas to "get away from people" (Dwyer 1982).

One of the major attractions within the urban forest, in both intensively managed parks and more natural settings, is wildlife. Trees may provide colors, shapes, sounds, and other sensory pleasures, but wild animals provide the animation that particularly delights most forest visitors. From the ubiquitous gray squirrel and pigeon of the central city to the shy deer or rabbit of the greenway, people delight in watching the wildlife that characterizes trees, forests, and their surrounding environs. In Minneapolis and St. Paul, Minnesota, for example, it was estimated in 1975 that more than 1,800 Canada geese shared an urban lifestyle with over two million people, largely because of the plentitude of lakes surrounded by parks and forested developments (Sayler and Cooper 1975).

Around our homes, mostly in association with treed lawns and lots, Americans prize the existence of songbirds and other urban wildlife. A 1974 study found Americans spend some $170 million per year on wild bird seed, and that some 20 percent of all households are involved in those purchases (DeGraaf and Payne 1975).

Noise Reduction

Noise is a pervasive and troublesome feature of the urban environment, and a great deal of literature is available suggesting that intense, persistent noise causes psychological disturbance that threatens peaceful community life. Trees can be a significant actor in reducing unwanted sound levels. The leaves, twigs, and branches absorb sound, particularly high-frequency sounds that are the most bothersome to humans. A belt of trees thirty meters wide and fifteen meters tall has been shown to reduce highway noise by from six to ten decibels—a reduction of almost 50 percent in terms of sound energy (Cook 1978).

In addition to reducing unwanted noise, trees produce alternative sounds that "mask" other noises and make them less noticeable. With the wind rustling through leaves and birds singing, the drone of a nearby freeway is less noticeable and less bothersome to people.

Human Health

Being involved in that urban environment and its quality has significant social, as well as environmental, impacts. A study on the sociology of urban tree planting found that residents who participated in a street tree planting project in a low-income neighborhood of Oakland, California, felt an enhanced sense of community, better understanding of their neighbors, and a greater degree of control over their environment (Ames 1980).

Researchers have found that recuperating hospital patients placed in rooms with windows facing out onto trees heal significantly faster, need shorter hospital stays, and require far less pain-killing drugs than those in rooms without an outside view (Ulrich 1984a, b). These findings have led to new hospital designs that provide patients with a better view of trees and the natural environment.

It seems logical to assume that the same health benefits might extend into the concept of "wellness," where people who live within constant view of the natural world enjoy better health. At this point, however, there is no research to demonstrate whether or not that claim is true, or to what degree any such benefit extends. What we do know is that the current interest in physical fitness has produced a huge volume of urban forest users who demand walking, jogging, and bicycling trails through parks, greenways, stream corridors, and other natural areas.

THE CONDITION OF THE CITY FOREST

An oak or maple tree that could live 200 to 400 years in a forest lives only thirty-two years in the average city—less than ten years when it is planted in a downtown planting pit. It scarcely has time to become environmentally valuable before it dies. Where these situations exist, it is small wonder that urban budgeteers look on city trees as a liability rather than an asset.

America's urban forests are in trouble—about four trees die or are removed for each new one planted in the average city. That number can go as high as eight or ten in some cities (Moll 1987b). The reasons are many. Experts estimate the biggest problem is lack of space, both above and, perhaps more importantly, below ground level. Another is that, in many cities, trees have been allowed to grow old without needed maintenance or replacement. Suddenly, the city finds itself awash in dead and dying trees. The budget for urban forestry is fully absorbed with cleaning up these problems, and nothing remains for the necessary planting and tree care needed to rebuild a healthy, productive urban forest.

Another problem in recent years has been insect and disease epidemics that have swept through many portions of the country. Dutch elm disease went through many cities in the 1970s, and where the stately elm was used almost exclusively because of its wonderful shade properties, the effect was disastrous. Today, few American elms remain in any city, and the rebuilding process has been both slow and expensive.

The gypsy moth, eating its way through the hardwoods (primarily oaks), and oak wilt are creating similar problems today. When these epidemics hit, the shady, pleasant communities created by our grand-parents can be converted almost overnight into another barren urban heat island.

MANAGING TREES IN THE CITY

The urban environment may be improved by a better urban forest, but getting that forest is not an easy task. In too many cities the space for trees to grow and thrive simply doesn't exist. Streets, sidewalks and building foundations take up most of the space, channeling available water into storm sewers and providing almost no open soil to take up air and water needed for healthy root growth. Urban soils often consist mainly of heavily compacted construction rubble and have little resemblance to a normal soil structure. Air and water movement through these soil conditions is abnormal, and normal root growth is restricted or prevented.

Air pollution concentrations are abnormally high for urban trees, containing high levels of ozone, one of the major products created in the air as the result of automobile exhaust and a pollutant that has definitely been linked to tree damage. Water running off of paved surfaces is often contaminated with a variety of pollutants ranging from asbestos fibers to road salts, while herbicides used on lawns and gardens may produce toxic vapors that affect surrounding trees.

So urban trees are almost always facing bad growing conditions. Drought is rampant, both because of the hotter temperatures in mid-city and because most of the available rain is channeled off by streets and sewers rather than soaking into the soil. Fertility may be nonexistent, both because urban soils are badly disturbed, and because there is no undergrowth or animal life to help produce litter and soil nutrients.

Construction designed to improve urban living conditions often does just the opposite. In 1975, a major project installed new paths, curbing, and sewers in the Boston Common. Not only did the construction kill more trees in one year than Dutch elm disease had killed in three years, but the excessive drainage caused by the new sewers required that the trees be artificially irrigated the following year (Foster 1978).

Mechanical damage from other sources is common, as well. Trees that are not destroyed by automobiles, trucks, bicycles, or children's toy hatchets may be bruised by lawn mowers, driven full of nails by political sign-hangers, or damaged by a variety of other hazards. A seemingly innocuous bump may produce an opening to the inner bark which allows disease or fungus to enter, spelling the beginning of the end for the tree.

A tree that lives to the average age of only thirty-two years is just beginning to reach the most valuable stage of its life when it dies. If this lifetime is stretched ten years by maintenance (a readily achievable goal), the value of the tree to the city is doubled. Yet a 1985 survey by Michigan State University found that, of 1,062 cities responding, only 409 (39 percent) had a systematic tree care program (Kielbaso 1988).

Urban trees, just like forests everywhere, respond to management. This demands a resource commitment on the part of local government, however. Kielbaso (1988) found that the national average for city tree care expenditures was $10.62 per street tree per year, or $2.60 per capita. To estimate what this might mean in terms of budget impact in a given city, multiply the street miles times the national average of 134 street trees per mile.

In an interesting historical sidenote, it has been theorized that the advent of air conditioning, which reduced the public demand for cooler urban micro-climates, and the flight to the suburbs, which allowed people to live on larger lots with more trees, have both been significant factors in reducing the public demand—and the political constituency—for urban forestry programs (Bartenstein 1982). These very factors, due to the rise in living costs caused by fossil fuel energy's gradual depletion, now make the improvement of urban trees and forests one of the more economical investments a city can make. The problem is to bring these new facts and opportunities to the attention of the public and, through public opinion, to elected officials.

A good management program can extend the lives of urban and community trees from their current average of thirty-two years to something far longer—and double or triple the benefits each tree confers on the community in the process. Good forest management costs money but, in towns like on tree farms, it pays significant dividends. But this message is seldom penetrating the decision-making fabric of urban governments. According to Moll and Gangloff (1987), "In 1984, the delegates at the national meeting of directors of parks and recreation identified trees as their biggest maintenance problem, a problem they have yet to communicate effectively to the public or their political leaders."

The management of urban trees has a significantly higher "public involvement" factor that is common in rural forests. In addition to knowing the physical characteristics of the urban forest, and being constantly aware of the legal and institutional constraints on management, the urban forester must also deal directly with the public and recognize the very direct and emotional attachment that city residents often develop with the trees and forests that share their habitat.

ADAPTING TREES TO THE CITYSCAPE

In planting trees into an urban environment, there are several things that must be taken into account. First, because the urban forest is an ecosystem like any other, it is important not to create a monoculture by planting too much of any one species. The communities that were dominated by the beautiful, but vulnerable, American elm learned that lesson when Dutch elm disease swept the country a few years back. Today, urban foresters feel it unwise to allow any single species to make up more than 10 or 15 percent of the tree population in an urban forest (Grey and Deneke 1986). Many foresters say that the target should be even more diversity, with no species adding up to more than 5 percent of the total. Selecting trees from adapted species, and mixing them to provide an adequately complex forest environment, is a major challenge in most cities.

The most critical problem with urban trees, of course, is space. Trees that have no root space, or growth room above ground, are not going to thrive. Placed in a small pit surrounded by the highly compacted soils common to street, sidewalk, and building foundations, most trees will suffer stunted growth as the roots are confined to the pit. Water either builds up and drowns the roots or is unavailable, and air supplies are likewise affected. Moving the "container" for the tree roots out of the ground into a raised pot creates all the same problems, plus the additional hazard of exposure to freezing temperatures that can kill the roots. While the city would be well served by having thrifty, healthy, large trees lining its streets and sidewalks, the space allotted for their growth often condemns the street to be characterized by small, stunted, short-lived, and expensive specimens.

Location is important, as well. Trees in urban areas have to be located so that they do not interfere with the human activities and functions of the city. There are intersections where sight lines are important, overhead power lines and underground utilities to be avoided, and curbs, driveways, and signs that must not be crowded or covered up. In addition, trees should be located where they will have the most beneficial effect in terms of energy conservation, pollution reduction, and beautification. As often as not, trees are an important visual element that must be integrated properly into the architectural design of the city. Obviously, planting trees correctly in an urban setting is a far more complex and demanding science than it might appear at first glance (Arnold 1980).

Tree geneticists have done considerable work in developing trees that are of a certain size, or shape, so that they fit well in particular spaces. In addition, they have led the search for trees that can withstand city heat, tolerate the lack of air in the soil when water is present, and suffer through the inevitable droughts that characterize downtown areas. While these efforts have been exceptionally helpful in improving the city forest under some very difficult conditions, the real answer for cities probably lies in the other direction—changing the city to fit the trees.

DESIGNING CITIES FOR TREES

Significantly, improving the ecology of the city is going to call for larger trees, not smaller ones. The cooling of the urban heat island, the reduction of air and water pollution, the provision of wildlife habitat, and the visual impact breaking up the urban scene requires trees that can grow large and live long lifetimes. That means that, instead of designing trees to fit inadequate urban spaces, we must design urban spaces to fit trees.

The best time to make a city fit into the natural environment, of course, is during the planning and development phase. Obviously, that time is long gone in many urban places, and the best strategy is to improve planting and management programs so as to mimic the natural world as well as possible. But new developments are constantly springing up in many communities, in downtowns as well as on the periphery. Are those new developments being fit into the environment skillfully or creating an environment in which trees will thrive for decades? Or are they just being "bulldozed in" as quickly as possible?

The difference reflects the attitude of city leaders, planners, and citizens toward the relationship of nature to the city. Do people feel that the city is to be built and maintained as a part of the natural surroundings, or is the city being designed to reject and conquer the natural world? If new communities and developments learn from the mistakes of older cities, it is possible to exploit the opportunities of the natural environment right from the outset. The result will be a better urban environment, at a lower long-term cost to the citizenry.

One example is the Pennsylvania Avenue Redevelopment effort in downtown Washington, D.C. Here, in the midst of an intensively developed urban area, the "nation's main street" has been landscaped with a variety of large street trees, in addition to landscaped parks and plazas in the middle of the boulevard. The development has converted a blighted urban street into a beautiful, tree-shaded avenue. But this accomplishment is no accident. Tree spaces are created both above- and below-ground. Sidewalks and plazas are covered with blocks and bricks that allow water and air to enter the soil below. An underground irrigation system exists to provide water when needed, and soil moisture monitoring tells when the water should be turned on. The underground has been "opened up" to allow tree roots to grow rather than being compacted.

So communities have options. They are not without costs, but sound investments that result in long-lived, healthy forests are nearly always more cost-effective than their alternatives.

New subdivisions in treeless areas can be required to plant trees—large trees—as part of their development plan. Properly placing trees in new construction is as logical a part of development as locating streets and sewers. By injecting the expertise of the urban forester into the planning and engineering design processes, a better urban environment can result for far less cost. In Milwaukee, for example, studies have shown that tree costs take only about 2.2 cents of each construction dollar.

In forested areas, developers can be required to preserve trees and to protect them from harm during development due to machine damage, soil compaction, root cutting, or over-filling soils that smother tree roots. Where old trees are doomed to death by development activities, severe economic and environmental losses for future homeowners are assured. New trees cost money, and they cannot develop the beneficial environmental effects of the old trees for decades. Saving old trees is clearly in society's interest, as well as in the monetary interest of the homeowners. But cities and towns let builders come in, damage the trees, leave with their money, and let the homeowners and future taxpayers pay the bills. Those abuses can be halted, as easily as we have halted other development abuses, through building codes and subdivision regulations.

Roadsides and highways can be planted with trees, creating significant environmental benefits to communities. A major problem today is the proclivity of lawyers to sue communities on behalf of clients who crash into roadside trees. One answer is to enact state legislation eliminating any municipal or governmental liability to anyone who hits a roadside tree. In many municipalities, motorists who lose control of their automobile and damage a roadside utility pole or road sign are liable for the cost of the replacement of what they destroyed. They should be similarly liable for damaging trees. Roadside trees are an essential part of the human-built environment. Destroying them in an act of reckless or uncontrolled driving is the fault of the motorist, not the fault of the tree or the unit of government that maintains the road.

Greenways can create ribbons of natural forest through a city, linking parks, stream corridors, forests, playgrounds, and surrounding natural areas with trails for people, as well as corridors for wildlife. The problem with greenways is that while they contribute greatly to the quality of life in an urban area, they do not create additions to the profit flows from urban development in the same way that office buildings and tract housing would do. Thus, these open lands are always a target for development. Only a strong set of city ordinances, developed as part of a long-term plan supported by a broad constituency of citizens, has a chance of resisting this pressure.

THE KEY: CITIZENS WHO CARE

Therein lies the key to better urban forests and more habitable cities. People must be mobilized to begin the positive actions that they can

take as individuals, join together into citizen's groups to address neighborhood challenges, and challenge political leaders to create and maintain effective public programs. That public action will only begin when
people are convinced that it is necessary, and that their actions can
make a difference.

The American Forestry Association has a program called Global Re-
Leaf that, as one of its goals, encourages Americans to plant new trees
in the estimated 100 million tree spaces that exist on private lands in
America's communities (Sampson 1988). That program has attracted the
cooperation of all fifty states and hundreds of communities and nonprofit organizations across the country.

Global ReLeaf calls upon Americans to join together in a massive environmental repair campaign. It encourages them to start with individual positive actions that they can do with readily available money and
technology. It is not presented as an environmental panacea, but as a
small step in the right direction. It is the epitome of thinking globally
and acting locally, as urged by ecologist Rene Dubos. It offers a simple,
positive response to the most commonly asked question that comes
from people who have been told that the world is suffering serious environmental abuse. "What can I do?" they ask. "Plant a tree," Global Re-
Leaf responds.

The potential environmental impact is significant. It has been estimated that planting the 100 million trees could, by the time they reach
full size, result in an annual savings of some $4 billion in air condition-
ing costs each year (Akbari et al. 1988). Urban heat island effects would
be reduced, energy resources would be conserved, and a small step toward reducing the greenhouse effect would be in place.

Perhaps even more important for the long-term, however, will be the
effect on public attitudes and political constituencies of getting so many
people involved in the task of environmental repair and enhancement.
People and companies who have been involved in planting trees and
improving forest management on their own lands, and in their own
neighborhoods, will be more insistent that local, state, and national leaders take appropriate policy and program actions as well.

The result could be a future in which individuals, companies, communities, and national governments cooperate in joint efforts to assure that
the productive ecosystems essential to the survival of the earth are managed, maintained, and used wisely.

16

LIVING ON THE CRUST OF THE EARTH: HUMAN ECOLOGY AND ENVIRONMENTAL PLANNING

SHELDON W. SAMUELS

INTRODUCTION

Contemporary studies in human ecology apply ecological principles, such as ecological succession, to enhance our understanding of human societies. Exogenous factors are recognized (Hawley 1986), but (inconsistent with reality) human environmental health factors seldom receive adequate (or any) consideration. Consequently, the application of human ecology to environmental planning has been slowed, and the potential for using its broad purview to organize the spectra of information and ideas necessary to *prevent* ecological disaster likewise has been slowed.

True interdisciplinary efforts are rare and require that we do more than apply the principles and the methods of one discipline to another. What is attempted here is an integration of disciplines using an early concept of human ecology: the study of "change in the ecosystem of which man is a part [especially those activities which] serve to accelerate the rate and widen the scope of natural changes in ways that lower the potential of the environment to sustain him" (Sears 1956).

Political, social, health, demographic, technologic, economic, and natural resource considerations are necessary to plan change successfully within the human ecologic system. Organizing the planning process is facilitated by recognizing the total burden of risk to the sustaining niche of the human community.

THE HUMAN NICHE

Human ecology focuses on the effect of the location of communities on other communities, or of individuals and institutions within a community on the community itself (McKenzie 1968). The analysis of environmental factors in community planning may be understood as an application of the science of human ecology through examination of human activity, and its sequelae, associated with communities.

The components of the human community are limited in large part by division of labor and by adjustment to physical habitat. Habitat adjustment can mean exploitation of natural resources (Repetto 1985). Dependence upon local habitat resources for our population as a whole has progressively declined, as seen most clearly in the decline in the proportion of the population engaged in agriculture. This change, accompanied by the adverse environmental effects associated with large-scale operations (as contrasted with land-caring family farming), may be attributable almost entirely to positive technologic-based changes in the division of labor.

The changes wrought by technology have not all been positive and are often viewed as the main factor in environmental decay (Commoner 1971). The significance of technology is not without challenge. Population growth and the multiplication of *per capita* impacts also can be seen, for example, producing overdevelopment, including a decrease in the quality of life which is magnified in affluent societies (Ehrlich and Ehrlich 1972).

Regardless of their relative significance in environmental change, there is a parallel alteration of the structure of our habitat associated with its industrial composition not necessarily related to changing technology or population growth, that is, a third factor, the relative importance of which may be accelerated (but not initiated) by technological and population change: fundamental social change through the reduction of the empowerment of a sub-population·associated with a reduction in size alone. This reduction in empowerment implies potential changes in the political process currently a characteristic of the North American community.

The decreasing numbers of family food producers (farmers and waterpeople) and supporting blue- and white-collar workers—the bulk of a society middle class in character, that is, in social values, spending patterns, mobility, and cultural values reflected in language, leisure time use, and mating behavior—impacts the essential character of the entire population. The mobility factor, social and geographic, is especially important. In America, there has been no working class in the Marxian sense because of our flexible class (as distinct from our relatively inflexible racial caste) structure. The traditional ability to move up and down a socioeconomic scale traditionally militates against rigid social class identification, acceptance, and conflict (Myrdal and Rose 1944; Warner 1953).

The massive elimination or downgrading (in earnings and skills) of more than thirty million jobs since World War II tends to create a two-tier society characterized by class inflexibility with a concentration of economic burden and other symptoms of *anomie* concentrated in the lowest tier. From a society with social mobility and loosely defined classes, we now tend toward a rigid cross-racial *caste* structure with a largely blue-collar lower tier (or caste) characterized by upper-tier-imposed and indigenous cannibalism, suicide, transgenerational poverty, worklessness, alcohol and drug dependency, socially bifurcated education and safety, institutionalized illegitimacy (no recognizable nuclear families), endemic violence, and decreased community communication (through radical changes in language, art forms, and leisure time use). Parallel with these radical alterations in the human niche are associated changes in (relativistic) moral values exercised with increasing unrestrained concentration of political power in the upper tier.

A result has been powers that enable the use of existing molecular biological technologies to select workers with socially forgiving, pollution-resilient genotypes. In this kind of society, the cutting edge of change historically is not found in the polling booth. It is found in the hands of a leader of a raging mob.

Consider just two of the typically unrecognized traits that dominate the emerging structure of human society: cannibalism and suicide.

Cannibalism did not disappear with the demise of a few primitive tribes. Nor is it only observed among other species (e.g., infanticidal rats) in unusual, stressed circumstances (e.g., while starving or living in crowded communities).

For example, in twenty-four states, 306 workers' compensation claims for injuries of children under age thirteen among 23,823 claims for children seventeen years or younger were filed in 1980 (Schober et al. in press). There is a conscious acceptance of hazardous child labor in our society, acts of cannibalism incorporated as mores in biologically aberrant social structures.

"Man," concludes Erich Fromm from his examination of cannibalism, "is the only primate who can feel intense pleasure in killing and torturing . . . [but] this destructiveness is neither innate, nor part of 'human nature,' and . . . not common to all men" (Fromm 1973, 181).

Cannibalism is only one consequence of our industrialized society. Mass man, in a crowd as lonely as he, deprived of meaningful supportive social structures, expresses the resulting *anomie* of his niche. His atomization traditionally is measured by rates of suicide that pace industrialization itself (Durkheim 1897). Earlier studies linked the two.

Masaryk (1970), whose German term for suicide, *selbstmord*, is an accurate commentary on the phenomenon, developed a calculus of factors in the etiology of suicide that included poverty, occupation, and age, among other factors, to explain "the great increase in suicide among children." Environmental factors we create, such as urban life, also were in the calculus. But, environmental factors, as he understood them, were the forces of nature and the external world that exists independently of us.

More than one hundred years later, we have yet to specifically investigate the role of environmental factors we create, such as toxic substances, in modern forms of cannibalism (or in suicide) except as part of mortality data sets. Is the existence of these intertwined threads farfetched, or golden?

A probe of factors in hazardous child labor underway in counties contiguous with the Chesapeake Bay (Samuels 1989) links poverty to hazardous child labor. Poverty and the current hazardous patterns of legal and illegal child labor, the probe suggests, are associated both with the environmental degradation that has destroyed traditional patterns of family employment, as well as the exposure to toxic substances in seemingly benign occupations.

A quarter century ago, in America, suicide was a minor cause of death. Today, suicide is the eighth leading cause of death for populations of all ages in the United States. Among minors and young people just entering the workforce, ages fifteen to twenty-four, suicide rates have undergone a dramatic change in a single generation. In 1960, the suicide rate for this population was half that of the nation as a whole. By 1979, the rate for minors and young people exceeded the general population. By 1986, in this age group, suicide became the third leading cause of death. In 1990, suicide was the second leading cause of death for such white males.

To remain human in the most essential sense, society takes biologically adaptive measures to control changes taking place, of which suicide and cannibalism are surrogate measures.

Within the human niche, as in all open systems, change may be irreversible or nonadaptive, but it takes new directions based on the past (Samuels 1988a). The trend toward a two-caste system denoted by occupation is countered by the force of democratic institutions still controlled by a middle class that has not yet disappeared either in fact or in the memory of those recently fallen. These institutions are community structures—participatory environmental, labor, and civic organizations—evolving in response to environmentally sensitive reindustrialization. Increasingly, the critical precondition to siting and housing new techniques in manufacture and agriculture is meeting the perceived needs of these countervailing institutions.

THE ECOLOGY OF COPPER

While manufacturing has declined in importance, so has the relative number of workers employed in agriculture declined. The historic movement of farm laborers into industrial employment has become more difficult. Hundreds of plants are permanently closed, ending hundreds of thousands of jobs.

Among the reasons for the decline are the short-term views of private interests that conflict with long-term industrial planning. Competing nations uniformly override these interests in the public interest, using government for both economic and environmental planning.

Not all of the decline in manufacturing can be blamed on failure in economic planning. The lack of environmental planning has meant that we often fail to consider environmental impacts on the direction of technologic change and, reciprocally, the impacts of technology on environment.

The mining and smelting of heavy metals provide good examples. These highly toxic elements have no "half-life." They never degrade or change physically in the manner of radioactive materials. In water-soluble form, they persist, accumulate, and concentrate adversely in the biosphere.

Copper, for example, persists as a necessary (historically and culturally impacted) metal. Mining, however, is no longer a necessary source of the metal. Smelting capacity for new copper in the United States exceeds demand. The need for new copper is decreased by recycling efforts stimulated by the rising costs of controlling the environmental burden of new copper mining and smelting.

The decreasing ratio of "new" to "old" copper production within the short but critical four years illustrated in Table 1 is economic because of rising control costs and because of technological changes that result in the very high and increasingly efficient recoverability of copper. At the same time the total need for copper is decreasing.

Table 1
"New" vs. "Old" Copper Production

	1979	1981	1983
"New" Smelters	1.313	1.295	0.888
"Old" Smelters	0.604	0.598	0.455
Ratio	2.174	2.166	1.952

* in million metric tons.
  Source: USDI Minerals Yearbooks

From an environmental perspective, copper production should be concentrated in mines and smelters selected for their use of the best possible control technology and, therefore, whose production results in the least ecologic disruption. Copper ore, for example, generally contains more sulphur than copper and when smelted results in massive sulphur oxide emissions.

The absorption of a mixture of copper and other heavy metals by children in smelter towns has been well-studied (Baker et al. 1977). These same children are exposed to other pollutants that result from smelting heavy metals. Thus Dodge (1980, 1983) found that children living in Arizona smelter communities with relatively high concentrations of particulates in the air experience significantly decreased pulmonary function. These same children were found with increased respiratory symptoms when they breathe high concentrations of sulfur dioxide. These effects can be expected in populations exposed to relatively lower concentrations of particulate and sulfur oxides, albeit at lower rates.

The total burden or combined effect on these children of the heavy metals, particulates associated with heavy metals, and the sulfur oxides is unknown. This is in part true because studies such as those of Baker and Dodge provide us with only a symptom of what may be a small portion of the total burden.

Copper at very low concentrations is a nutrient about which the Paraceltic wisdom that "dose makes the poison" may hide subtle and difficult-to-measure effects that may manifest in very large populations at very low levels among those at the low end of the spectrum of sensitivity found in any normal population.

Copper has been found, for example, to induce hemolytic anemia in "susceptible" populations (Calabrese et al. 1980). Copper also appears to have an etiologic role in Wilson's Disease (hereditary hepatolenticular degeneration). This disease, characterized by copper deposits in the liver and central nervous system leading to progressive and fatal changes, has been found in every racial group in which it has been sought. The abnormal genes are inherited by one in about 200 people, and, thus, are rarely observed in small populations (NRC/NAS 1977).

Table 2 lists the results of studies showing the inhibiting effects of varying levels of copper on the production of six enzymes, rarely inherited deficiencies which are associated with hemolytic anemia induced by environmental conditions.

What are the implications for environmental planning of either gross contamination by heavy metals, particulates with heavy metals and sulfur oxides on children (and adults), or less easily observed effects of genetic differences phenotypically expressed by low concentrations leached from soils impacted by "acid rains" and precipitated particulates ingested by whole populations through the food chain? Must we

Table 2
Copper-Induced Inhibition of Enzymes

Preparation	Copper (ug/ml)
Hexokinase	0.95 - 6.3
Phophofructokiinase	"
Phosphoglyceric kinase	"
Pyruvate kinase	"
6-Phosphogluconate dehydrogenase	"
Glucose-6-phosphate dehydrogenase	3.15 - 6.3

Source: NRC/NAS

unravel the mechanism of each exposure of each agent individually or collectively before taking action?

From a planning perspective, the control of one contaminant in the mixture of contaminants, as in the case of smelter emissions, forces control of the total. Thus the total burden on the community may be abated by surrogate control, that is, abating the effluence as a whole by monitoring and controlling one factor. The degree of control, including zero emissions through ending an industrial operation, takes into account either the necessity of the product or the necessity of production at a particular site. In the case of copper, both avenues of control need to be explored.

INDUSTRY, LAND USE, AND HISTORY

The consequences of *not* shaping the industrial process to human and physical environmental limits needs no reiteration. Most of the existing literature on the work, community, and natural environments consists of a compilation of negative impacts. From these data alone, however, a planning process can not be conceived. Implicit in each option in the process is a set of human values generated over time (Samuels 1986).

Planning consistent with the values of a democratic society is stereotypically a local non-governmental and governmental function. The society may be democratic, but the stereotype is wrong.

Civic and neighborhood groups—especially in private communities that share land titles qualified by covenants governing architecture, land use, conservation, and facilities used in common—often plan with successful implementation. It is a myth, however, that they depend upon voluntary action. They do not function, typically, through social pressures alone. They act *as if* they are governments in fact. They often enforce covenants and collect mandatory "fees" (taxes) through the courts.

Another myth, the popular conception that governmental land use control is an essentially local activity, is belied by the fact that there are at least 137 separate, largely uncoordinated federal program land use criteria administered through a multiple veto process (Noble et al. 1977). Most of these inputs (Table 3) are environmental constraints. Perhaps our best established, most socially acceptable tool for environmental planning, they are reactions to public and bureaucratic perceptions of potential environmental insults emanating from industrial processes.

Two hundred years ago, when our federal government was structured, what we would now call environmental regulation protected individual rights, especially the right to protection itself (Samuels 1988b). Pollution and degradation of the community environment were controlled if public health was an issue. Otherwise the focus was on endangered property rights to land, air, and water in the community and workplace. Known, broader effects were ignored, despite a preview in the British and European experience and the pleas of leaders as eminent as Thomas Jefferson (who was concerned about working conditions and land erosion). Understanding of the issues was limited, but the popular will to regulate was even more limited.

The depletion of natural and human resources was not perceived in a nation that had only begun to scratch the earth for minerals, whose forests and waters seemed infinitely abundant, and whose harbors were packed with ships bearing immigrants who begged to indenture themselves for work.

As our nation grew westward, it also grew in population density and industrial activity. The demands for raw materials for factories and construction, and food for burgeoning, uncontrolled population growth, were multiplied by changing technologies and an increasingly better standard of living.

A distinctly American way of life, incorporating significant leisure time and money to be spent in its enjoyment, resulted in the establishment of the world's most extensive public park, recreational, and wilderness system. This developed side-by-side with land-hungry systems of transportation and energy production and distribution.

By the turn of this century, today's basic land use patterns were established. Open space began to rapidly decrease, creating a demand not only for land use coordination, but for coordination of existing and emerging technologies for air and water resources associated with land. Concurrent with these demands is the need to coordinate state-to-state shifting of plants and distribution centers in a manner that recognizes changing markets and resources, while preventing the creation of pol-

Table 3
Federal Environmental Planning Decisions

Siting Factors	Regulatory Constraints
Land Availability	DOA, DOI, FAA, DOE, DOD, Land Use Zoning. Public Housing and VA Hospital Encroachments. DOA Farm Land Use.
Water	EPA, Corps of Engineers, Potable/ Industrial Process Standards (Surface/ Drinking Water Quality, Minimum Stream Flow Requirements)
Transportation	Hazardous Materials Transport (Road, Rail, Air, Waterway)
Human Resources	OSHA, MSHA, NRC, DOT, DOE, DOD, EPA Work Environment Limits
Natural Resources	DOA, DOI, DOE, DOD Land Reclamation, Dam Siting, Wetlands Re-creation, Open Space
Industrial Infrastructure	Allied Industry Requirements, Industrial Standards (FTC)
Hydrology/Geology	Aquifer Protection (EPA) Soil Erosion (DOA) Building Standards (FDIC, VA, FHA, S&L, Farm Home)
Air Quality	EPA requirements to prevent significant deterioration of clean areas and ambient standards.
Waste Disposal	EPA waste water, RCRA and CERCLA requirements.

luters' havens and unhampered exploitation of the nation's natural resources.

The ability of the federal government to provide coordination is strained as states compete for industry and federal policies shift with political changes. In spite of its historic lethargy, the central government has become stronger, and uniform regulations uniformly applied have become more frequent as environmental problems burst out of political boundaries. Enlightened elements of the environmental and labor movements and industry increasingly support strong uniformity for long-term economic and ecological reasons.

Area after area of environmental regulation has yielded to the need for strong uniformity, radically changing the role of the states. Less recognized has been the need within the states for uniformity among state agencies and within municipalities. Conflicts on land use policies as a tool of environmental management, for example, are found in the persistent differences in how to control air pollution between the City and State of New York or the County of Los Angeles and the State of California.

Some state environmental programs simply serve the federal government as administrative agents, some enforce federally cast regulations, some compete with federal enforcement, some assume a relatively passive role of regulatory research, education, and program monitoring.

A web of red tape has been woven that prevents reindustrialization from proceeding on a rational basis. Modernized factories need to expand or be relocated with environmental controls and waste control facilities that often require as much space and energy as the industrial process itself. This process must take place in the context of 137 separate, largely uncoordinated federal program inputs on land use authorized by twenty-seven federal statutes implemented by nineteen federal agencies, overlaying the mandated and unmandated multiple veto system involving thousands of states, villages, towns, cities, counties, and special districts responding to millions of citizen voices.

Reindustrialization that protects our croplands, forests, and fisheries—and fragile groundwater recharge areas, deserts, and wetlands—may need to focus on the redevelopment of existing industrial areas simply to avoid the adverse impacts of providing new housing, social infrastructures, and public services, in addition to the communications, transport, and energy necessary to industrial enterprise.

THE ECOLOGY OF URBAN HEALTH

It is difficult to find in history a time when an awareness of the relation between health and environment did not exist. Hippocrates noted that "whoever wishes to investigate medicine properly should proceed thus: . . . when one comes into a city to which he is a stranger, he ought to consider its situation, how it lies as to the winds and the rising of the sun." But awareness is not understanding.

Investigations establishing an effect on health associated with urbanization have been plagued with many problems, including a difficulty analogous to that of determining physiological causation, in which the tendency towards equilibrium in the internal milieu often obscures clear-cut single cause and effect relationships, let alone the multi-factorial biological reality.

In the external environment, this kind of homeostatic phenomenon produces the same kind of obscurity among entire populations (Allee et al. 1949). This ecologic effect is evident in the disappearance of quantitative limits to our cities, but without a total loss of heterogeneity (Landsberg 1956; Mumford 1956). A dose-response relationship—a key relationship in establishing causation in populations as well as in individuals—has been demonstrated in a number of studies establishing a rural-urban gradient of adverse effects.

An early study establishing this gradient took place in New York State. Pneumonia (chiefly bronchopneumonia) and emphysema deaths were measured (Brightman, Rihm, and Samuels 1962). Bronchopneumonia death rates for the years 1949 and 1959 were shown to be associated with rates of air pollution measured by concentrations of an air pollution surrogate (suspended particles) in non-metropolitan areas, in eleven upstate cities, and in New York City. Increases of these death rates from 1949 to 1959 was associated both with increase in air pollution, as measured by the surrogate, and increasing urbanization.

Increasing urbanization and air pollution in the same time span appeared to also result in increased emphysema death rates: New York City figures showed significant increases (from 0.9 to 3.0 per 100,000 from 1949 to 1959) for deaths recorded from emphysema alone. In upstate New York, covering many rural as well as urban areas, the rate changed from 0.1 to 2.2. While the rate level was lower than for New York City, a greater rise in rate occurred, reflecting the rate of urbanization.

Broad-stroke studies such as these provide us only with rough correlations on the basis of which hypotheses are framed for further study of these and other ecologic factors. We undertook them because knowledge of these factors is the basis for planning and control. But the factors we choose for study often come to our attention simply by a broad awareness of what is occurring in a population's niche and then casting a net into the waters of several disciplines to find explanations.

Even the rough measurements of reality necessary for planning as a social science are difficult to achieve. In part, this is because critical toxicological and epidemiological data are most often derived from studies of single agents.

In nature, as we noted in our analysis of the ecology of copper, the toxic agents of concern are seldom found alone. Heavy metals tend to be found together. However, they can be measured and controlled as an aggregate (e.g., total suspended particulates in community air pollution control and the benzene-soluble fraction of total participate matter in in-plant coke emission control).

Environmental planning, then, is not necessarily a captive of the methodological limitations of inquiry felt by other scientists in other disciplines.

PHYSICAL PLANNING FACTORS: TOPOGRAPHY
AND METEOROLOGY

The first systematic consideration of environmental planning appears to have been John Evelyn's *Fumifugium* published in 1661. Reacting to the widespread use of soft coal and peat in London, despite a law forbidding the practice decreed three centuries earlier prescribing the death penalty, Evelyn advocated better fuels and effective urban zoning that considered weather and landscape features prior to site or source location.

Environmental planning as a tool in air quality control has not advanced much further than Evelyn in examining basic urban factors as a vector system with an air pollution resultant. It is clear, as usual, that even the little we know is not being used.

We know that any change in natural ground cover has significant effects on local climate. Every farm, village, even every road, produces a new microclimate. This new climate is the result of surface alterations that affect the aerodynamic and moisture systems, heat production, and changes in atmospheric composition.

The city is often located in areas that, for topographical reasons, accentuate the inherently poor urban-induced climate. The infamous Donora disaster and the continuous Los Angeles smog illustrate the important contribution valley topography makes to the accumulation of pollutants because of poor ventilation in the atmosphere—resulting in smog episodes.

Even when topography favors good ventilation and, therefore, the rapid dispersion of pollutants, as in Buffalo or New York City, other factors create a poor microclimate. Cloud nucleation from pollutants increases precipitation. Higher temperatures are caused by self-screening, rough-surfaced obstacles with high conductivity. The diminished cooling powers of the wind field—caused by arterial orientation, building height and contours, construction materials and the location of major sources of pollution in the wind field that result in diminished air flow speed—leads to increased temperature inversions (air lids) and, therefore, air stagnation.

In New York City, where inversions are very common, wind speed is about 19 percent slower in Central Park than at LaGuardia Airport. Where sources of pollution are most concentrated, the ventilation possibility is poorest. Cities in general have fewer clear days and less illumination and ultraviolet radiation that their rural environs (Landsberg 1956).

Two possible urban patterns reduce potential air pollution. LeCorbusier's (1948) core city with triple level streets, alternating skyscrapers and parks, and extremely concentrated population and activity may result in the same pollution potential as the dispersed pattern of Wright's (1948) *Broadacre City*. In Broadacre City, pollution would be advantageously diluted and dispersed. In a core city, the pollution plume or packet would have a relatively short distance to travel before leaving the confines of the densely populated area. Adverse air quality appears not to be inherent in the pattern, but rather in the content. On the other hand, a combination of the two forms could result in a cancellation of the benefits of either.

ENVIRONMENTAL PLANNING IN NEW YORK

At least one state has attempted to use statewide comprehensive planning as a regulatory tool. In 1964, the New York State Air Pollution Control Board adopted a system of air zoning based on existing land use patterns that encompassed about 85 percent of the state's population. In 1966, the legislature increased the Board's powers to establish ambient air quality and emission standards to make the zoning system an effective means of air pollution control. The federal Air Quality Act of 1967 effectively pre-empted the state system, before it was widely enforced, with another system of planning.

Under the federal act, eight atmospheric areas (or air "sheds") were defined on the basis of air flow and associated pollution problems within administrative and political boundaries rather than land use. It was possible under the federal system to consider land use because ambient standards could have differing values on a regional basis, and clean areas were to have been protected by special provisions to prevent their significant deterioration. The air sheds themselves, however, were too large to coordinate with land use. Although strengthened by the Clean Air Act of 1977, the federal system has never been fully implemented. To date neither the federal nor state system has been given a full trial.

The New York system was grounded on extensive data gathering: source inventories, air monitoring, economic activity, topography, meteorology, demography, recreation, and conservation. Present and future atmospheric loadings were modeled and predicted. There was an attempt by the Board not to simply accept the *status quo*, but to determine future urban composition by combining within a regulatory program zoning and industrial site selection, ambient air quality standards and emission limitations.

Site selection was seen as a tool for environmental planning. There was an understanding of its importance as an effective method of locating contaminant sources in areas that would minimize their effects on the community and preserve clean areas for agriculture, recreation, and conservation. Prevailing wind direction, natural air drainage, and other meteorological factors were to be considered in the location of large sources—an expansion of the usual list of land values, transportation, markets, labor, and raw material sources considered in industrial siting.

Enforceable zoning was seen as a way to prevent the incursions of industry into residential areas (and of residential into industrial zones), as well as to provide for growth and community development, control traffic patterns and transportation, designate green belts, and limit the quantity or proximity of structures. Waste disposal and water quality regulation were to have been integrated with air pollution control.

CLOSING THE BIOLOGY-TECHNOLOGY GAP

Thus far we have considered segments of information that fall into two categories: human biological data and concepts, and data and concepts associated with the technology of urbanization (artifacts of human culture). While analogies can be drawn on the processes of change between and within both categories, they remain, as Gould (1987) (and Huxley before him) pointed out, mere analogies (albeit often fruitfully drawn) unless an isomorphism can be established. This does not appear to be the case.

Fundamental biological change appears to be primarily Darwinian in nature (natural selection operating upon *undirected* variation). Fundamental change in human culture appears to be primarily Lamarckian in nature (new characteristics, i.e., "discoveries," passed from one generation to another by communication, e.g., teaching and writing, used to direct variation). Thus, while human culture may have a biological base, change is transmitted environmentally within a universe of discourse. By this means cultural variation can be *directed*. The universe of discourse is the community and communities in communication. Communication, when effective, is a conscious act that closes, albeit never completely, the gap between biology and technology.

Delineating the external and internal boundaries and structures, the form of the human niche, depends upon communicating known and relevant information in accordance with a plan or set of purposes for which the biological data can provide criteria for biological limits.

The manner in which the form of the human niche is set surely draws upon cultural considerations tempered by physical realities: geographical, technological, political, economic, historical, and future purposes or intentions. All of these factors are guided by the values of our culture.

A critical issue is how we use biological criteria, deductions from biological data about the consequences of future change based upon our perception of past consequences, to direct change.

The cultural planning device of architecturally sequestering and designing structures in designated land use zones, for example, without calculating the total biological burden on the community emanating from activities *in* such structures, clearly is inadequate. Process and agent standards (that ideally embody both biological and cultural considerations) that when achieved protect the community from the combined effect of unnecessary environmental insults are needed for use within the zone.

By what method can standards be set, utilizing data from a myriad of disciplines, in the planning process? Our success in answering this question is a test of our ability to usefully integrate a multidisciplinary set of data. To accept current practice is to accept our current failure in environmental planning.

One answer given by some environmentalists is the attempt to ignore all but the biological, for example, human health considerations. The argument is made that we ought to achieve the "safety" claimed to be the goal of their opponents.

Disconcerting to policymakers who attempt to follow this advice is the fact that environmental standards can not be based on purely biological data because of the inability to achieve safety, that is, find a no-effect threshold in a population (Rall 1975; DeNevers 1979).

To mask this mistake, most environmental standards, including those which use the artifice of limits below *observable* effects or of an "acceptable risk," have a surreptitiously inserted, largely unexamined, simplistic (implied or explicit) economic or technological base. While current agent-by-agent, and even process-by-process, traditional clinical, toxicological, and epidemiologic research (the bulk of our environmental research effort) may yield the reason to control, standards for control are still based upon guesswork.

What *should* be equally disconcerting to policymakers are two additional facts. The economic and technologic portions of the data bases for each microenvironment are different. What we know (which in part is a function of what questions we ask) and how we organize what we know about the work environments is radically different from what we know and how we organize our knowledge about ambient environments. Yet it is the high-risk worker populations that provide most of the useful health effects data.

Moreover, the biological portions of the data bases are different for each subpopulation, for example, populations defined by age. We know very little about work environments for workers below age sixteen and over age sixty-five largely because our data gathering systems tend to ignore the existence of these populations which number in the millions). We are captives of the data we collect.

The consequence is that while risk is distributed throughout all populations, and collectively there is a total burden of risk, the examination of that burden is hampered by confining our studies to subpopulations and by arbitrary averaging and separating effects. This may be heuristic for methodological purposes, but the result is a game played by carrying the methodological exercise of "as if" too far.

The resulting mean values are man-made constructs that obscure the uneven distribution of real risk among biologically different individuals within a population. They lack "statistical compassion" (Selikoff 1989).

Reality in the natural community of the human niche is heterogeneous. But the data we use in planning the community is unreal: homogenized, artificially limited and defined data bases skewed for convenience. The policymaker has become dependent upon not truth, but a shifting approximation of truth. Perhaps necessary to suit limited methods, convenience is confused with ecological reality.

Equally unproductive is our systemic failure to understand and use population thinking in multidisciplinary research: the heart of human ecological study. We can not continue the endless and nearly fruitless isolated examination of each factor in the causal calculus of the human niche. A different approach must be taken.

If we conclude that we need new ways to assess the human ecological reality, then we must identify observable *critical* effects among communities, signal effects that express the integrated, total burden of *technology* (which itself integrates cultural phenomena) on the quality of community life.

The gap between traditional biological research and the investigation of factors of technology may be bridged in the planning process by methods, common to both, selected by understanding that technology is essentially a tool that, like all tools, extends the ethical, social, economic, political, and biological potential of the human population who uses it.

17

CONCLUSIONS

DUANE G. LeVINE AND ARTHUR C. UPTON

There are numerous interactions between planning the built environment, improving transportation, and shaping patterns of land use. For instance, spatial location of populations affects the type of alternatives available to improve transportation. A very interesting, very complex set of contradictions and tradeoffs were discussed in the previous chapters. In the United States, many of us desire the advantages of relative separation, safety, and status associated with life in the suburbs—a somewhat lower density lifestyle. A more dense, integrated land use pattern supports greater numbers of people who are closer to jobs, stores, and other amenities. This directionally reduces their use of the automobile for daily errands, cutting down on street congestion, noise, and emissions. It is also easier to provide bus service and utilities for higher density communities. This decreases the cost of housing, as well as public transportation, and allows for more open space. Unfortunately, efforts to make housing more affordable are often neutralized by rising costs, landscaping, and handicapped access requirements. Hence, societal needs to enhance community aesthetics and provide all citizens with equal access thwart equally important efforts to provide basic housing needs. Assessing and understanding these interactions and the needs and priorities of a community is essential to developing a planning scheme that will shape patterns of land use in a desirable fashion, ensuring space for housing, offices, shops, factories, public places, transport routes, utilities, and historic structures.

Some changes needed for planning the built environment include: (1)

technologies to improve the quality of indoor environments; (2) strategies to improve the quality, quantity, and affordability of housing in communities; (3) inventories and surveys to determine features of value in cities so that they can be protected; and (4) behavioral research to properly define what enhances "livability" of the environment and what makes people react negatively to their environment.

Changes needed for improving urban transportation include: (1) better technology so that telecommuting utilization can be increased— moving information rather than people; (2) cleaner energy sources that are affordable and efficient; and (3) arrangements to permit transportation planning on a more regional (metropolitan, as opposed to municipal) level.

Changes needed for shaping patterns of urban land use include: (1) behavioral research to determine how various land use patterns affect the public; (2) modeling to determine the potential costs associated with specific patterns of land use; (3) creative use of tax incentives to promote desired land use patterns; and (4) acceptance of more integrated land use patterns that include industry, housing, shops, and public spaces to achieve a more self-sustaining, energy-efficient community.

Real public participation in the planning stages of any community development projects—transportation, housing, public health, etc.— rather than general pro forma approaches will improve the quality of the urban environment. Decisions that affect the everyday life of a community should not be made without input from those whose interests are at stake. There is often suspicion of decisionmakers and other authorities when citizens do not understand the issue at hand or how they can effectively work with officials to form a constructive alliance. Only an education program can serve community needs at such a time. Frank, public informational meetings are helpful to explain and clarify an issue for citizens before the actual decision-making process begins. The problem should be clearly outlined, and all available alternatives should be defined. Only if citizens are made to feel their input is meaningful will suspicion and distrust be put aside.

Citizens play a vital role when attempts are made to improve the urban environment. Working closely with civic leaders can ensure community support for a project and can achieve a specific goal. Leadership and incentive on the part of the government, industry, and the public can ensure that less and less time and energy is wasted on projects that are not appropriate for a given location. This fact has not been lost on government offices or utilities or industry. Currently forty-four states have designated People's Counsels to represent consumers before public service commissions. Of the forty-four, thirty-seven are funded by tax dollars and seven through assessments on utilities. There are also several local government consumer offices in the United States, and some state insurance commissions, specifically in Texas and South Carolina, are including public advocates of people's counsels. Still many attitudes need to change if the public is to be given a voice where and when it can be most helpful.

BIBLIOGRAPHY

Akbari, H., J. Huang, P. Martien, L. Rainer, A. Rosenfeld, and H. Taha. 1988. "The Impact of Summer Heat Islands on Cooling Energy Consumption and CO_2 Emissions." Presented at the American Council on an Energy Efficient Economy's Summer Study on Energy Efficiency in Buildings, Asilomar, CA, August.

Akbari, Hashem, Art Rosenfeld, and Haider Taha. 1989. "Recent Developments in Heat Island Studies: Technical and Policy." Presented at the Heat Island Workshop, Lawrence Berkeley Laboratory, Berkeley, CA, February.

Allee, W.C., et al. 1949. *Principles of Animal Ecology*. Philadelphia: Saunders Co.

American Forestry Association. 1989. *Save Our Urban Trees: Citizen Action Guide*. Washington, D.C.

Ames, R. G. 1980. "The Sociology of Urban Tree Planting." *Journal of Arboriculture* 6(5):120–23.

Arnold, Henry. 1980. *Trees in Urban Design*. New York: Van Norstrand Reinhold Co.

Baker, Edward L., et al. 1977. "A Nationwide Survey of Heavy Metal Absorptions in Children Living Near Primary Copper, Lead and Zinc Smelters." *American Journal of Epidemiology* (106)4:261–73.

Bartenstein, F. 1982. "Meeting Urban and Community Needs through Urban Forestry." *Proceedings of the Second National Urban Forest Conference*, 21–26. Washington, D.C.: American Forestry Association.

Bernatzky, A. 1978. *Tree Ecology and Preservation*. New York: Elsevier Scientific Publishing Company.

Brightman, I. Jay, Alexander Rihm, Jr., and Sheldon W. Samuels. 1962. "Air Pollution and Health: New Facts From New York State." *American Pollution Control Association Journal* 12(6).

Calabrese, E. J., et al. 1980. "Low G-6-PD Activity in Human and Sheep Red Blood Cells and Susceptibility to Copper-Induced Oxidative Damage." *Environmental Research* 21:366–72.

Commoner, Barry. 1971. *The Closing Circle.* New York: Knopf.

Congress of the United States. 1988. *New Directions for the Nation's Public Works.* Washington, D.C.: Congressional Budget Office.

Cook, D. I. 1978. "Trees, Solid Barriers, and Combinations: Alternatives for Noise Control." *Proceedings of the First National Urban Forest Conference,* 267–83. Washington, D.C.: USDA Forest Service.

DeGraff, R. M. and B. R. Payne. 1975. "Economic Values of Nongame Birds and Some Urban Wildlife Research Needs." *Transactions of the 40th North American Wildlife and Natural Resources Conference,* 281–87. Washington, D.C.: Wildlife Management Institute.

DeNevers, N. 1979. "Human Health Effects and Air Pollution Control Philosophies." *Lung* 156:95–107.

DeWalle, David R. 1978. "Manipulating Urban Vegetation for Residential Energy Conservation." *Proceedings of the First National Urban Forest Conference,* 267–83. Washington, D.C.: USDA Forest Service.

Dodge, Russell. 1980. "The Respiratory Health of School Children in Smelter Communities." *American Journal of Industrial Medicine* 1:359–64.

———. 1983. "The Respiratory Health and Lung Function of Anglo-American Children in a Smelter Town." *American Review of Respiratory Disease* 127:158–61.

Dubos, Rene. 1968. *So Human an Animal.* New York: Scribner's.

Dubos, Rene and Barbara Ward. 1972. *Only One Earth.* New York: W.W. Norton & Company.

Durkheim, Emile. 1897. *Le Suicide.* Paris: F. Alcan.

———. 1947. *The Division of Labor.* Translated by Simpson. New York: Glencoe.

Dwyer, J. F. 1982. "Challenges in Managing Urban Forest Recreation Resources." *Proceedings of the Second National Urban Forest Conference,* 152–56. Washington, D.C.: American Forestry Association.

Ehrlich, Paul and Anne Ehrlich. 1972. *Population, Resources, Environment.* San Francisco: W. H. Freeman.

Evelyn, John. 1661. *Fumifugium.* London: Printed by W. Godbid for Gabriel Bedel and Thomas Collins.

Federal Highway Administration. 1987. *Highway Statistics.* Washington, D.C.

Federer, C. A. 1971. "Effects of Trees in Modifying Urban Microclimate." *Trees and Forests in an Urbanizing Environment.* University of Massachussetts Cooperative Extension Service Monograph 17: 23–28.

———. 1976. "Trees Modify the Urban Microclimate." *Journal of Arboriculture.* February: 121–27.

Foster, Ruth S. 1978. "Bio-Engineering for the Urban Ecosystem." *Metropolitan Tree Improvement Alliance Proceedings,* 15.

Fromm, Erich. 1973. *The Anatomy of Human Destructiveness.* New York: Holt, Rinehart and Winston.

"Getting Warmer, The Search for Super-C." 1988. *The Lamp* 70(2):14–17.

Gottman, Jean and Wolf Von Eckardt. 1964. *Megalopolis.* New York: Macmillan.

Gould, Stephen Jay. 1987. *An Urchin in the Storm.* New York: W.W. Norton.

Gray, Gene and Frederick Deneke. 1986. *Urban Forestry.* 2nd ed. New York: John Wiley & Sons.

Hansen, James E. 1988. "The Greenhouse Effect: Impacts on Current Global Temperature and Regional Heat Waves." Statement to United States Senate Committee on Energy and Natural Resources, Washington, D.C., June 23.

Hawley, Amos H. 1986. *Human Ecology.* Chicago: University of Chicago Press.

Heisler, Gordon M. and David R. DeWalle. 1984. "Plantings that Save Energy." *American Forests.*

Hippocrates. *Ancient Medicine.* (Regency edition, 1919).

Keith, John P. 1988a. *Participatory Planning.* New York: Regional Plan Association.

———. 1988b. "Conserving Cities." *Regional Development Dialogue* IX(3):4–14. Nagoya, Japan: United Nations Centre for Regional Development.

Kelly, Marcia M. 1988. "The Work-At-Home Revolution." *The Futurist.* November-December: 28–32.

Kielbaso, James. 1988. "Trends in Urban Forestry Management." *Baseline Data Report* 20(1). Washington, D.C.: International City Management Association.

Landsberg, H.E. 1956. "The Climate of Towns." *Man's Role In Changing the Face of the Earth.* Chicago: University of Chicago Press.

LeCorbusier, Charles. 1948. *New World of Space.* New York: New York Press.

Lehner, F. 1969. *Regional Organization of Transport and Urban Development.* Report 1a for the 38th UITP Congress in London. Brussels: UITP.

Lenski, Gerhard and Patrick D. Nolan. 1984. "Trajectories of Development: A Test of Ecological-Evolutionary Theory." *Social Forces* 63(1): 1–23.

McKenzie, Roderick D. 1968. *On Human Ecology.* Chicago: University of Chicago Press.

Masaryk, Thomas G. 1970. *Suicide and the Meaning of Civilization.* Translated by William B. Weist and Robert G. Batson. Chicago: University of Chicago Press.

"The Metropolis Speaks." 1974. *Regional Plan News* 95 (August). New York.

Miller, Robert W. 1988. *Urban Forestry: Planning and Managing Urban Greenspaces.* Englewood Cliffs, NJ: Prentice Hall.

Moll, Gary M. 1985. "How Valuable are Your Trees?" *American Forests.* April: 13–16.

———. 1987a. "The State of Our City Forests." *American Forests.* May–June: 61–64.

———. 1987b. "Improving the Health of the Urban Forest, Part I." *American Forests.* November–December: 61–64.

———. 1988. "Improving the Health of the Urban Forest, Part II." *American Forests.* January–February: 45–48.

———. 1989. "Designing the Ecological City." *Americn Forests.* March–April (Part I), May–June (Part II).

Moll, Gary M. and Deborah Gangloff. 1987. "Urban Forestry in the United States." *UNASYLVA 39* 1:36–45.

Moll, Gary M. and Sara Ebenreck, eds. 1989. *Shading Our Cities: A Resource Guide for Urban and Community Forests.* Washington, D.C.: Island Press.

Motor Vehicles Manufacturers Association. 1988. *Motor Vehicle Facts & Figures*. Detroit.

Mumford, Lewis. 1956. "The Natural History of Urbanization." *Man's Role in Changing the Face of the Earth*. Chicago: University of Chicago Press.

Myrdal, Gunnar and Arnold Marshall Rose. 1944. *American Dilemma*. New York: Harper.

Noble, John H., John Banta, and John S. Rosenberg. 1977. *Groping Through the Maze*. Washington, D.C.: Conservation Foundation.

NRC/NAS. 1977. *Copper*. Washington, D.C.

Owen, Wilfred. 1966. *The Metropolitan Transportation Problem*, revised edition. New York: Doubleday & Company.

———. 1972. *Accessible City*. Washington, D.C.: The Brookings Institution.

———. 1976. *Transportation for Cities*. Washington, D.C.: The Brookings Institution.

———. 1987. *Transportation and World Development*. Baltimore: The Johns Hopkins University Press.

Parker, John H. 1983. "Landscaping to Reduce the Energy Used in Cooling Buildings." *Journal of Forestry* 81(2):82–83.

People's Bank Study. 1987. Bridgeport, CT.

Phillips, Ali and Deborah Gangloff, eds. 1987. *Proceedings of the Third National Urban Forestry Conference*. Washington, D.C.: American Forestry Association.

Pisarski, Alan E. 1987. *Commuting in America: A National Report on Commuting Patterns and Trends*. Westport, CT: Eno Foundation for Transportation.

Pucher, John. 1988. "Urban Travel Behavior as the Outcome of Public Policy: The Example of Modal Split in Western Europe and North America." *APA Journal* 54(509).

Pushkarev, Boris and Jeffrey Zupan. 1977. *Public Transportation and Land Use Policy*. Bloomington: Indiana University Press.

Pushkarev, B., J. Zupan and R. Cumella. 1982. *Urban Rail in America*. Bloomington: Indiana University Press.

Rall, D.P. 1975. Article in *Regulation of Atmospheric Sulfates*, 99. Washington, D.C.: Environmental Protection Agency.

Regional Plan Association. 1962. *Spread City*. New York.

———. 1974. *Regional Energy Consumption*. New York.

Renner, Michael. 1988. *Rethinking the Role of the Automobile*. Worldwatch Paper 84, 46. Washington, D.C.: Worldwatch Institute.

Repetto, Robert. 1985. *The Global Possible*. New Haven: Yale University Press.

Rowntree, R. A. and R. A. Sanders. 1983. "Executive Summary, Dayton (Ohio) Climate Project" (in-service document). Syracuse, N.Y.: USDA Forest Service, NE Forest Experiment Station, SUNY College of Environmental Science and Forestry.

Sampson, R. Neil. 1988. "Cool the Greenhouse, Plant 100 Million Trees . . . ." *Los Angeles Times*. October 16: V–3.

Samuels, S. W. 1986. "Dialogue as a Tool of the Real World." *American Journal of Industrial Medicine* 9: 3–7.

———. 1988a. "Ethical and Metaethical Criteria for Emerging Technologies."

Living In a Chemical World, 920–27. New York: Annals New York Academy of Sciences.

———. 1988b. "The Arrogance of Intellectual Power." In *Phenotypic Variations in Populations,* eds. Avryl D. Woodhead et al., 118. New York: Plenum.

———. 1989. *Children At Risk.* Workplace Health Fund Research Reports. Washington, D.C.

Sayler, R. D. and J. A. Cooper. 1975. "Status and Productivity of Canada Geese Breeding in the Twin Cities of Minnesota." 36th Midwestern Fish and Wildlife Conference, Indianapolis.

Schaeffer, K.H. and E. Sclar. 1975. *Access for All.* London: Penguin Books Ltd.

Schober, S.E. et al. (in press). "Work-Related Injuries in Minors." *American Journal of Industrial Medicine.*

Sears, Paul B. 1956. "Changing Man's Habitat: Physical and Biological Phenomena." In *Current Anthropology,* ed. William L. Thomas, Jr. Chicago: University of Chicago Press.

Selikoff, I.J. 1989. *Statistical Compassion,* Presented at the Conference on Ethics in Epidemiology, Birmingham, AL, June.

Shigo, Alex. 1986. *A New Tree Biology.* Durham, N.H.: Shigo & Trees Association.

Smith, W. H. and S. Dochinger. 1976. "Capability of Metropolitan Trees to Reduce Atmospheric Contaminants." In *Better Trees for Metropolitan Landscapes,* 49–59. USDA Forest Service General Technical Report NE-22.

Sopper, W. E. and S. N. Kerr. 1978. "Potential Use of Forest Land for Recycling Municipal Waste Water and Sludge." *Proceedings of the First National Urban Forest Conference,* 392–409. Washington, D.C.: USDA Forest Service.

Spirn, Anne Whiston. 1984. *The Granite Garden.* New York: Basic Books, Inc.

State of the World. Worldwatch Institute Report. 1987, 1988, and 1989. Washington, D.C.: Worldwatch Institute.

Transportation Research Board. 1987. *Research for Public Transit.* Special Report 213. Washington D.C: National Research Council.

———. 1988a. *A Look Ahead—Year 2020.* Special Report 220. Washington, D.C.: National Research Council.

———. 1988b. *Transportation in an Aging Society: Improving Mobility and Safety.* Special Report 218 (I). Washington, D.C.: National Research Council.

Transportation Systems Center. 1987. *National Transportation Statistics.* Cambridge, MA.

Ulrich, Roger S. 1984a. "View Through a Window May Influence Recovery from Surgery." *Science* (224). 27 April: 420–21.

———. 1984b. "The Psychological Benefits of Plants." *Garden Magazine* November: 16–21.

U.S. Council on Environmental Quality. 1984. *Environmental Quality—15th Annual Report of the Council on Environmental Quality.* Washington, D.C.: Government Printing Office.

Vuchic, V.R. 1981. *Urban Public Transportation Systems and Technology.* New York: Prentice Hall.

———. 1986. "Metro Systems in the Year 2000: Modernization, Expansion, Diversification." *UITP Revue.* April: 307–44. Brussels.

———. 1991. "Recognizing the Value of Rail Transit." *TR News 156.* September-October: 13–19.

Warner, W. Lloyd. 1953. *American Life-Dream and Reality.* Chicago: University of Chicago Press.
World Future Society. 1989. *Future Survey* 11(2). Washington, D.C.
Wright, Frank Lloyd. 1948. *Broadacre City.* New York: Taliesin.
Zwicker, Denise Allen. *The Changing Nature of Gasoline.* New York: Exxon Corporation.

INDEX

Acid rain, 50, 59, 91
AFL-CIO Tritrades Agreement, 7
Air pollution, 78, 90, 125, 160, 165, 181–84
Air Quality Act of 1967, 183
American Association of State Highway and Transportation Officals (AASHTO), 113–20
American Forestry Association, 170

Barnes, K. R., 39–46
Bay Area Residential Investment and Development Group (BRIDGE), 21–22

Cannibalism, 173–74
Categorical Highway Program, 116
Citizen action, 28
Class: inflexibility, 172; lower, 128; middle, 17, 30, 154, 172, 174
Clawson, D., 113–20
Clay, L. D., 113
Clean Air Act Amendments of 1990 (CAAA), 99
Clean Air Act of 1977, 183
Community Development Corporations (CDCs), 29–38

Community Reinvestment Act, 22
Compressed natural gas, 92
Congestion: pricing, 77, 88–89, 92, 94; relief, 91
Conservation, 55–59, 62–63, 160, 177, 183
Consumer Price Index (CPI), 19
Copper, 19, 157, 175–77, 181
"Corporate average fuel economy"(CAFE) legislation, 93
Council on Affordable Housing, 18, 19

Direct intervention, 137–38
Dubos, R., 74, 170
Dutch elm disease, 164–65, 167

Eisenhower, D. D., 113
Electricity, 48, 50–52, 55–57, 59
Emissions, 85, 91–93, 95, 176–77, 187
Emphysema, 181
Energy: efficiency, 55–63, 65–68, 110–11; needs, 159; use, 47–53, 56, 85, 93
Enterprise Zone legislation, 10
Environmental planning, 175–76, 178–79, 181–84

Exclusivity, 135
Exurbs, 97

Fair Housing Act of 1985, 18
Father Panik Village, 16
Federal Home Loan Mortgage Corporation (Freddie Mac), 36
Federal Urban Development Actions Grants (UDAG), 147
Fiscal zoning, 135
Five E's, 74, 110–11
Fixed-guideway transit, 88
Flexible Highway Program, 116
Freeman, L. M., 55–70

Gentrification, 143, 145–46, 154–55
Global ReLeaf, 170
Greenhouse effect, 53, 59, 92, 170
Grogan, P. S., 29–38

Hackensack Meadowlands Development Commission (HMDC), 139
Heat island, 158–60, 165, 168, 170
Heating, 48–53, 55, 160
High Occupancy Vehicle (HOV) lane, 122, 127
Highway pricing, 89, 94
Homeless, 30, 39, 42–45, 149
Housing: cluster, 24–25, 95; infill, 26–28; private sector, 42; rental, 36, 40, 43–44; transitional, 44–45
Housing and Urban Development (HUD), 5, 10–11, 13, 23–24
Hovnanian Enterprises, 19–20
Human ecology, 171–72, 186
Human niche, 172–74, 184–86

Intermodal Surface Transportation Efficiency Act of 1991 (ISTEA), 99
Interstate system, 113–14, 116, 121

Joint Venture for Affordable Housing (JVAH), 23–24

Keith, J. P., 133–40

Land controls, 134
Land development policies, 134

Landmarks Preservation Commission, 152
LeVine, D. G., 187–89
Levitt, W., 14–15
Levittown, 135
Light rail transit, 106–7, 109
Load management, 56–59, 61–63, 65–68
Local Initiatives Managed Assets Corporation (LIMAC), 36–37
Local Initiatives Support Corporations (LISC), 34–38
Logue, E., 16
Low-Income Housing Fund (LIHF), 22
Low-Income Housing Tax Credit, 34

Methanol, 92
Metropolitan Regional Council (MRC), 137–38
Mining, 175–76
Mt. Laurel, 19–20

National Energy Conservation Policy Act (NECPA), 56, 68
National Environmental Protection Act, 9
National Equity Fund, 36–37
National Housing Task Force, 13
National Preservation Act of 1966, 142
NEHEMIAH, 14–16
Neighborhood Development Support Collaborative (NDSC), 36
Neighborhood disinvestment, 32
New York City Partnership, 5
New York State Air Pollution Control Board, 183
NIMBY (Not In My Backyard), 9
Noise, 78, 125, 163, 187
Nonprofit housing developers, 21

Operation Breakthrough, 5
Overdevelopment, 172
Owen, W., 73–82

Pneumonia, 181
Profit-oriented developers, 40
Pushkarev, B., 83–96

Radial capacity, 123
Rapid transit system, 123
Regional form, 137
Regional Plan Association (RPA), 133–34, 138–40
Regional rail systems, 107–8
Reindustrialization, 174, 180
Revenue Act of 1976, 145
Robbins, I. D., 15
Robinson, J. D., 5
Rockefeller, D., 5

Sampson, R. N., 157–70
Samuels, S. W., 171–86
Secondary displacement, 15
South Street Seaport, 147–50
Stein, R. G., 47–54
Suburbia, 135
Suicide, 173–74
Surface Transportation Assistance Act of 1987, 113–14

Tax incentives, 40, 143–45, 188
Tax Reform Act of 1986, 14
Tax sharing, 137, 139

Taylor, E. F., 55–70
Topography, 25–27
Transportation Alternative Group (TAG), 114–16
"Transportation control measures" (TCMs), 101
Tri-State Regional Planning Commission, 137

Upton, A. C., 187–89
Urban: forestry, 165–66; population, 74, 162
Urban Renewal District, 147–48

Vuchic, V. R., 105–12

Water quality, 161–62
West Side Renaissance, 146–47
Wilson, W. J., 30, 38
Wright, M. A., 97–104
Wylde, K., 3–12

Yost, Z., 13–28

Zoning, 23

ABOUT THE CONTRIBUTORS

KERRON R. BARNES, Office of Community Development, Dutchess County, New York.

M. CHRISTINE BOYER, Professor, School of Architecture, Princeton University.

DAVID CLAWSON, Program Director, American Association of State Highways and Transportation Officials.

MATTHEW A. COOGAN, Vice President for Transportation, Rackemann Environmental Services.

RUTH A. EBLEN, Executive Director, The Rene Dubos Center for Human Environments.

WILLIAM R. EBLEN, President, The Rene Dubos Center for Human Environments.

LUISA M. FREEMAN, Vice President, Applied Energy Group.

PAUL S. GROGAN, President, Local Initiatives Support Corporation.

JOHN P. KEITH, Senior Associate, Institute of Public Administration.

DUANE G. LeVINE, Manager, Science and Strategy Development, Environment and Safety, Exxon Corporation.

WILFRED OWEN, Former Senior Fellow, The Brookings Institution.

BORIS PUSHKAREV, Vice President for Research and Planning, Regional Plan Association.

R. NEIL SAMPSON, Executive Vice President, American Forests.

SHELDON W. SAMUELS, Executive Vice President, The Ramazzini Institute.

RICHARD G. STEIN, Principal, The Stein Partnership.

MAURICE F. STRONG, Chairman and CEO, Hydro Ontario Canada; Secretary-General, United Nations Conference on Environment and Development.

EARLE F. TAYLOR, JR., Vice President, Marketing, Kemper Management Services, Inc.

ARTHUR C. UPTON, Former Professor of Environmental Medicine and Director of the Institute of Environmental Medicine, New York University School of Medicine.

VUKAN R. VUCHIC, Professor, Transportation Engineering, University of Pennsylvania.

MARK A. WRIGHT, Editor, *Passenger Vessels*, Bostrom Corporation.

KATHRYN WYLDE, President, Housing, New York City Partnerships, Inc.

ZANE YOST, President, Zane Yost and Associates.